SANDILE ZULU

COLIN RICHARDS

DAVID KRUT
PUBLISHING

Published by David Krut Publishing with funding from
The National Arts Council of South Africa (NAC)
The Royal Netherlands Embassy
The Arts & Culture Trust
David Krut Arts Resource (DKARTS)
The French Institute of South Africa (IFAS)
The French Embassy

Cover image: Detail, *Involution 2* (2001)
photograph by John Hodgkiss

David Krut Publishing cc
PO Box 892
Houghton 2041
Johannesburg
Tel: 011 880 5648
Fax: 011 880 6368
dkrut@icon.co.za
www.taxiartbooks.com
www.davidkrutpublishing.com

ISBN 0-958-4688-7-7

NATIONAL ARTS COUNCIL
OF SOUTH AFRICA

Ambassade van het
Koninkrijk der Nederlanden

ARTS & CULTURE TRUST

DAVID KRUT
ARTS RESOURCE

Institut Français
d'Afrique du Sud

Liberté • Égalité • Fraternité
RÉPUBLIQUE FRANÇAISE
AMBASSADE DE FRANCE
EN AFRIQUE DE SUD
Service de Coopération
et d'Action Culturelle

CONTENTS

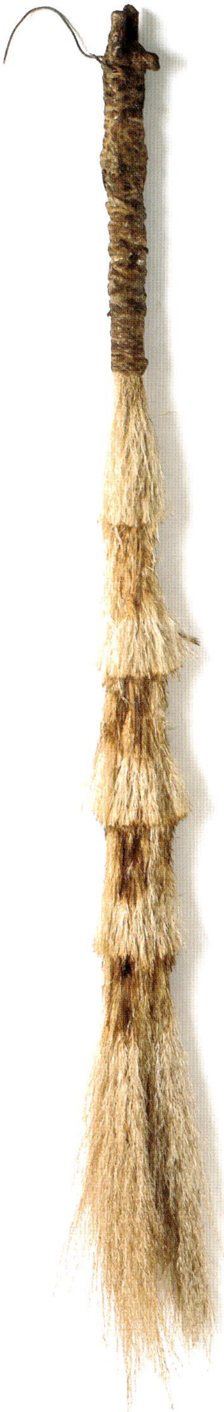

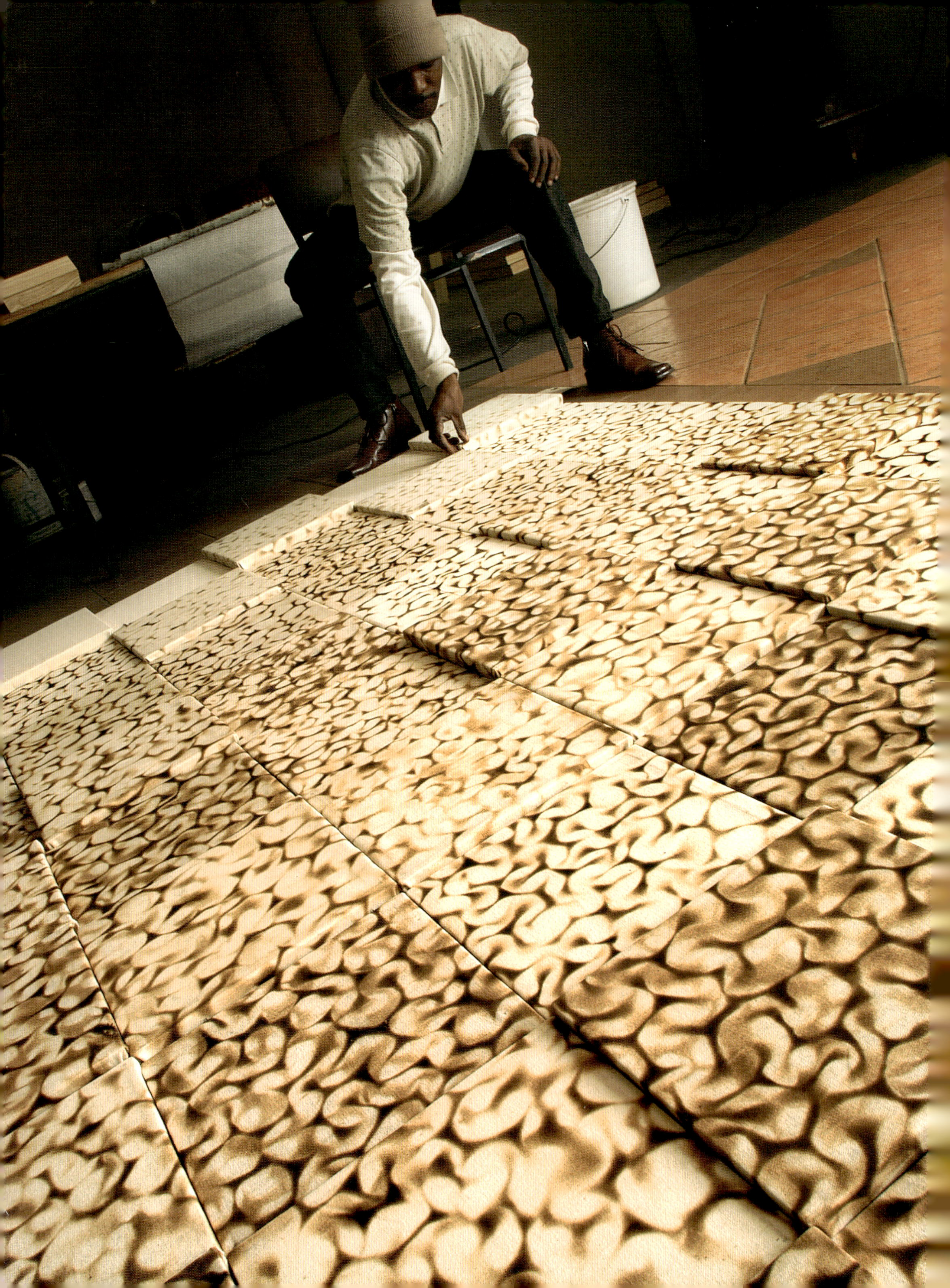

I have dreamed of restoring our love... It was not to be. Our cake was consumed by fire with our house... Love. Death by fire.

(Njabulo Ndebele, *The Cry of Winnie Mandela: A Novel*)

Drought and fire, and rumour of locust, earthquake and unrest on the scorching inland air – then, then we know on what continent we are settled.

(Peter Blum, "News From the Interior")

Does it please you when before you, still like death I stand like ghosts of the dead, and weep fire onto your white face

(Sandile Zulu, "Not Forever")[1]

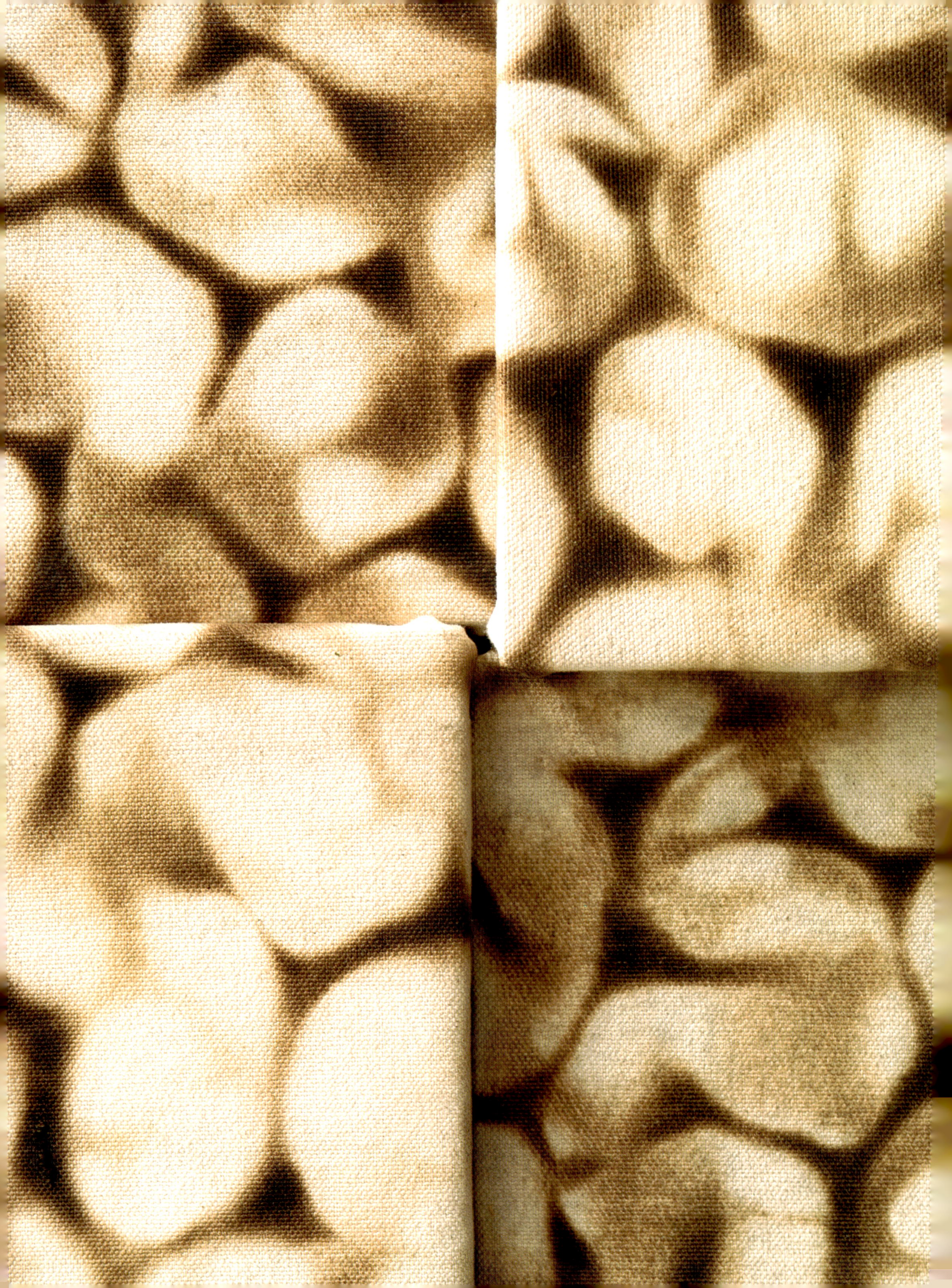

PORTRAIT OF THE ARTIST BURN! AS YOUNG FIREBRAND

01. STARTING OUT

Sandile Zulu uses natural energies and everyday, organic materials to create his artworks. Fire, wind, water, earth,[2] the skins of animals, seeds, roots, grass, glue, cardboard, paper, canvas. But his is not a pure nature. Zulu also scavenges urban waste, recycling barbed wire, glass beads, plastic, string, rope, industrial moulds, metal, sponge rubber and metropolitan debris of every kind.[3] His art is as much a synthesising collateral creativity of a decaying urbanism as it is of rural nature. The aesthetic tone is ritualistic and repetitive, mantric and mesmerising

His creative method – if we can trap what he does in a 'method' – is mostly additive and cumulative. In many works, simple, primary units and marks systematically mutate and multiply, creating intricate, iconic wholes. Elementary aesthetic 'atoms' evolve into building blocks for elaborate image fields in, for example, *Camouflage 1* (1998), *Indluyengwe (Leopard's Lair)* (2000) and the aptly named *Elementary Units and Relationships 1* and *2* (2003). Zulu's creative practice is patterned on natural processes involving constancy and change. Such patterning is also part of our man-made, urban habitats, something to which he is also sensitive.[4] Not for nothing was his father a builder and his mother a designer of clothes.[5] Both supported their son's creativity in every way.

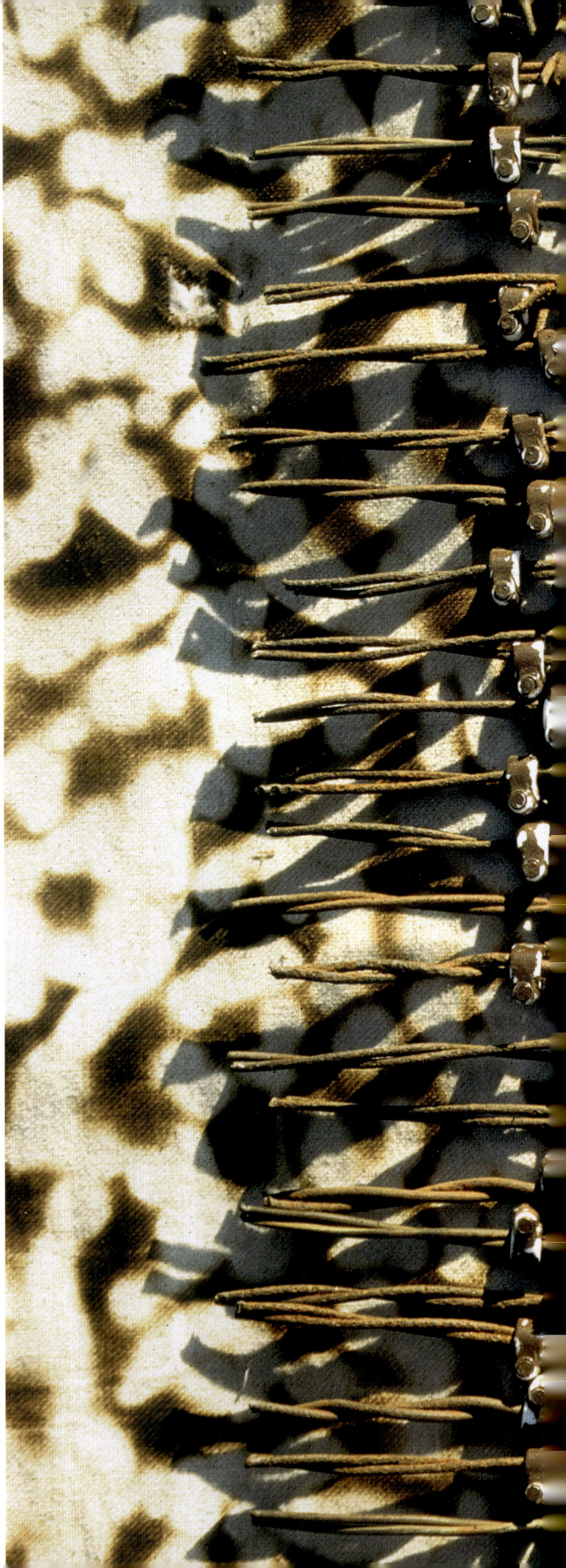

Detail, **Camouflage 1** (1998)

fire, water, air, earth, barbed wire, grass and canvas | 114 x 60 x 20 cm

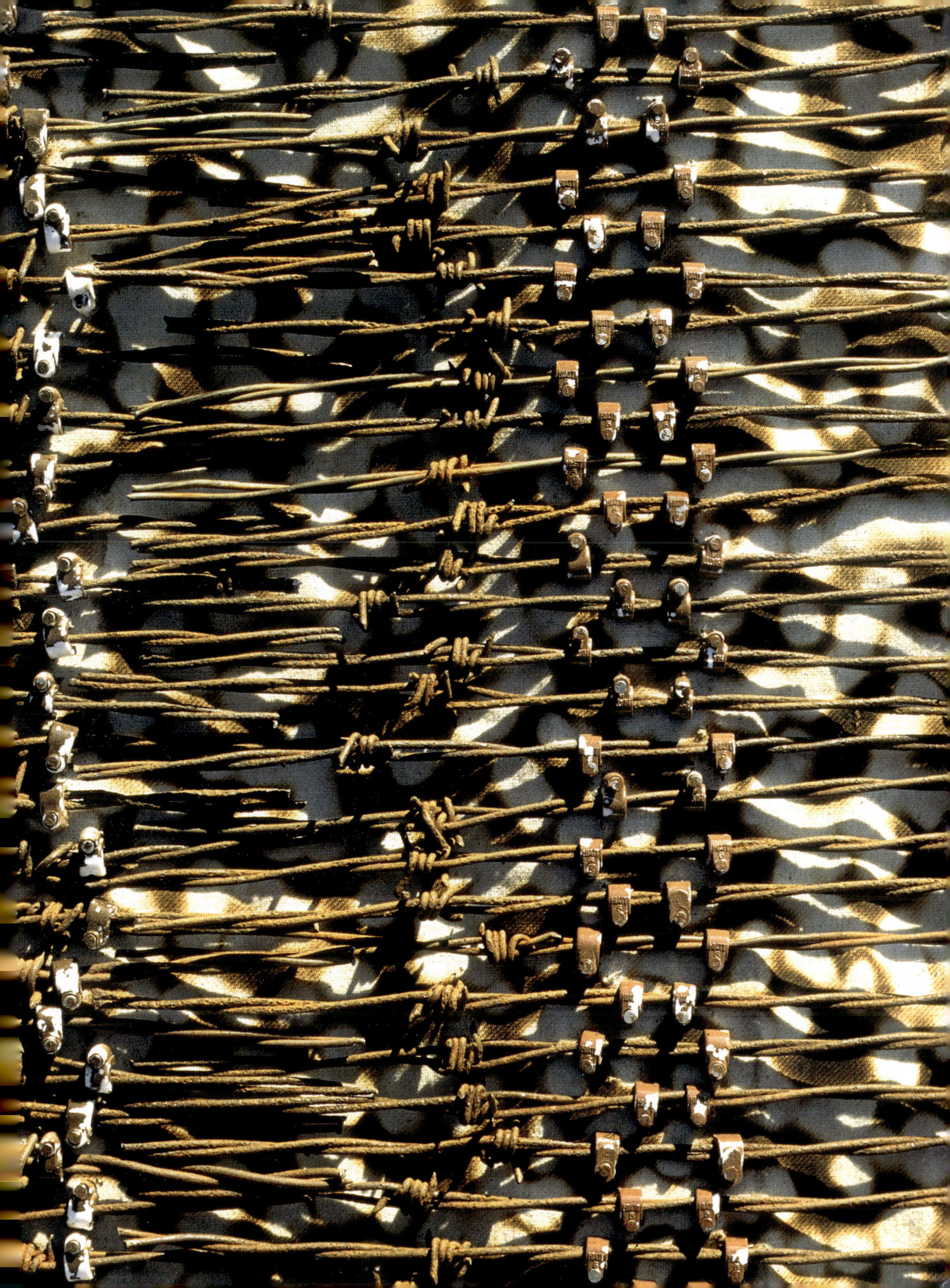

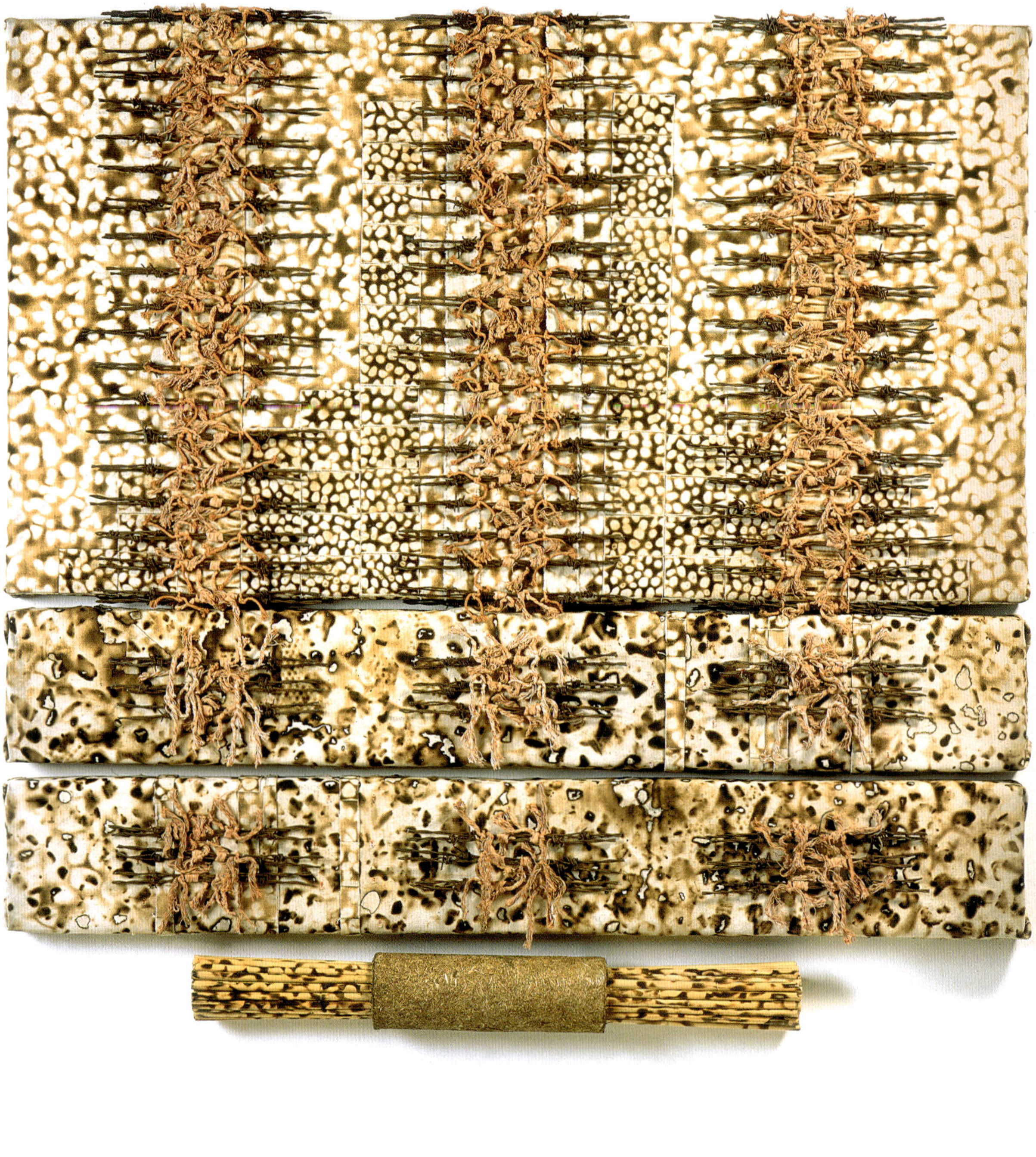

10 | **Indluyengwe (Leopard's Lair)** | (2000) | fire, water, air, earth, barbed wire, canvas and string | 154 x 142 cm

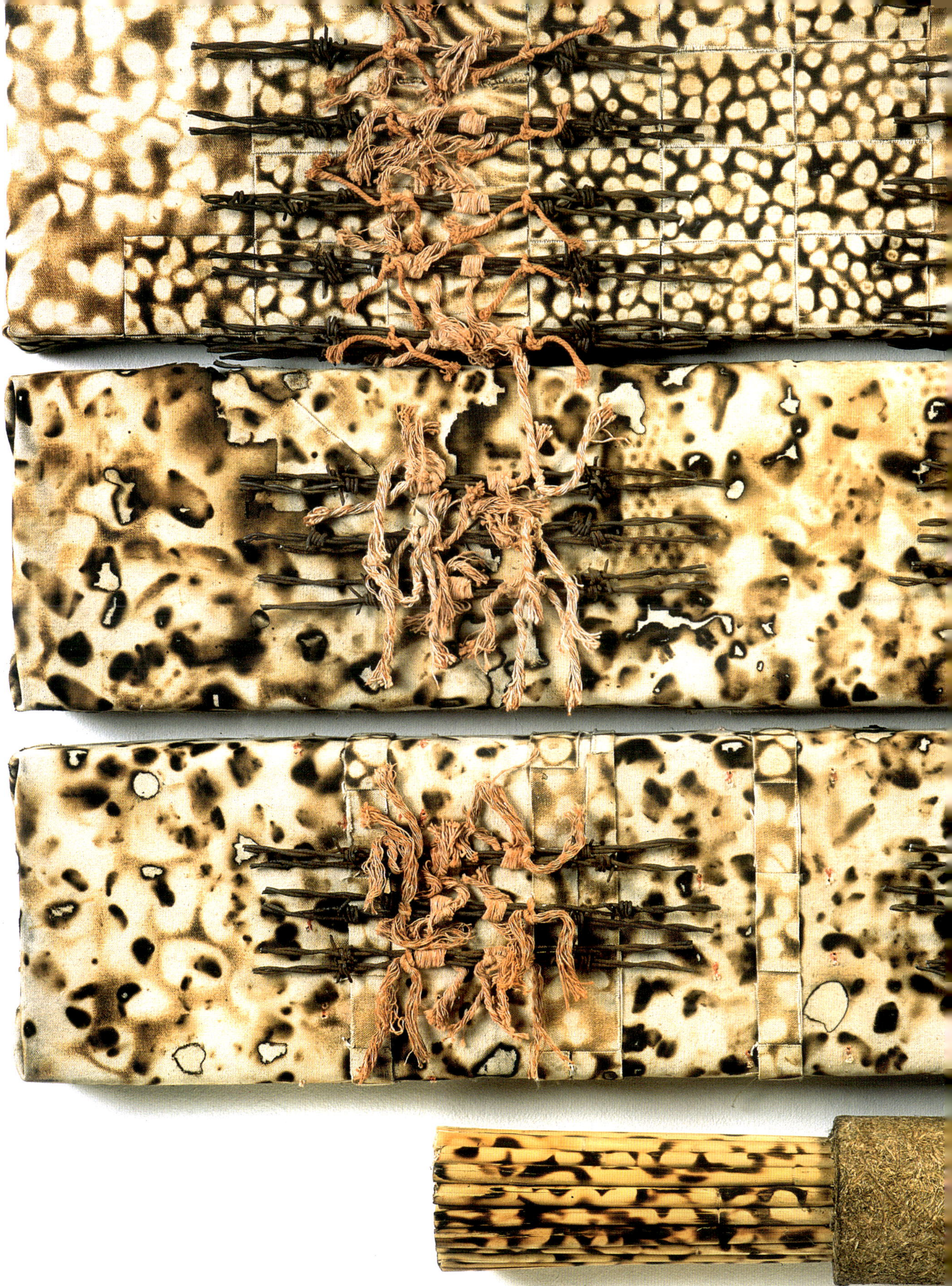

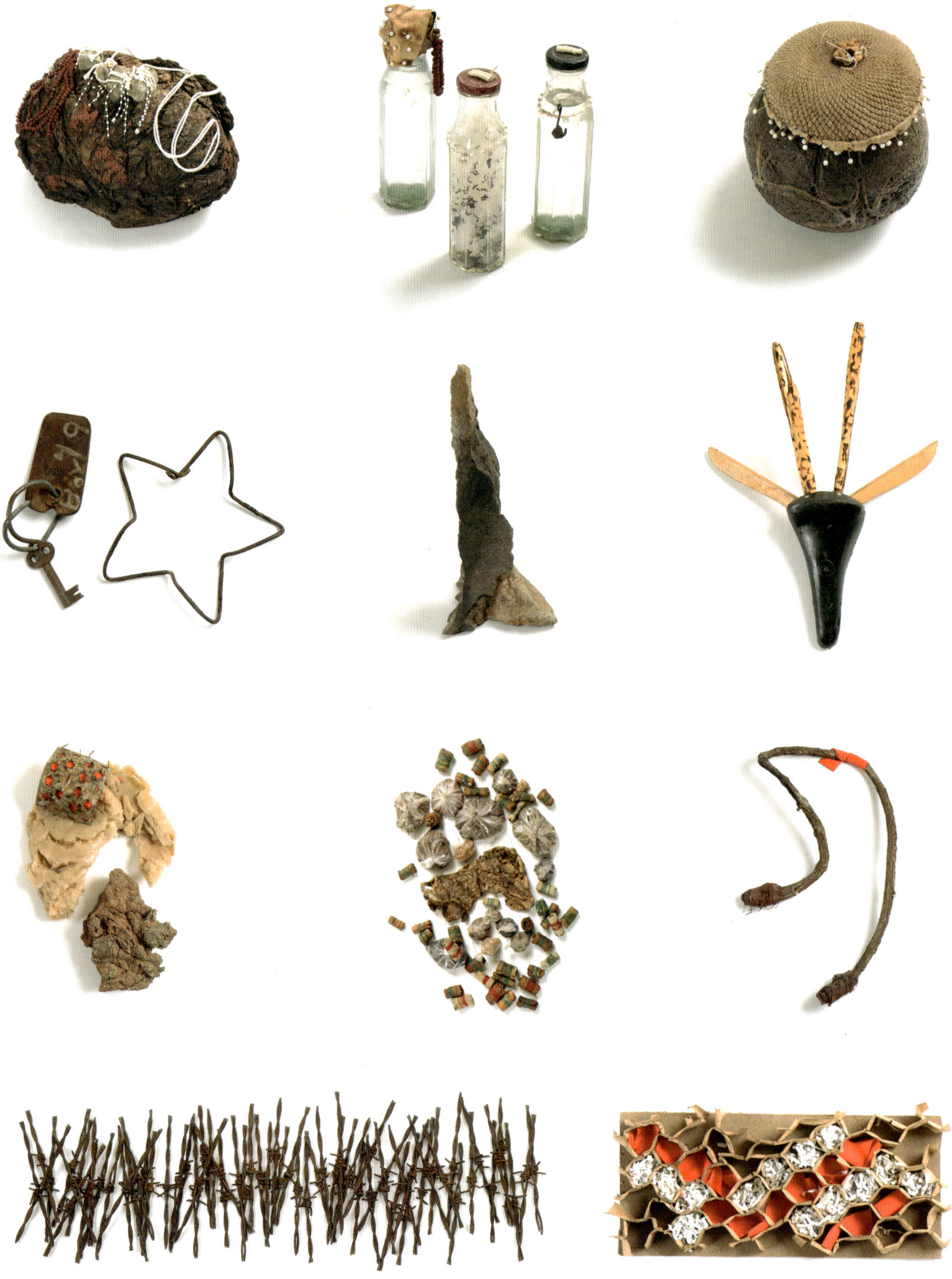

Objects from the artist's studio

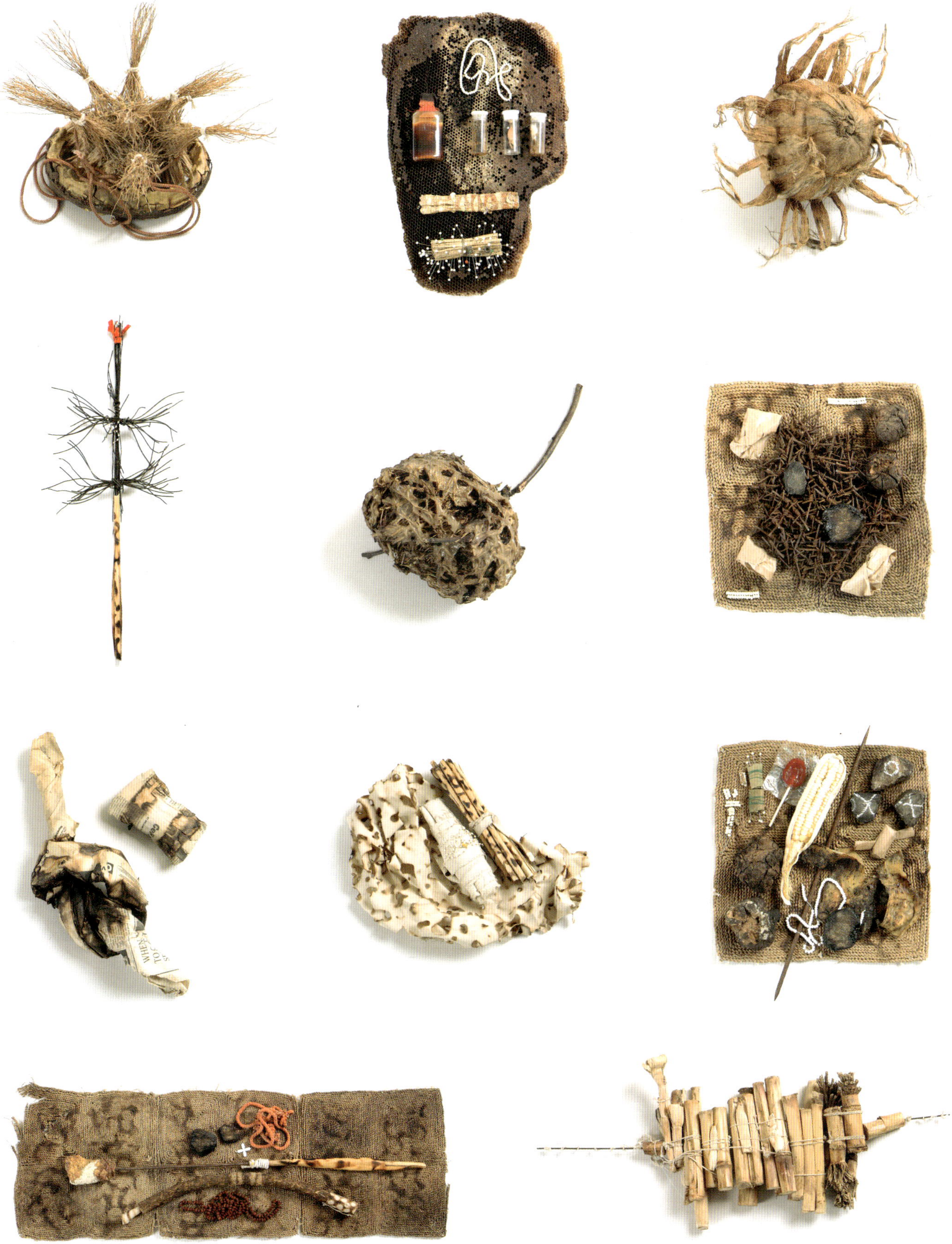

02. THE STUDIO (INSIDE)

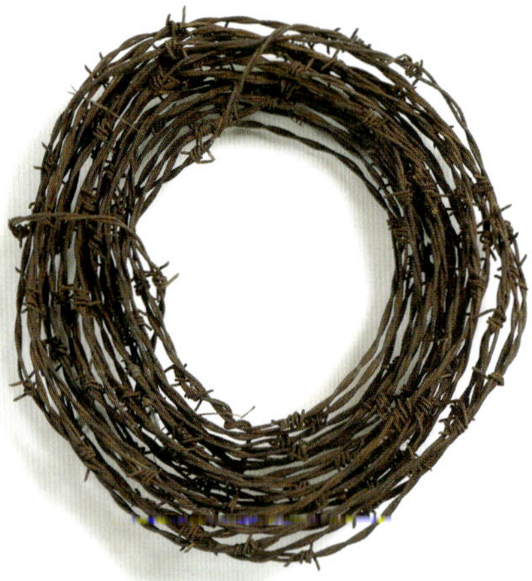

Sandile Zulu is a pyromancer. His work is a wellspring for ever-expanding social meanings and aesthetic energies. This much is clear if you have the good fortune of visiting his studio in downtown Fordsburg. There, you will enjoy an unrivalled vision of his remarkable creative cosmos. Set out on the industrial floor, itself a scuffed and scarred landscape as if seen from high above, a loose, grid-like encyclopaedia of objects and materials is arranged in an oddly 'haphazard' order.

A long line of short, single cut lengths of blackened barbed wire rests next to the same wire carefully bundled and bound with white string. These barbed bouquets look like beheaded roses and appear in *Study for Abduction* (1997) and *Abduction* (1997). The short, carefully arranged single lengths of wire recall amongst other things the patterns on 'traditional' Zulu battle shields as well as the ribbed fronts of British dress-tunics of the nineteenth-century colonial military.[6] The violent conflict enjoined in these works finds wider expression in the Dachau installation, which included *Procession of Stones* (2004) and *Procession of Ambers 1* and *2* (2004).

Some surpassingly strange and beautiful things include the rusted upper rim of a paint-tin, with the once-liquid contents forming a petrified ring of drips, like solid fire. Inside the rust-tinged ring of hardened fluid, a cut-off coconut shell nestles. The wiry fibres of the coconut shell have been patiently separated and knotted as one might hair, pointing to the importance of body-dressing in our culture[7] and to our tendency to anthropomorphise natural, non-human phenomena, including fire, so central to Zulu's creative project. Stephen Pyne writes "it is testimony to the immense significance of fire that humanity has for so long chosen not only to anthropomorphise it but to grant it a substantive identity it does not deserve."[8] The traces of fire are evident everywhere; singed foam rubber, pieces of cold lava from the Island of Réunion, a sinister, fleshy, fire-scarred growth from a gum tree. Two exquisite sunflower heads – one dimmed and dried by sun and fire – tell of the regularity and constancy of nature, but also its violence and indifference.

A tawny, woven rope of flax resembles a hangman's noose, burned bundles of bamboo or reeds in a quiver, or a rocket, as we see in Zulu's *Involution 1* and *2* (2001) or *Imiqangala Yemvunge Yomhlanga (Black Mud Reed Sound)* (2001). Grassroots, shrunken and shrivelled sweet potatoes, perhaps not quite dead, lie scattered in another area; "when a sweet potato has been thrown into the ash-heap it becomes uneatable."[9] The sweet potato is a staple food in some parts of this region and finds a place in, for example, *Endangered Roots* (1997). A mealie lies on a mat, alongside a lollipop, the first also a staple food, the other a sweet reward for a good deed.

Nearby lies a weather-blackened piece of machined intricacy – part of a radiator? – from a mine near the Amakhono Art Centre. Amakhono was where Zulu had his first professional studio, becoming part of a community of artists who lived and worked there. Fragments of bleached, fire-resistant ceramic stick to a single coiled spring holding energy in an object that is almost invisible on the grey-brown floor. Other bits of blackened wire are tied in loose knots, scribbled lines in three dimensions. Elsewhere twisted metal cables are patiently picked apart. Some structures – a twisted metal matrix of nails – echo more than anything a DNA molecule. The same twisted double helix comprises a hinge, or spine in, for example, *Involution 1* and *2* (2002). The helix here comprises wax-stiffened string. Also familiar in many of his works are carefully burned and trimmed fronds of 'weeping love grass' (*Eragostis curvula*) and stiff, hardy pampas grass (*Cortaderia agentea*), both used in *Frontline with Centurion Models* (1997) and later *Camouflage 1* (1998).

Violence seems to have touched and marked many of the things arrayed on the concrete floor. Near the shaved, cut-grass structure, a length of tightly rolled newspaper rests, scorched while tied in a knot and then untied. A singed woven mat "only for food, not for sitting"[10]

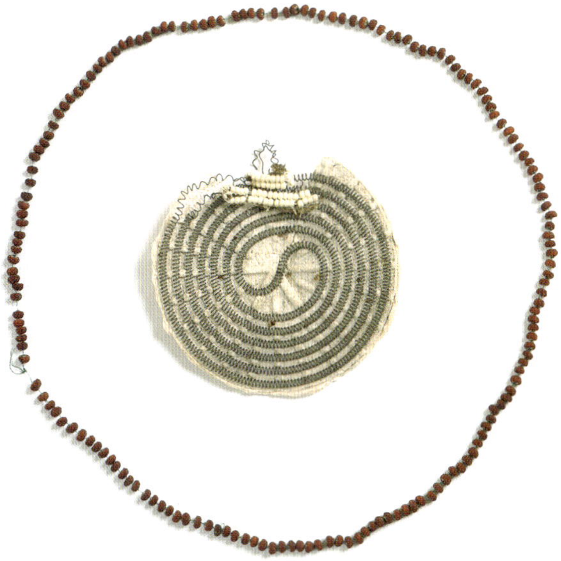

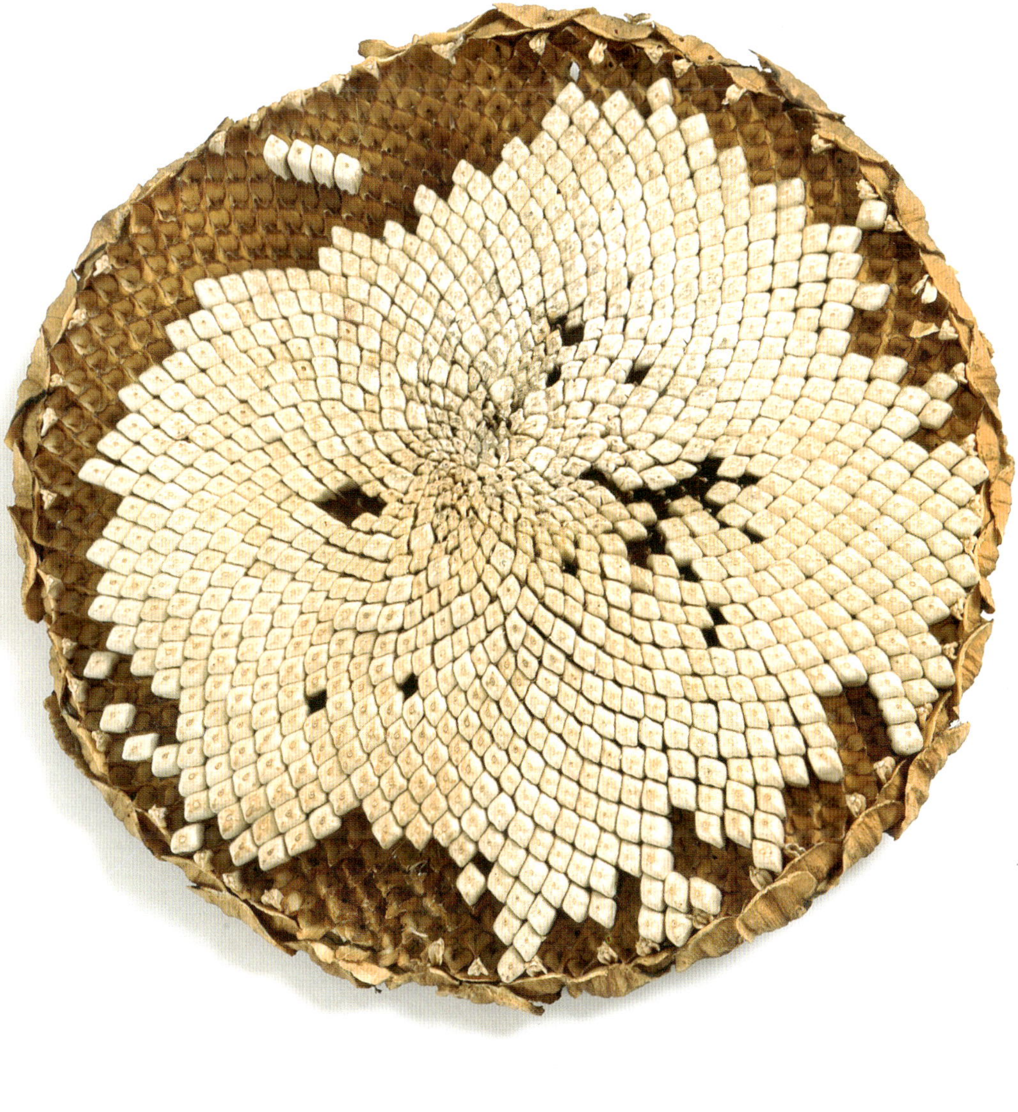

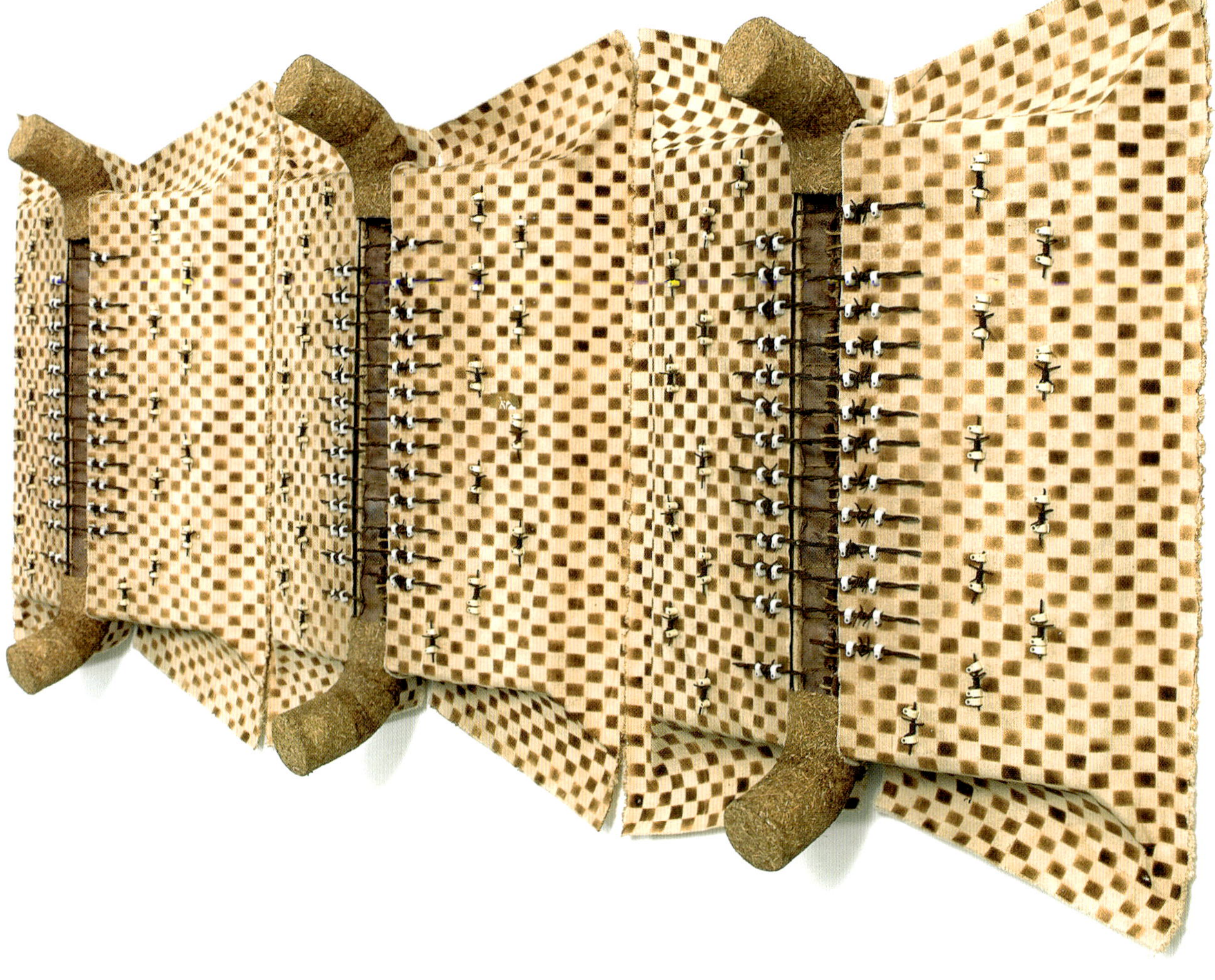

16	**Involution 2**	(2002)	fire, water, air, earth, metal, barbed wire and canvas	240 x 90 x 23 cm

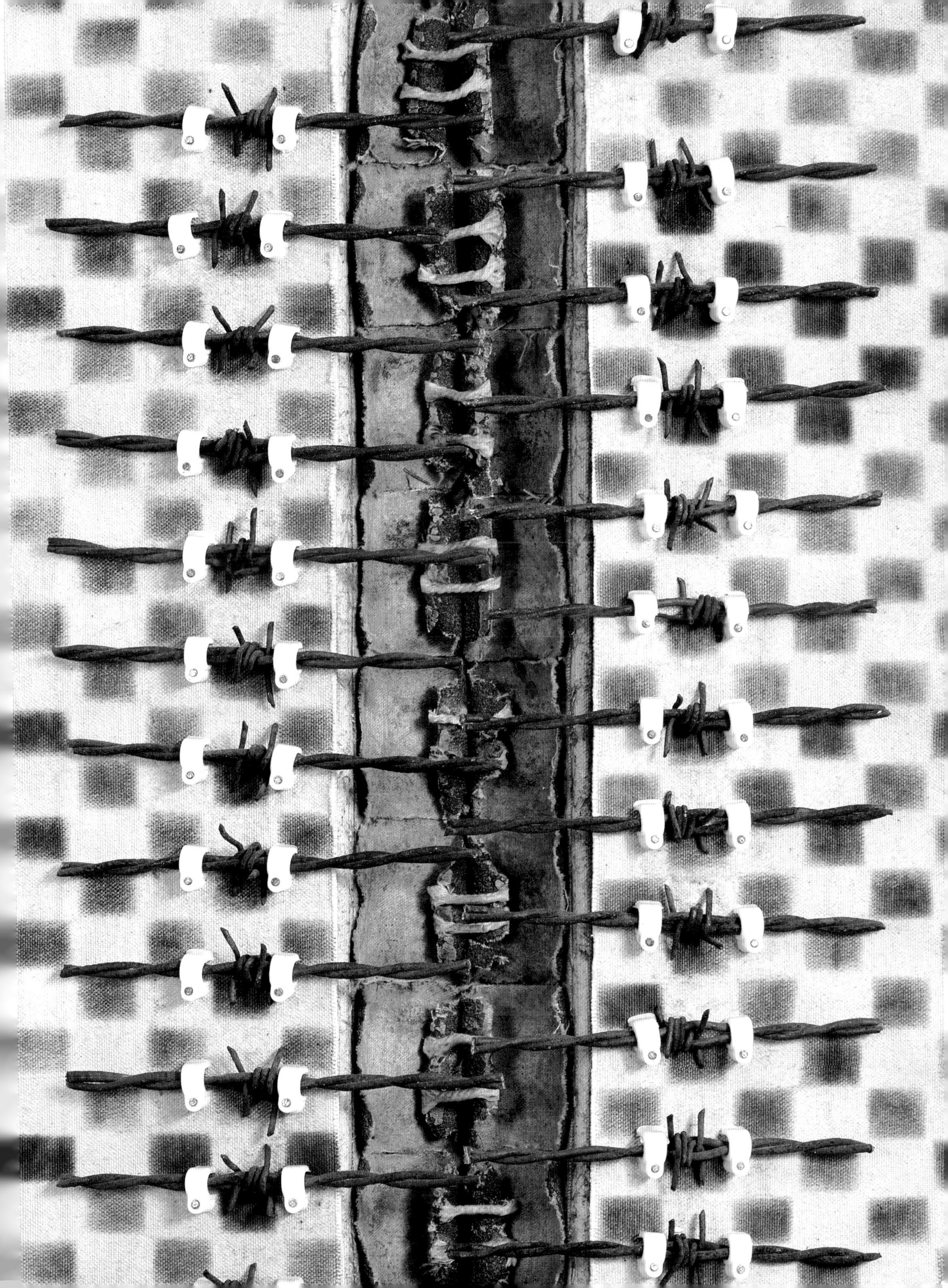

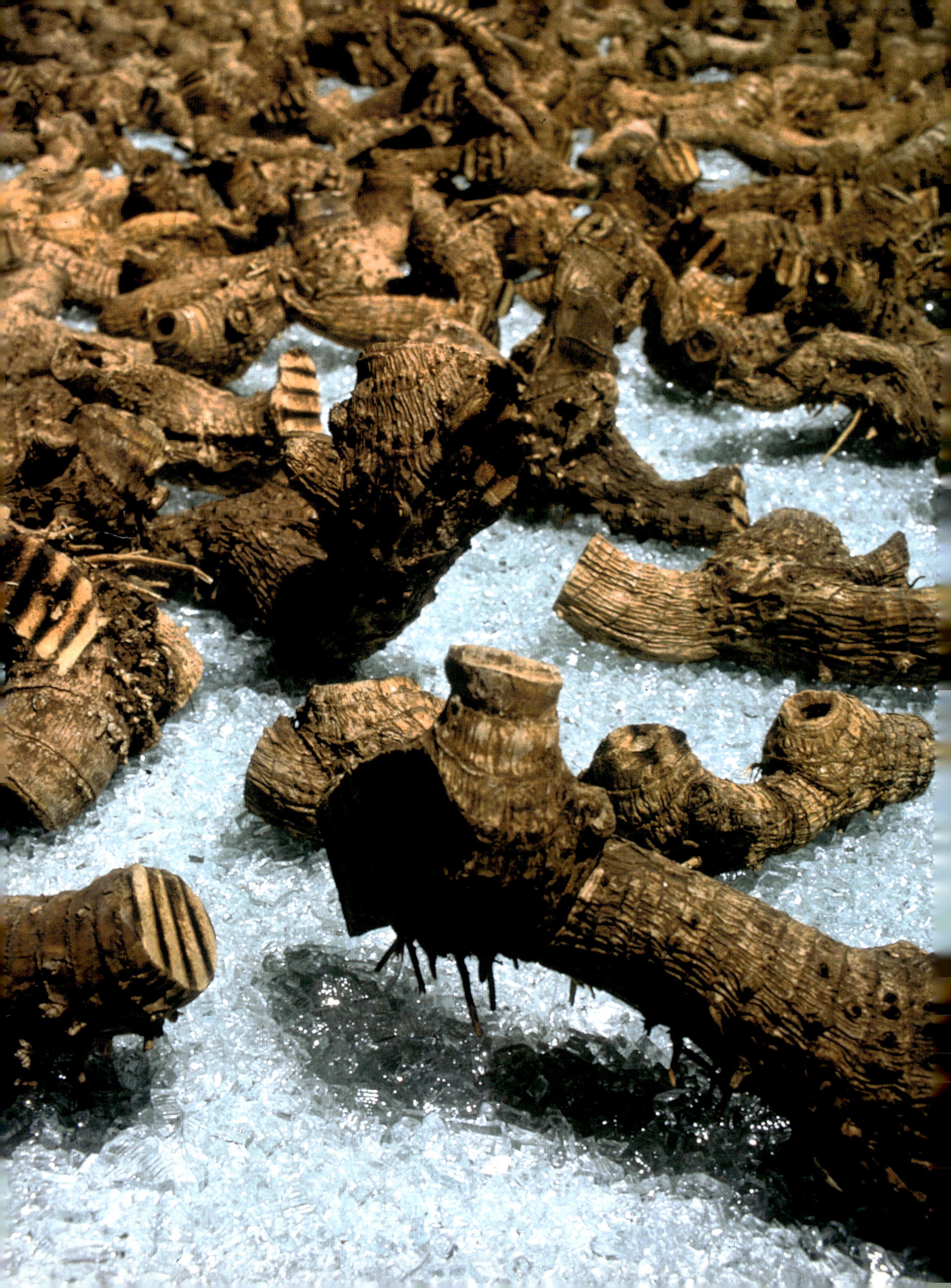

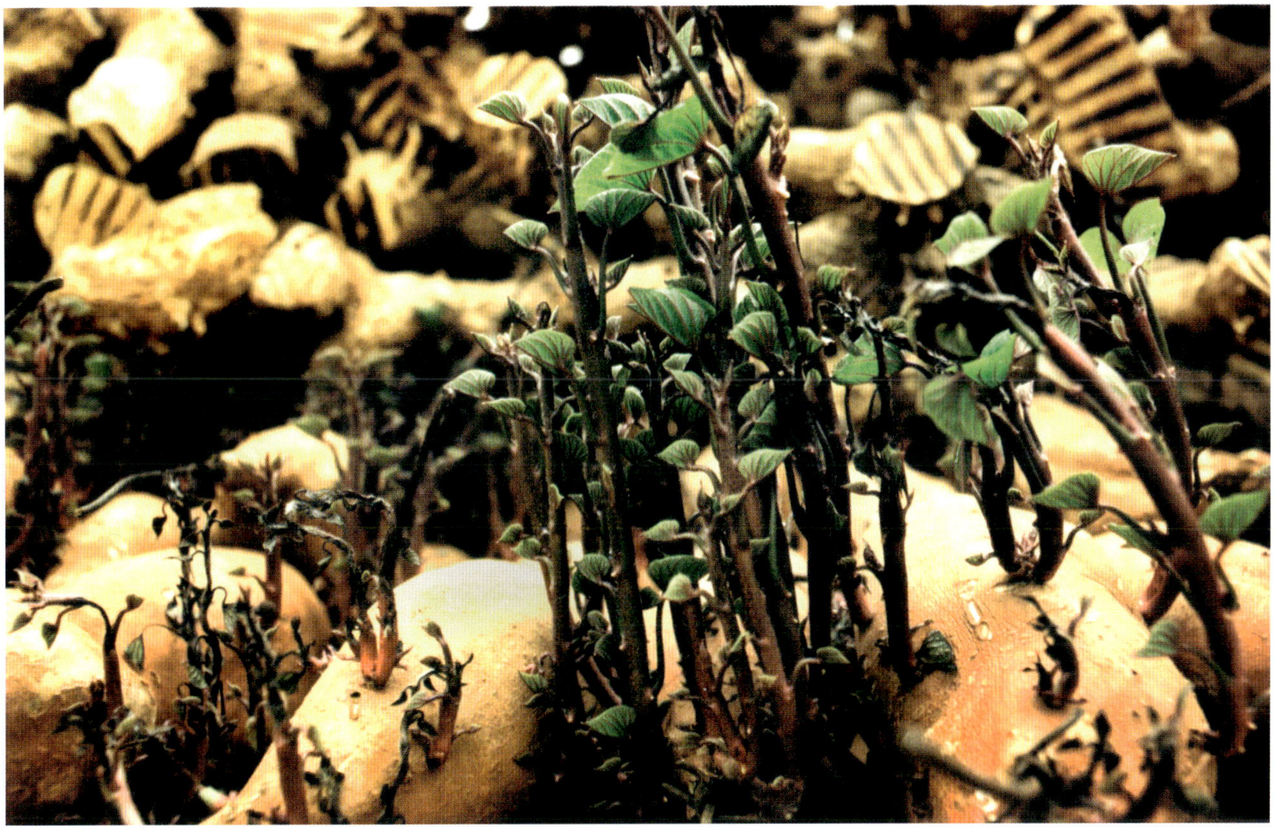

Endangered Roots | (1997) | fire, water, air, earth, glass, bamboo roots, barbed wire and sweet potatoes | 250 x 150 x 70 cm

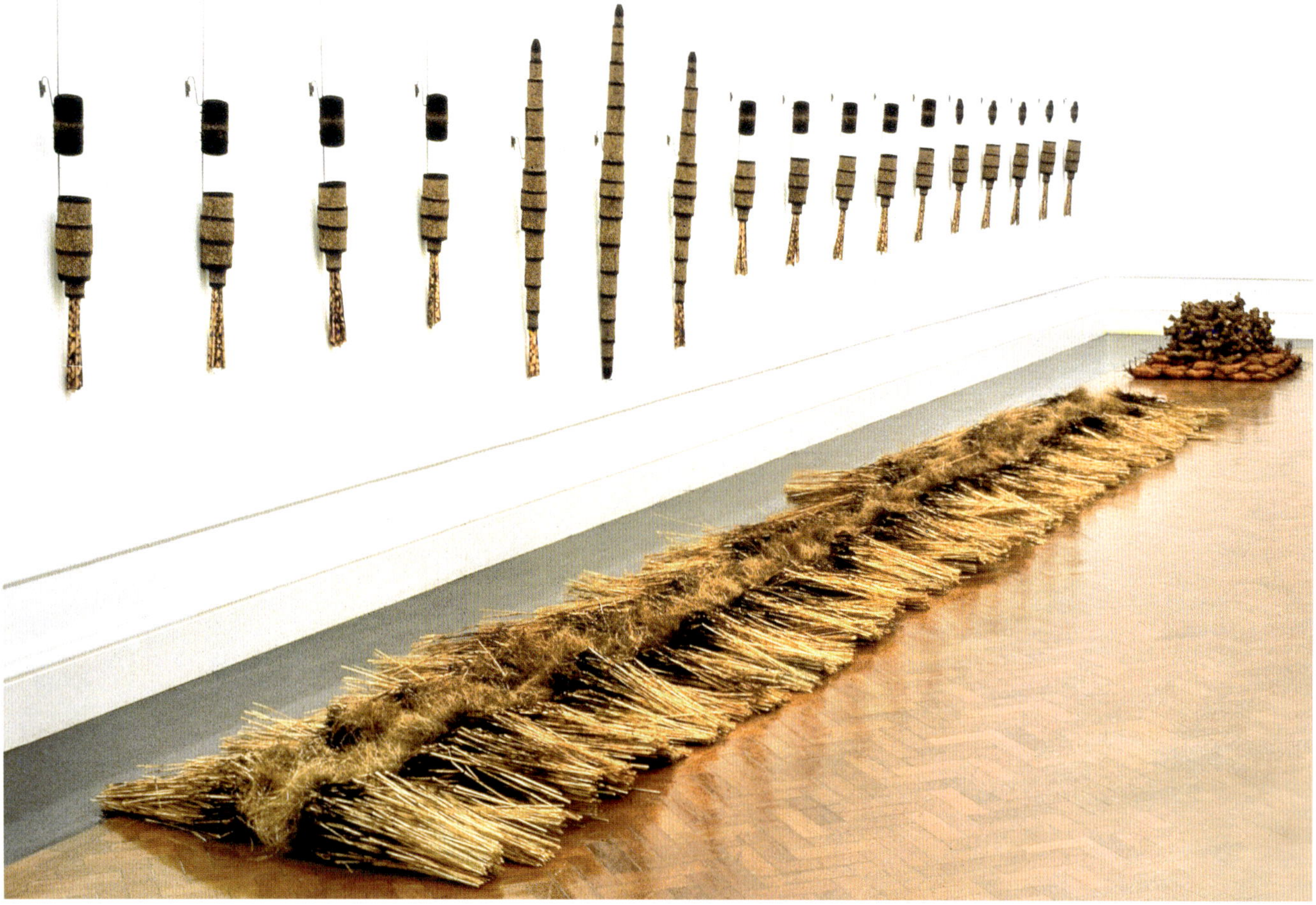

is placed next to a collection of string-bound stones. These look like slingshots. Stones have a wide symbolic reach, from sources of warmth to stone throwing;[11]

> It was winter, so we used to hold these stones. We used to put them inside the stove and then they get warm. Now inside the stove, there was this... tray where ashes could fall. So we'd put them there. So my sister had to put her stone there, or my brother has his stone, just like that. In the morning one would take out [his] stone... wrapping it with paper and going... down to [Nghungunyane Junior Secondary School].[12]

Other stones bear a chalk cross, an 'X' which resurfaces in, for example, *Elementary Units and Relationships 1* and *2* (2002). A wire star, fashioned from a chain link fence accompanies a key to nothing. These stars, according to Zulu, are easily mass-produced.

Melted puddles of sterile plastic mimic scalded skin. Other pieces of warped, stained gelatine suggest burned flesh; "the fat of the land, the fat of the animal – *umhlwehlwe* – slaughtered for ritual purposes, licked and 'eaten' by the *amadlozi*. For cleansing. Also *impepho* [incense] for the spirits/ancestors."[13] All this molten material looks like it was collected after a veld fire in an abandoned urban lot. The forms are often pure contingency, like the fire at the core of Zulu's work; "fire's wild properties are what make it valuable... People let it loose, like a cheetah trained to the hunt and allow it to roam."[14] Near the edge of the floor spread, smoked, singed chunks of dark honeycomb are the ground for stark white beads, the beads speaking of the adorned body. Manufactured honeycomb cardboard structures from industrial packaging follow the pattern of the evacuated home of bees; as happens in, for example, the hide and cardboard *Untitled* (1996).

Packages lie everywhere. Capsules – like the glass and plastic pill containers which so many of us know – are arranged in a row. Each has different contents: a flower in brandy, the foot of a dead bird with a different flower, the fine white silken seeds from a pod that looks like a human uterus and other things. Alongside these 'mock' medicines is a collection of small cellophane bags of sand retrieved from underground by communities of ants. The sand is clean and carefully sorted by these industrious non-human social creatures. There is soil too from moles, and Zulu reminds us that "moles... are thought to heal mad people, people with head sickness."[15]

Not far away again, we notice more dry gelatine, solidified wax (for hardening, polishing and preserving animal skins) and stones seared on the edges. These stones, according to Zulu, were masks for creating the burnt patterns in a number of works, ranging from *Study for Monumental Shield* (1998) to *Amatshehlathi (Stones of the Forest)* (2004). According to historian Clifton Crais in a recent interpretation of modern South African history, one way of fighting evil is by fire, with those designated as evil being stretched on the ground "and tortured by stinging ants and hot stones."[16]

Distributed parallel to the capsules I referred to earlier are newsprint parcels of indigenous medicines of the type that make up, for example, *Abduction of the Text – Main Theme Grassroots Frontline* (1998). The folding of these paper parcels is unusual and more elaborate than pure utility demands, and finds a parallel in bunches of leaves nearby, all tightly bundled. These abut a parcel of boards that looks for all the world like a book of manuscripts retrieved from some sinister library auto-da-fé.[17] A time-stained, smoke-blackened bird nest in congealed gelatine rests near coils of barbed wire.

Picking his way through this magical, macabre assemblage, the artist speaks of the wonder of wind-waves in grass, of burning fire-breaks around the home for fire protection, of hearth and warmth, ploughing and planting, of city life and its creative opportunities.The hot vapour of flame Zulu uses time and again encourages these thoughts in a formally spare but symbolically saturated aesthetic universe.

These objects, some extraordinary in their enigmatic slipperiness, remind me of the vagrant readings of poplarwood slips described in J. M. Coetzee's *Waiting for the Barbarians* (1980). Late in the book, Colonel Joll charges that the inscriptions on the inner surfaces of the string-bound white poplarwood slips found in the wooden chest in the Magistrate's apartment contain messages between the Magistrate and "other parties." The Magistrate has "no idea what they stand for," but offers a number of readings:

> Now let us see what the next one says. See, there is only a single character. It is the barbarian character *war*, but it has other senses too. It can stand for *vengeance,* and, if you turn it upside down... it can be made to read *justice*. There is no knowing which sense is intended. That is part of barbarian cunning. It is the same with the rest of these slips... They can be read in many orders. Further, each single slip can be read in many ways. Together they can be read as a domestic journal, or they can be read as a plan of war, or they can be turned on their sides and read as a history of the last years of the Empire – the old Empire, I mean...[18]

The referential avenues opened by Zulu's works seem to function in just these "many orders" and "many ways." Sometimes his expression is direct, sometimes distinctly allegorical. The wider frame for reading is largely the history and prehistory of colonial domination, and is shot through with what Homi Bhabha named "sly civility."[19]

Frontline with Centurion Models | (1997) | fire, water, air, earth, reed and metal | 1000 x 150 x 15 cm

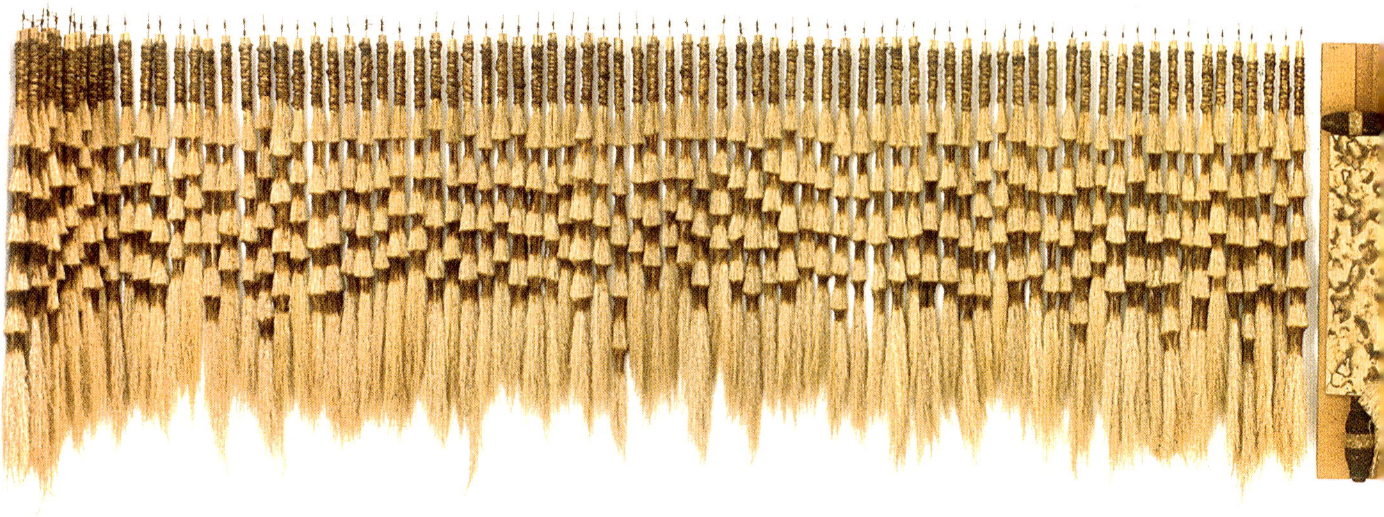

03. THE STUDIO (OUTSIDE)

In its elaborate austerity, Zulu's work sparks myriad associations. It is profligate in this contagion of connected meanings. Moving out of the studio, the artist speaks eloquently of the visual experiences which opened, illuminated and directed his aesthetic pathways. Zulu remembers, for example, this image from his early years in his home district and birthplace of Ixopo in the midlands of KwaZulu-Natal.

When the land was enclosed in Ixopo, his father's fortune – measured in cattle and goats – faltered. The relentless, forced fencing of land encroached on land for grazing. The artist vividly remembers particularly a barbed wire border between a white farmer's ever-expanding and his own father's ever-contracting land. Borders are deeply, painfully embedded in the South African imagination. For poet Breyten Breytenbach "Borders are as many scars, in places still sensitive to touch, likely to erupt unexpectedly, over which one is never too keen to linger."[20] Inevitably, Zulu's father's cattle overgrazed the depleted grass on his side of the fence, and soon strayed to the greener pastures as cattle do. And when an animal strayed, it ended up shot, stolen or detained. Many an animal starved to death in detention.

The stunningly beautiful Ixopo region is in fact the setting for ancient and very current rural conflicts over land, settlement and pasture. The Midlands area lies at the heart of Jonny Steinberg's remarkable book *Midlands*, published in 2002. The author describes a "countryside clattered with the noise of its cruel politics, each new scene a micro-world of stubborn memories and pernicious games."[21] The divide between different symbolic and economic worlds, different entitlements, different ideas of being, belonging, possessing is decisively drawn across this fractured, bounded world, a land of cultivated grievances and unhealed hurts, wounds dressed in barbed wire.

Zulu goes on to describe his father's land as increasingly arid, barren and overgrazed, while the land was watered and fertile on the other side. His father's land became a depleted, ungiving island in a sea of colonial and neo-colonial social engineering. What Zulu recalls here uncannily echoes the opening words of arguably the best-known South African fable of the 1950s, Alan Paton's *Cry the Beloved Country.*[22] Paton's novel, set in Ixopo, opens,

> The grass is rich and matted, you cannot see the soil. It holds the rain and mist, and they seep into the ground, feeding the streams of every kloof. It is well-tended, and not too many cattle feed upon it, not too many fires burn it, laying bare the soil... Where you stand the grass is rich and matted, you cannot see the soil. But the rich green hills break down. They fall into the valley below, and falling, change their nature. For they grow red and bare; they cannot hold the rain and mist, and the streams are dry in the kloofs. Too many cattle feed upon the grass, and too many fires have burned it.[23]

Paton repeats these words again in the second book[24] of the novel. And, the word *Ixopo* mimics the sound the hooves of cattle, or human feet, lifting out of mud. It is an aesthetic, expressive word that, with Paton's words and Zulu's recollections, orientates us in appreciating more deeply the imaginative world the artist inhabits.

 Frontline 1 | (1997) | fire, water, air, earth, grass, paper, metal and barbed wire | 600 x 100 x 15 cm

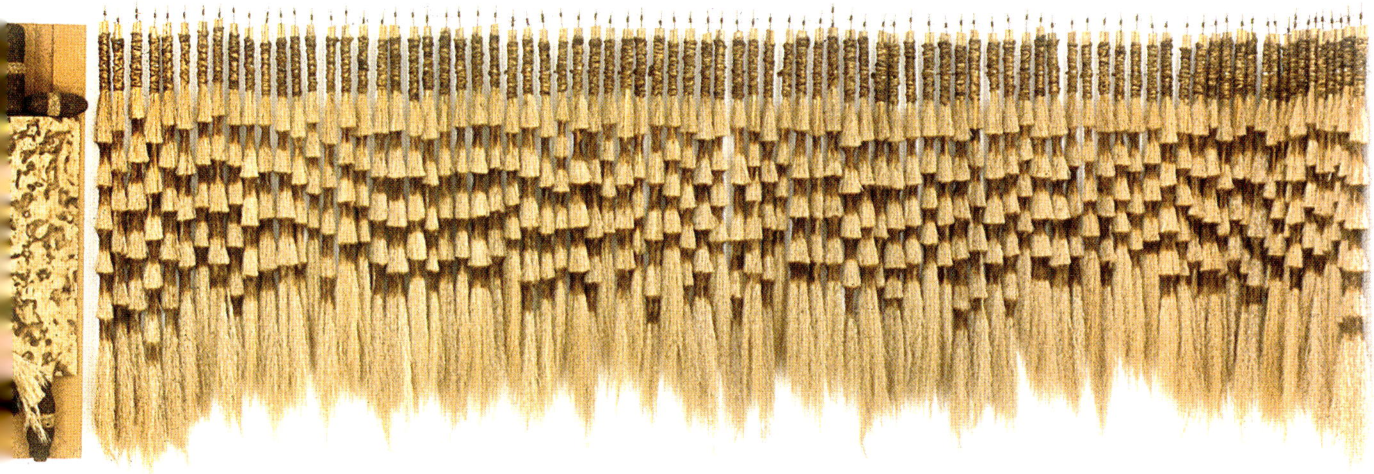

Whatever else we may need by way of orientation can be gleaned from another site: Zulu's studio at the Amakhono Art Centre, now abandoned. West of Johannesburg, south of the suburbs of Florida, Amakhono is an old mine property, a many-roomed house complete with derelict formal garden, empty pond, *khakibos* (blackjack) and mounds of junk. Alien species of bluegum trees – gluttons for already scarce water, shedding candle-bark like peeling skin – line the once-grand avenue to the entrance of the property. An ornate wrought iron gate between heavy brick posts stands chained and stranded in a ruined perimeter wall. Outside this wall – a useless sign of some past insecurity and need for separation – the grassy veld opens onto distant mine dumps. The dumps are shades of bilious yellow, stained with cyanide and powdered iron pyrites. Pyrites is better known as fool's gold.

Poet Lionel Abrahams, in memory of a poetry reading held at a mine dump during a storm, constructs a desultory poetics of the industrial sublime in his poem "Place." The storm is "the drama of cloud and wind, lightning flares, bombs of thunder and sudden sniping drops,"[25] and the place "shallow, violent, bleak, a drained and shadeless wedge of earth, uncultivated, mired by money-miners... sterile and brilliant with residual poison and gold."

Some dumps are gridded with the hardy pampas grass Zulu uses in a number of works. This grid is meant to stabilise the fine toxic dust that blows into the air and onto surrounding suburbs when winds are high. Some of the dumps are currently being reprocessed for the gold that escaped earlier, technically cruder, extraction processes. The residue of man-made sand – the remaindered dust of the dead labour of so many workers – is then dumped back into the abandoned mine shafts. Workers have actually been entombed deep beneath the surface, lost in a landscape already scarred by too many unmarked graves,[26] something that gives Zulu's *Shaft Street Runs Through Stormhill* (1995) a sombre edge. Zulu's unpublished "Miner's Prayer" gives concrete form to his consciousness of the conditions under which miners work; "here we sink / drown down the intestines / in dungeon dark pit /... shall we see the sun / rising again dear Lord?"[27] The open mouths of the disused mine shafts are fringed by barbed wire and verdant vegetation. Dank mist from the heated bowels of the earth stains the wire black and sustains the greenery. The hot air produces an eco-system doubtless peculiar to the mouths of shafts.

On the surface around Amakhono veld fires, controlled and otherwise, periodically rage through the parched winter grass. The intentional fires are meant to drive the snakes away and create firebreaks. The ground itself is often reduced to ash and blackened dust, revealing what the dry grass hid, what had been abandoned, what had been dumped, what had lived, what had died. Burned to a stubble, the veld discloses discarded rubble, domestic debris, industrial rubbish and a million forms of human waste. The rusting, obsolescent machinery of goldmines fallen on hard times is also exposed. The themes, materials and processes that make up Zulu's work are visible in both Ixopo and Amakhono; repetition, resistance, desire and violence, barbed wire, soil, grass, black and white ash, industrial castaways, cattle capital, cultural breakdown and economic hardship, desire. And fire. In his poem "The Will" Zulu writes "an African art aesthetician / all my scripts should be deployed / to orchestrate / a continental rebellion."

04. SMOKE SIGNALS

Sandile Zulu is bedazzled by fire, perhaps like all of us, by its richness and riskiness: "Once paper gets on fire it is very fascinating to me. I can control fire to create ordered designs."[28] The artist draws a quiet vitality from this fascination. Fire mediates radical contingency, chance, chaos; "Fire is a difficult medium to control... I use flame as an alternative approach... I want to feel the relationship between the material, the medium and me."[29] These words capture the often-precarious relation between medium and body, order and disorder, enchantment and banality, reflection and risk in his work. Firebrands are volatile. Spreading like wildfire is dangerous. Fire is literally contagious. Firebreaks – the controlled burning of veld – reduce the contagion, that danger, fire fighting fire. Firewalls are part of the virtual e-world, defending against data pillage and viral sabotage. As Paul Edmunds points out "Zulu's management of organic processes leaves one with the sense that they are just barely restrained, threatening to break the geometry he imposes."[30]

Zulu situates his use of fire in a strong sense of human community in both deep and present time. As philosopher Friedrich von Schlegel put it, "nothing is more common than fire."[31] A sense of the time before traumatic historical time, of pre-lapsarian idyll, is also bodied forth by fire; "Before there was a Europe, there was fire."[32] In the introduction to a scientific book on wildland fire management Stephen Pyne and his colleagues write about fire's African source:

> Africa is a fire continent... Africa sparkles with more routine fire than any landmass. The significance of African fire, however, derives not only from its extent but its antiquity. Here anthropogenic fire originated and has resided longer than anywhere else... Fire flourishes because most of sub-Saharan Africa has the environment to sustain it... Wet seasons grow fuels; dry ones ready them for burning.[33]

Fire is a social and spiritual phenomenon for Zulu, cementing human communities across time and space. The pre-Socratic Heraclitus most comes to mind here, "Fire is exchanged for all things, and all things for fire."[34] A shared purifying energy,[35] warming and animating us in what Zulu calls "cultural conflagration."[36] Zulu also links fire to lightning, a metaphysical and sometimes fatal phenomenon in parts of South Africa. The phenomenon is mythologised in the "lightning bird," an agent of magic and evil.[37] Historian Clifton Crais cites a case from 1856, where "the witch-finder discovered small amounts of fat in the hut of the accused witch, perhaps the fat of the impundulu, the magical lightning bird that serves witches in their evil work."[38] But in the main Zulu links lightning – the spontaneous non-human source of fire – with revelation, life, death and (re)birth, and resurrection, perhaps expressed most explicitly in Zulu's *Birth of a New World* (1996).[39]

Fire is a violent energy. The anarchic ambivalence of fire, at once a creative and destructive force, parallels a similar ambivalence in violence itself.[40] M. B. Pranger confronts what he considers the paradox of violence: while "we are inclined to think of civilization as a process in which physical violence is gradually banished... do we not," he asks, "pay with a certain life-lessness [sic] for the exclusion of violence from our works of art?"[41] Zulu grapples with this uncomfortable question in his use of fire and other natural energies.

Probably the most widely known use of fire in European art is in the work of the French artist Yves Klein, examples of which include *Fire Wall* (1961) and his investigations into *Pneumatic Architecture.*[42] Many other works in Anglo-American post-war art can be cited here: Jan Dibbets's *TV as a Fireplace* (1969), John Baldessari's *Cremation Project* (1970) and Ana Mendieta's *Firecracker Silueta* (1973-77).[43] For more expressly ritual fire, we could consider Joseph Beuys's *Hearth 1* (1974) and *Hearth 2* (1978), Mary Beth Edelson's *Where is our Fire?* (1979)[44] and Bill Viola's *The Crossing* (1996).[45]

Fire was and is used in so-called traditional southern African poker-work on mat racks.[46] As an image, or icon, fire features in numerous South African artworks. The almost paradigmatic colonial image by Frederick I'Ons, *Kaffirs Watching for the Return of Their Dead Warriors* (n.d.), depicts a landscape at sunrise, with figures around a burning tree on the crest of a koppie. The work represents one view of what happened on 18 February 1857, when the Xhosa peoples waited for the rising sun to herald the fulfilment of the healing prophecies of Nongqawuse and Mhlakaza.[47] Figures of fire also occur in the work of many 'modernist' artists, including Gerard Bengu's *Untitled* (three men fighting a fire at night) (ca. 1940) and Simon Mnguni's *Untitled* (witchdoctor outside his hut with lightning) (ca. 1943).

Contemporary examples would include Durant Sihlali's *The Fire Place* (ca. 1985), Nthubu David Koloane's *Blaze* (1994), Kim Berman's *Fires of the Truth Commission* (1998/9) and Bernie Searle's recent "Vapour" (2004), "Heat" (2004) and "Torch" (2004) series, all of which picture fire.[48] Fire as process and medium of depiction has been used extensively by Clive van den Berg in *Mine Dump Project* (1995), *Small Excavations* (1996) and *Metal* (1998).[49]

There is also Kagiso Patrick Mautloa's *Brazier* (1992), in which Mautloa constructs an assemblage from an actual brazier. Writer and scholar Andries Oliphant describes the brazier (the *mbaula*) as "a makeshift, improvised grid... a vessel, which can both contain and radiate the heat of fire," a vessel which is both a "fire-place for the homeless and a stove for shack dwellers." But Oliphant also points to the important social dimension of the brazier as a "mobile gathering point as well as an appliance in informal fast-food trading." Like the heat it radiates and contains, the brazier also has a darker aspect; "the vapours of the burning coal and other toxic materials can be asphyxiating and deadly in sealed places."[50] Fires, kindled

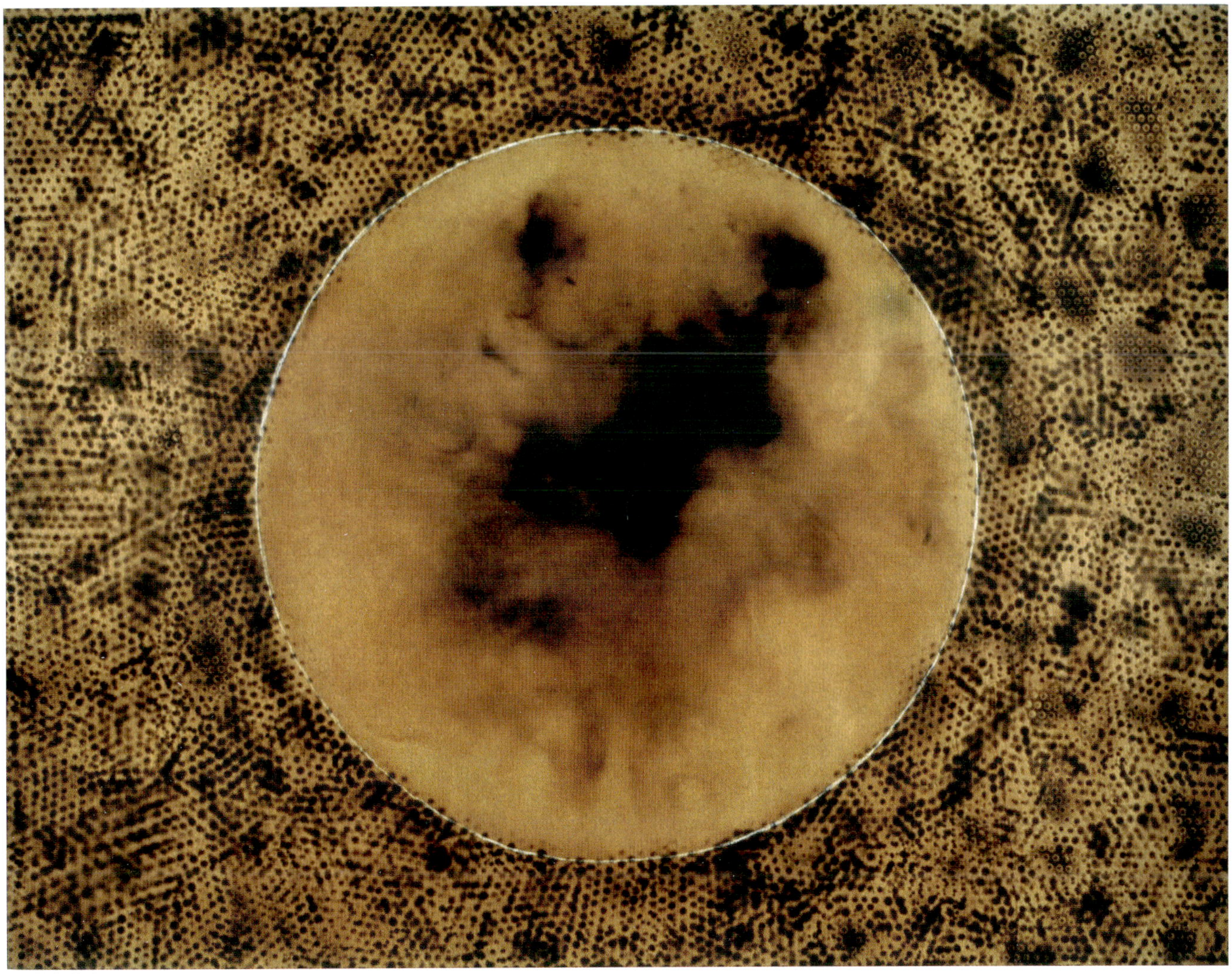

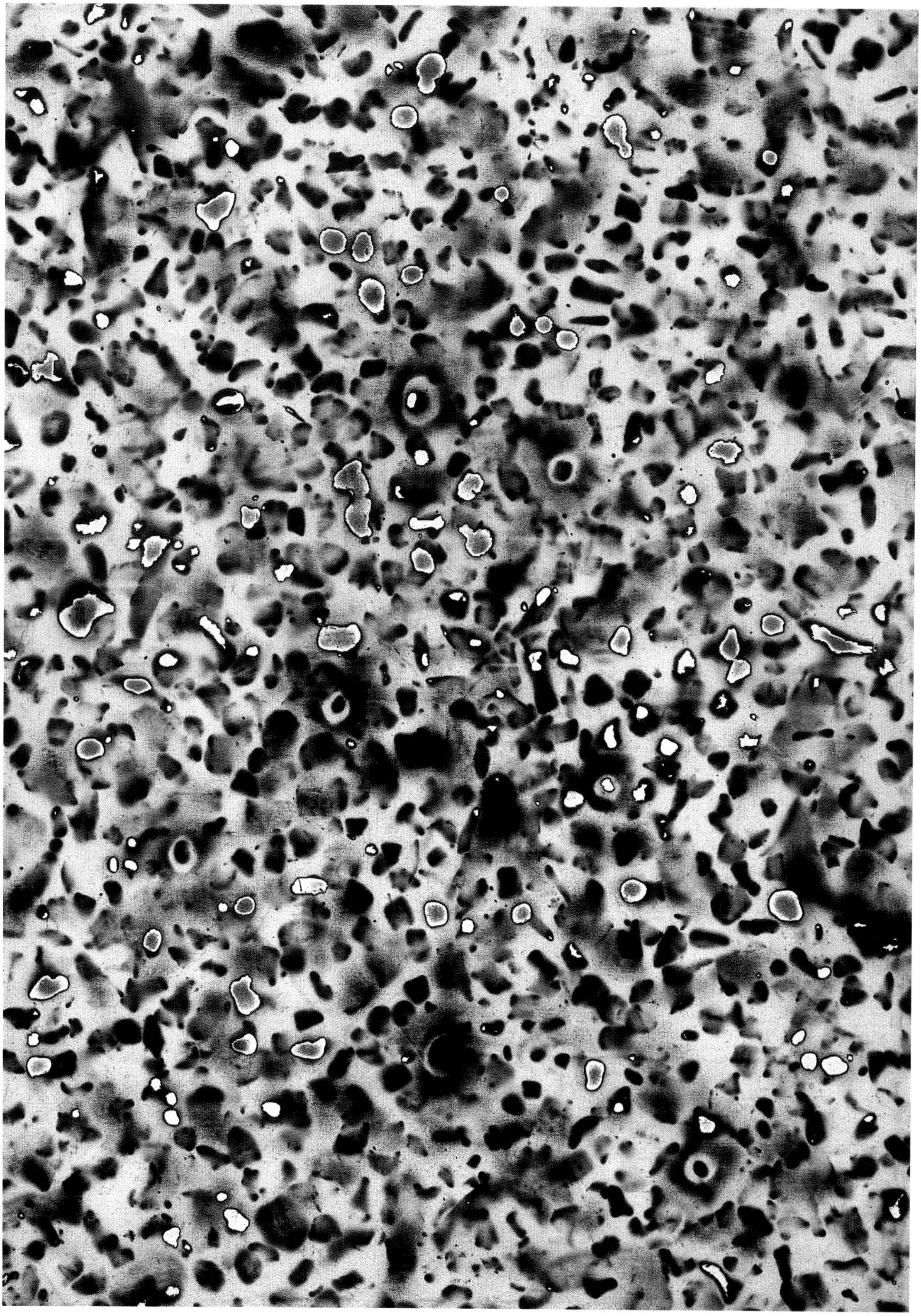

26	Artomic 2	(1997)	fire, water, air, earth, stones and canvas	180 x 100 cm

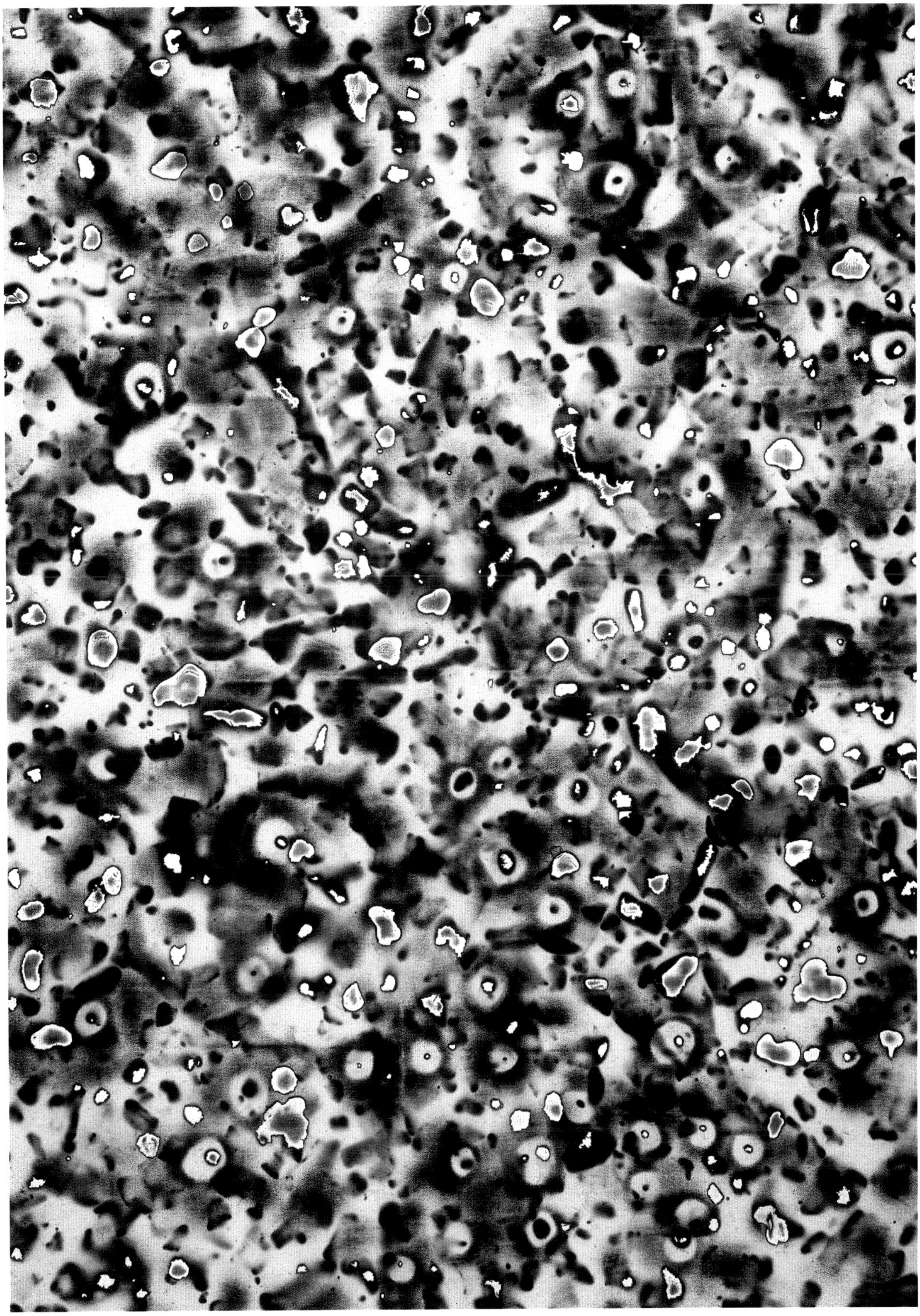

Artomic 3 | (1997) | fire, water, air, earth, stones and canvas | 180 x 100 cm

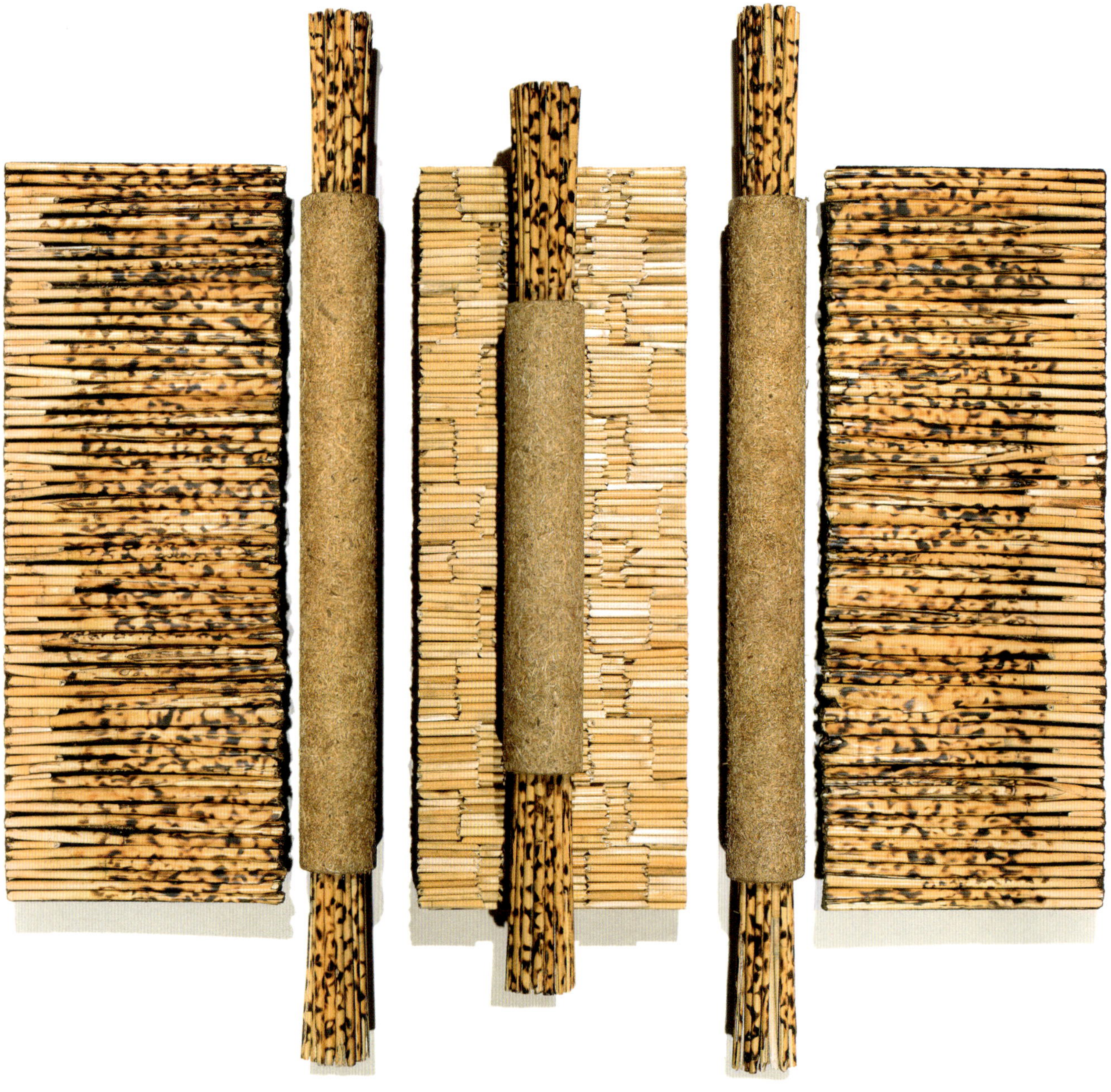

05. SYMBOL AND SENSATION

from untended candles and other sources of light and warmth in the absence of electricity, often rage through the shacks of informal settlements, destroying lives and property.

In Zulu's hands both fire and violence function almost homoeopathically: *similia similibus curantur* (like cures like).[51] Peter Pesic, in a remarkable narrative of the hidden quest in ancient science, observes that fire "applied moderately and in due measure, can induce magnetic behaviour in an otherwise indifferent rock. There is some delicate interconnection that moderate fire promotes and extreme fire disrupts."[52] Zulu fights fire with fire in a way which recalls this "delicate interconnection," and it is here that part of the psychosocial impulse to redemption in his creative work lies. The artist takes an explicitly homoeopathic position when he states that "a little bit of the poison cures," and when he implies that historical hurt and violence can service beauty, vitality and intellectual growth;[53] "I aspire to make works that stand for life."[54]

Fire burns deep within our cultural imaginary, our metaphors, our material lives. In using fire as his primary medium, Zulu draws on a rich pan-human legacy of ideas, objects and events. Fire is protogenic for creation and destruction, appearance and reality, history and the present. A few significant and better known ancient narratives of fire come readily to mind here: Heraclitus's view of the soul as fire, vital breath inspired (inhaled) at birth and expired (exhaled) at death,[55] Plato and his cave of shadows[56] and Prometheus,[57] who allegedly stole fire from the gods, gave it to humanity and was punished. Fire signals the onset of human control of nature and perhaps the first spark of an expressive, imaginative mental life.

The history and phenomenology of fire offers much insight into Zulu's work process. Myths of the control of fire like the one of Prometheus abound in originary fables of becoming. A good example here is Credo Mutwa's "The Sacred Story of the Tree of Life: The Self-Created";

> Of time and Nothingness,
> A most tiny nigh invisible spark
> Of living Fire was born
>
> This tiny, so tiny spark of Fire could think
> And grew conscious of its lonely state...
>
> There was nothing for the spark to feed and grow,
> So it fed upon itself....[58]

Fire, according to Susan Stewart, is "the ultimate image of consumption," echoing Mutwa's words here and indeed those of Leonardo da Vinci; "The light above the candle is fire in a chain; consuming that it consumes itself."[59]

The South African works that figure fire confirm fire's presence in South African visual history and culture.[60] Zulu engages this history and culture in his work, sometimes directly, sometimes obliquely. Selected moments in his igniting of the fuse of history and culture are illuminating.

During the infamous and much mythologised Battle of Blood River,[61] on 16 December 1838, the Zulu army set fire to the veld and wagons by setting alight the grass plaited around their throwing spears.[62] Leaping ahead a century, we find, in 1938, a ceremonial re-enactment of the Great Trek and the keeping of the vow of Blood River taken at the battle. This spectacle included massed flaming torches "like a river of fire,"[63] recalling the inflamed romantic symbolism of fascism:

> From a fire lit at the former headquarters of the defeated Zulu commander, a relay team of boys brought torches through the countryside. Arriving in Pretoria, they were surrounded by women who hovered over the flames, burning the fringes of their handkerchiefs and bonnets, to have lasting mementos of the event... The Great Trek gave our people its soul... It will always show us the beacons on our path and serve as the lighthouse in our night.[64]

The Voortrekker Monument itself houses a constant flame that "symbolises the flame of Civilization in South Africa." The 'barbarism' (personified by Dingane's warriors) yielded to 'civilization,' and this yielding became a key element in the vow the Voortrekkers first made on 9 December 1838, anticipating Dingane's attack at Blood River.[65]

Delving deeper back into prehistory, we find that control of fire was one of the technical innovations of *Acheulean hominids.* According to Peter Mitchell the charcoal deposits argued to be hearths in Pomongwe Cave, Bambata and the Cave of Hearths may have natural rather than cultural origins. The black staining observed by Professor Raymond Dart in the late 1950s at Makapansgat, not too far from Amakhono Art Centre as the crow flies, encouraged Dart to name the humans from the site *Australopithecus prometheus,*[66] but Mitchell suggests natural origins for these stains. Aeons later, at Makapansgat, the boers, avenging an alleged massacre, reportedly killed a large group of Ndebele seeking refuge in the caves by asphyxiating them, an incident which has been heavily mythologised in narratives of Afrikaner nationalism.[67]

If at Makapansgat the origins of fire are unclear, the "ash, charred bone and fire-shattered stone throughout the *Acheulean* levels at Wonderwerk" are, Mitchell argues, likely to show evidence of hominid activity. Even before this – the late Lower Pleistocene period – Swartkrans revealed bone fragments darkened by carbon residues, but how much these were the product of "fire management extended to making fire at will" was also unclear. It was archaeologist C.K. Brain who discovered signs of the tending and control of fire by the earliest hominids at these caves. Brain speculates "that the early stages of fire-management would have relied on gathered fire from naturally occurring conflagrations," and while "the gathering of fire is not as impressive an intellectual achievement as deliberate fire-making, it must nevertheless have been an immensely important milestone in the manipulation of the natural environment by early hominids."[68]

What did fire do for those who controlled and harnessed it? For Peter Mitchell,

> As well as extending the range of edible foods, fire must have offered added security from predators, warmth and the possibility of making fire-hardened artefacts. It may have assisted the territorial expansion of *Acheulean hominids* which is evident by at least 1 million years ago.[69]

Much later in historical time, around 1632, Autshumao, the head of a group of cattleless Khoikhoi, lit crucial signal fires "to attract those wishing to forward or receive letters" on the infamous Robben Island.[70]

From here the leap to the notorious farm burning associated with the invention of the concentration camp during the second South African War (1899-1902) is not great. In this war Lord Kitchener (1850-1916) "vigorously pursued [Lord Roberts's] 'scorched-earth' policy and greatly extended the scope of what were started as refugee camps for burghers loyal to Britain, and their families,"[71] but which became something quite different.

Another signal moment in our history of fire was the voice of Sol Tshekisho Plaatje, founding member of the precursor to the African National Congress, journalist, linguist, writer and court interpreter. Plaatje wrote an indignant response to the screening of that "inflammatory bioscope film" D.W. Griffiths's *Birth of a Nation* in Johannesburg in 1931.[72] The movie was released in 1915 and was essentially a whitewash of Ku Klux Klan history (an emblem of which is the burning cross).[73] Plaatje asks

> Why should a film, banned in the country of its origin, be licensed to fan the embers of race hatred in [Johannesburg] South Africa? Some of us who saw it in England are surprised at the alleged *Immortal Masterpiece* and wonder whether the t in the first word of the title [was] dropped into the type by the carelessness of some printer. Ugly black peril scenes are shown until emotions of white people are worked up to fever heat.[74]

Some two decades later, in 1951, the so-called War Veteran's Torch Commando organised massed torchlight rallies against the then Government's strategy to disenfranchise 'coloured' voters.[75] In the late 1950s one of the more incendiary acts of resistance was the spectacular public burning of the 'dompas' by Chief Albert Luthuli, Nelson Mandela, other leaders and countless numbers of ordinary people during the defiance campaign.[76]

But it is the Soweto uprising of 16 June 1976, when Zulu was a young man, which becomes the red-letter day in our archive of historical fire. Fire flares in rage in Mandla Nalazi's poem "June's blaze."[77] The conflagration of the uprising provoked and stimulated many poets and writers, all seeking to tap the rhetorical and poetic potency of the phenomenon. One striking image, for example, is expressed in Mbuyiseni Oswald Mtshali's "Hector Peterson: The Young Martyr" published ten years after the uprising; "the ghetto was ablaze, rising flames were gigantic tongues, licking the soft bellies of hovering helicopters."[78] Artist and writer Matsemela Manaka also turned to incendiary metaphors to express resistance; "the flames of your fire reared and raged on, your enemy could not douse only daze the blaze."[79] Poet Nolizwe Mnyaka's view of fire[80] is to turn away from the violence of the historical moment, a violence traceable through a jungle of mediations to the enlightenment project in Europe. Enlightenment and racist colonialism were, after all, not strangers.[81] A mural made as a backdrop for a play by the Imvaba collective in 1989 for the June 16 rally shows Sam Nzima's iconic photograph of the fatally wounded Hector Peterson against a background of flames.[82] The work suggests the iconography of Christian martyrdom.[83]

But the most significant icon of the harrowing decade of the 1980s was the burning tyre. Winnie Mandela, in Njabulo Ndebele's eponymous novel, utters her incendiary words of the 1980s, words which echoed around much of the world. "We have no guns – we have only stones, boxes of matches, petrol. Together, hand in hand, with our boxes of matches and our necklaces we will liberate this country."[84] The burning tyre associated with necklacing branded South Africa's liberation struggle[85] in its final decade, burned into the consciousness of millions. From the painted clay figure made by a nine-year old of "something seen recently"[86] to William Kentridge's early *Luncheon Party* (1985), the burning tyre (explicit or otherwise) has become part of the South African imagination. We need only consider Billy Mandindi's harrowing *Necklace of Death* (1986), Kendell Geers's *Eeny Meeni Miny Mo* (ca. 1988) and Minette Vári's pristine, exsanguinated *Firestone* (1995).[87] Geers's inflammatory *The Terrorist's Apprentice: Bastard* (2002) also refers to necklacing, and comprises a simple, glass-covered installation of a match. The work has many incarnations, this one being 18 carat gold. The original is a one-off, common wood and sulphur match.[88]

Detail, **Abduction of the Text – Main Theme Grassroots Frontline** | (1998) | fire, water, air, earth, newsprint, grass and roots | 1200 x 300 x 30 cm

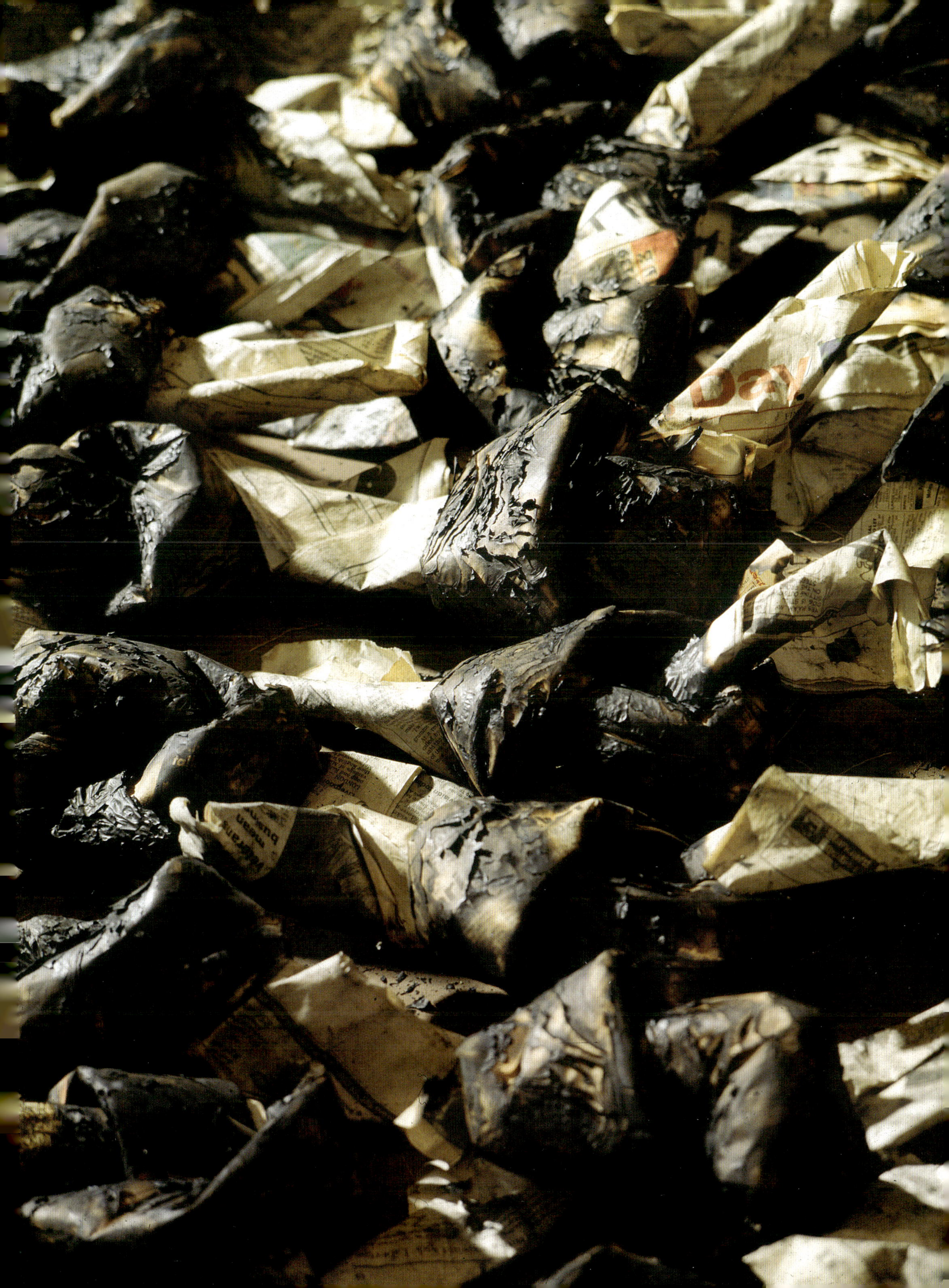
Day

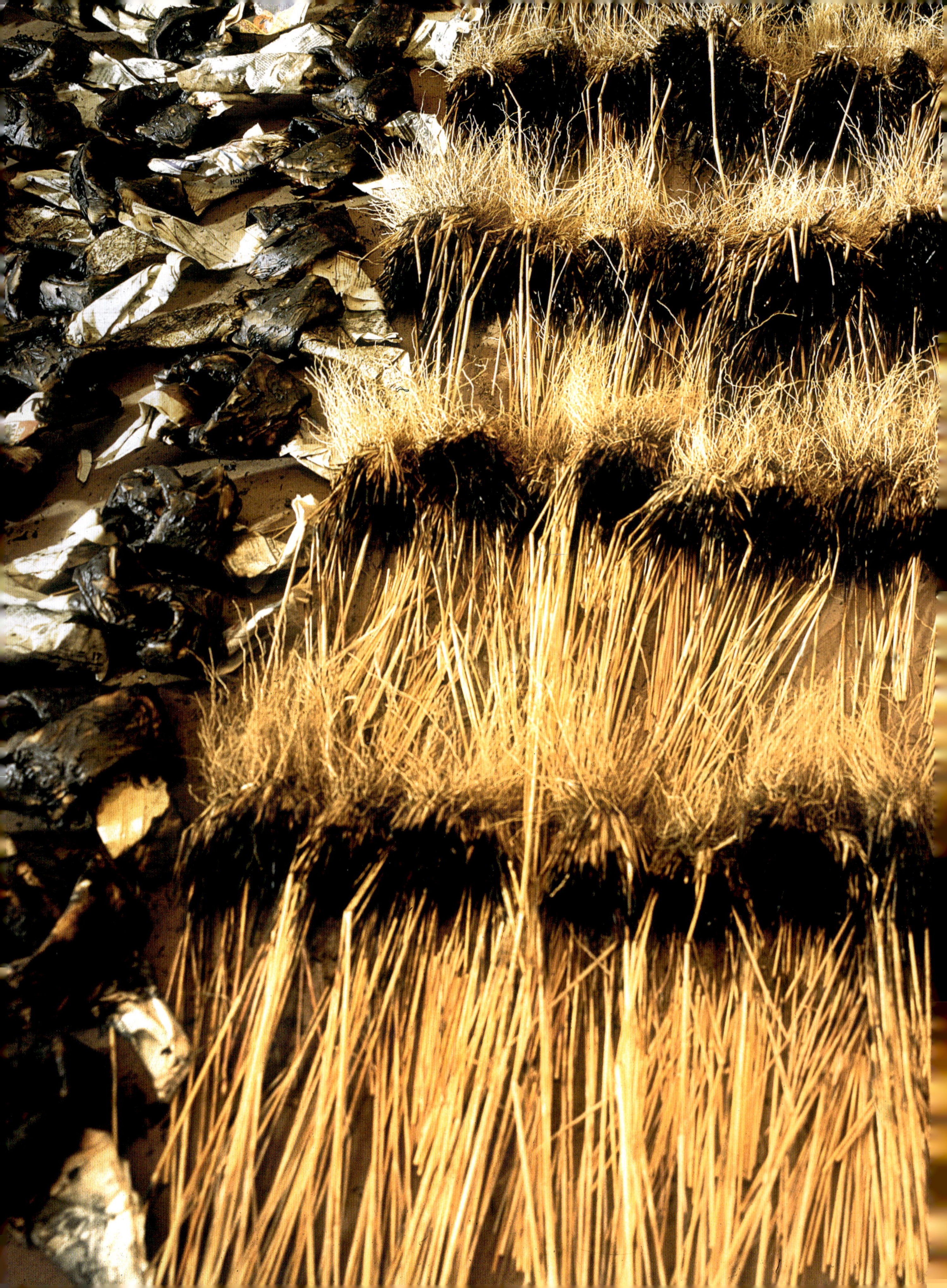

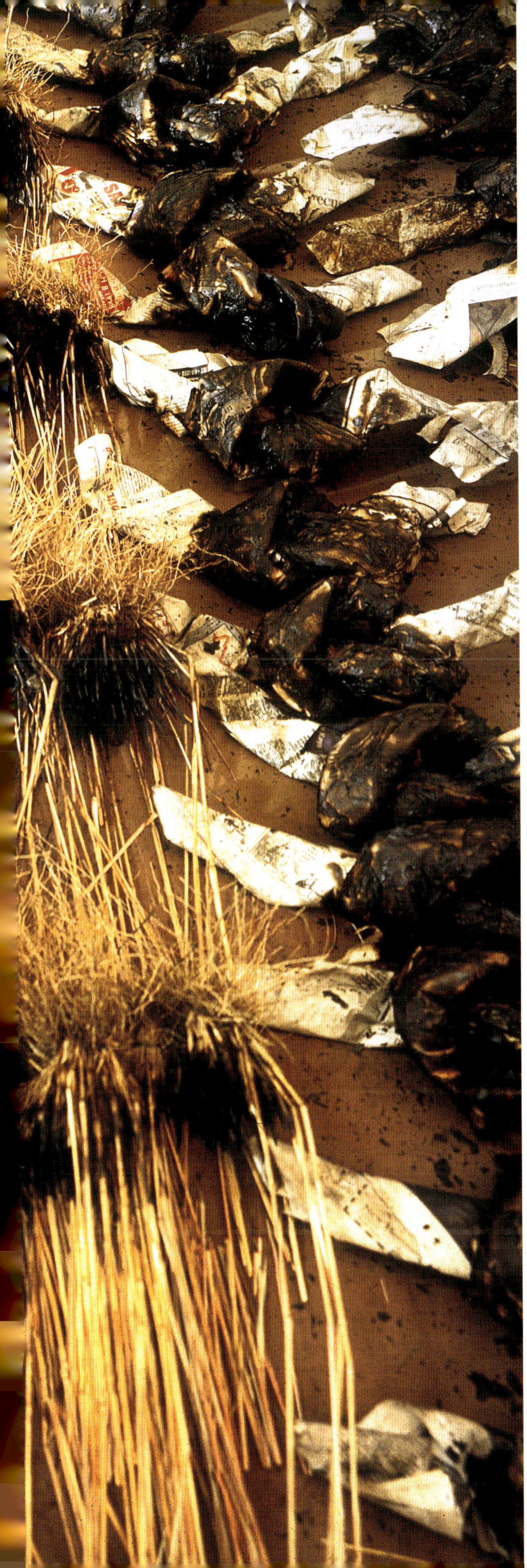

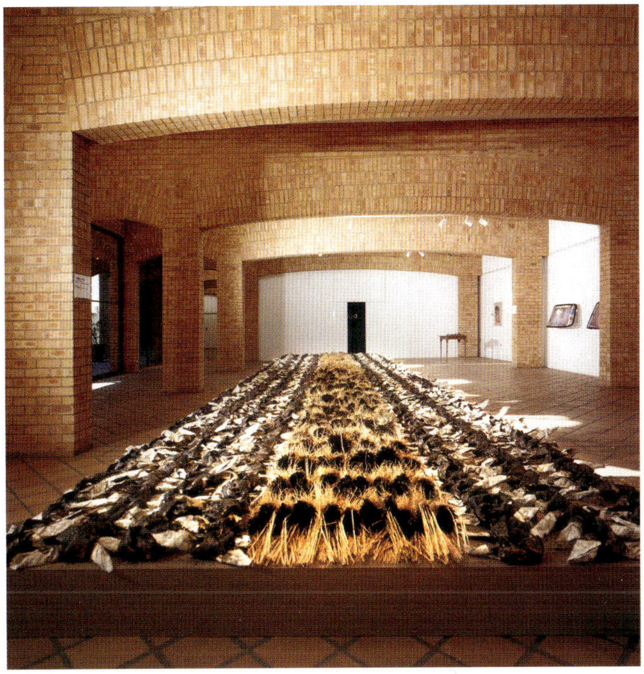

The incendiary part of the necklacing phenomenon had a frightening echo in the talk of other burnings during the Truth and Reconciliation Commission in the late 1990s. In one now notorious account, a distraught mother cries "They braaied my son while they drank and laughed."[89] Jacques Pauw recounts this scene:

> In a dry ditch on the slightly elevated river bank, a shallow grave was dug with bushveld wood and tyres. The two corpses were lifted onto the pyre and as the sun set over the Eastern Transvaal bushveld, two fires were lit, one to burn the bodies to ashes, the other for the security policemen to sit around, drinking and grilling meat... It was just another job to be done. In the beginning it smells like a meat braai, in the end like the burning of bones. It takes about seven to nine hours to burn the bodies to ashes. 'We would have our own little braai and just keep on drinking.'"[90]

Artist Johannes Segogela produced a small tableau titled *The Devil's Party* in 1991.[91] This work presents the horror of hell, be it religious or social, made all the more horrifying because the scene feels like a three-dimensional cartoon. A figure is tied to a spit being turned

Abduction of the Text – Main Theme Grassroots Frontline	(1998)
fire, water, air, earth, newsprint, grass and roots	1200 x 300 x 30 cm

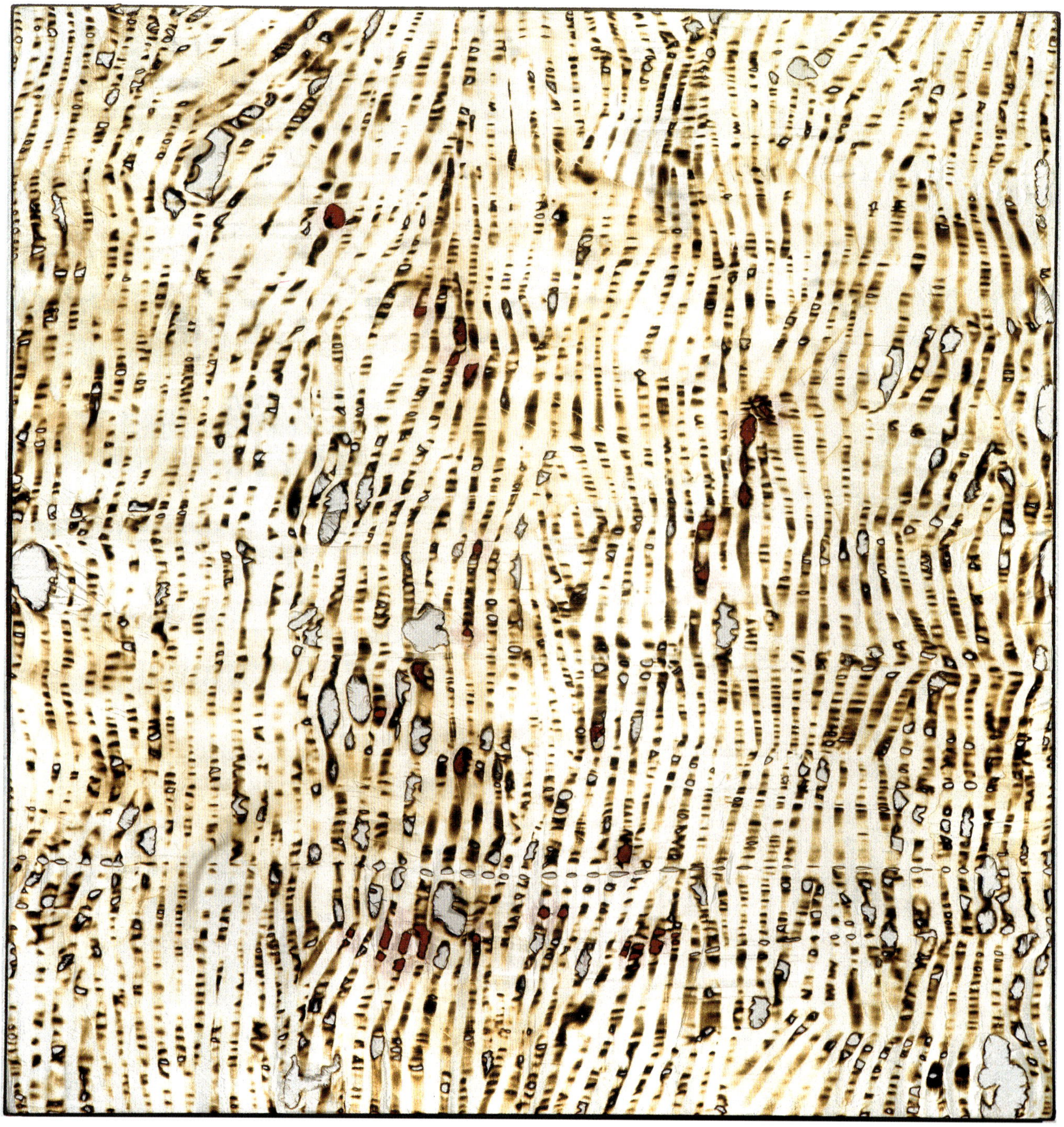

by two otherworldly night figures, the fire burning below. The subtext is surely a version of Christian eschatology that intersects unhappily with what happened at Vlakplaas. The infernal hell of each is cut from the same cloth as the other.

The hell that Vlakplaas was begins to be extinguished by the 'flame of freedom' lit by Nelson Mandela in his Robben Island cell on the first day of the new millennium. Addressing himself to Thabo Mbeki, Mandela proclaimed, "I hand over this flame of freedom to you. You are the only person in this country who should receive this flame and keep it burning and pass it on to younger generations."[92] Fire in Zulu's practice invokes this traumatic history, but also goes beyond trauma to deeper time, a time where fire and civilization are intimately entangled.[93]

A recent popular history of our journey to democracy opens with a long prologue on fire. The author, Michael Morris, describes the passage of fire in our history, observing that, unlike fleeting smoke,

> the leftovers of fire itself are more lasting – tempered steel, blackened rocks, charred wood, refined gold, memories of intimacy, memories of pain, scars, wealth, industry, monuments, ash.[94]

From this discussion it is easy for us to appreciate that embedded in fire and its relation to visual art is a force and symbol of profound and deeply destabilising ambivalence. The works of Sandile Zulu, where fire is image and process, encourage us to meditate on this ambivalence. Fire is not the source of illusion to be dissipated as when the chains of Plato's prisoners are struck. Fire offers more than a device for dispelling illusions. An active force, fire in Zulu's work resonates with the qualities spelled out by Gaston Bachelard in his remarkable ruminations on the phenomenon:

> Fire and heat provide modes of explanation in the most varied domains, because they have been for us the occasion of unforgettable memories, for simple and decisive personal experiences. Fire... can explain anything... It is intimate and it is universal. It lives in our heart. It lives in the sky. It rises from the depths of the substances and offers itself with the warmth of love. Or it can go back down into the substance and hide there, latent and pent-up, like hate and vengeance. Among all phenomena it is really the only one to which there can be so definitely attributed the opposing values of good and evil. It shines in Paradise. It burns in Hell. It is gentleness and torture... it can contradict itself.[95]

In his *Study for Attire* (1995), made during an artist's workshop on Réunion Island, Zulu used volcanic rocks to pin the canvas down while he manipulated the flame of a blowtorch to create blackened marks on the visual field. In *Artomic Passage 1, 2, 3, 4* and *5* (1999) and *Abduction of the Text: Total Eclipse* (1999) we find the scorched surface contained in a circle, suggesting a cold sun, or the dead, perhaps once-living, surface of the moon. An historical dimension to the eclipse returns us to the battle of Isandlhwana on 22 January 1879.[96] In this historic battle, the Zulu armies led by Chiefs Ntshingwayo kaMahole of the Khoza and Mavumengwana kaNdlela of the Ntuli defeated Lord Chelmsford's army during a British expansionist campaign.[97]

During the battle there was a partial eclipse which was taken as an omen by the Zulu armies.[98] The nearly 20,000 Zulu soldiers mustered for the attack had in fact being lying in wait for the new moon, in the belief that it was dangerous to fight when the moon was 'empty.'[99] The omen of *umnyama* [mystical force] was, according to John Laband and Paul Thompson "a time of darkness... because the moon was new and evil influences more potent."[100] According to one commentator, the partial eclipse, taken with the presence of many dead made "the dull day darker still."[101]

Isandhlwana is within striking distance of Rorke's Drift, another significant battle site (22 January 1879),[102] and, eventually, the site of the artistically very influential Evangelical Lutheran Art and Craft Centre known as Rorke's Drift started in 1963. Zulu himself became a student at this centre in 1982. Many local artists have produced work related to this battle, one striking example being one of the teachers at Rorke's Drift, Jules van de Vijver, who produced a suite of prints titled "Isandhlwana 1879-1979" which he described "as a picture of violence and silence."[103]

The general visual impression of war, the structured mass formations of troops, the lay of the land, the weaponry and dress, are also discernible in many of Zulu's works. Luke Sofikhasho Zungu of the iNgobamakhosi describes the uMcijo regiment under fire as lying "down in the grass like a strong wind,"[104] while in the *Natal Mercury* (January 1879) we read of the "beautiful precision" of two companies of "the enemy,"[105] all formal qualities common in Zulu's works. At the level of content the manifold resonances of Isandhlwana and its aftermath register in Zulu's work strongly, if obliquely, in, for example, the combative *Frontline with Centurion Models* (1997). The temper and tone of his interest in history is captured in some poems penned by the artist; "I carry the scent of your body mother / wear the mask of your image Afrika / on my breast / pin the identity symbol / like a belligerent soldier."[106] Elsewhere, he writes of what he calls 'futurists'; "The day shall dawn / when the young generation / shall march in unity! / when the new breed of futurists / will manoeuvre / like rolling restless machines / of the mines / like rolling guns coughing fire bullets / like rumbling black clouds / of burning mountain fires".[107]

06. SENSE AND STRUCTURE

The aesthetic architecture of Zulu's constructions comprises internally differentiated, elementary forms: lines, planes, circles, triangles, rectangles and grids in some variation. This visual syntax is cumulative and repetitive,[108] a concrete form of digital materialism.

Time and space are also a critical part of his aesthetic language; space usually as a grid and time as genesis and gradualism. The grid sometimes structures a work quite directly, as happens in, for example, *Wavelength* (1997), *Untitled Ivory Painting* (2002) and *Involution 1* and *2* (2002). The grid also characterises the arrangement of his studio objects I described in Section 02. Through the display in the studio, a different aesthetic economy linked to a literal economy becomes explicit, echoing the often exquisitely formal displays created by informal sector street vendors found in most of our major cities. These displays, like artworks, are meant to be noticed in a noisy, cluttered visual field.

The calm orderliness of Zulu's artistic structures acts as a counterpoint to the drastic contingency and symbolic intensity of his iconography of fire and conflict. It is as if the artist wishes to calibrate, measure and ultimately offset the temperature of feeling; feelings of fire in the blood, of love and hate, of the humours of temperament.

One aspect of finding and creating a usable past for the present involves a strong consciousness of time. We might want to recognise, for example, a dialectic between time advancing in a linear way, one thing after another and time returning to itself in a circular or spiral movement, a strict, hypnotising repetition. This dialectic can be detected in Zulu's elementary iconography, in his processing of material, and, importantly, in the number of multi-part or serial works in his output. The dialectic between movement and stasis, linearity and circularity, evolutionary and random change recognises and complicates modern obsessions with progress and novelty so common in our art world.

Zulu's work also touches on other, related orders of time, understood as immediacy and duration.[109] Repetition, seriality, the structure of the diptych, triptych and multi-part work all involve the interaction between simultaneity and duration. Here his use of fire merges with structure, pointing to specific, almost ritualistic, articulations of our experience of time. For Stephen Pyne and colleagues

> There exists... a chronic rhythm of wetting and drying. Seasonality flows [as] a cadence of rainfall... Wet seasons grow fuels; dry ones ready them for burning. Across this annual rhythm, longer waves of drought and deluge rise and fall. The formula is ideal for fire, and the onset of the rains will typically bring scattered thunderstorms laden with dry lightning. Long before humans arrived, fire thrived, and will continue to do so – bar only the driest and wettest sites – if people leave.[110]

Time as simultaneity and sequence structures Zulu's aesthetic. Time is compressed into space, into an iconic all-at-once presentness. Simultaneity and sequentiality involve repetition, the spatialisation of time and the temporalisation of space. Annette Michelson makes an important point about space/time in American artist Robert Morris's sculpture: "Cognitive in its fullest effect, then, rather than 'meaningful', comprehension not only demands time; it elicits the acknowledgement of temporality as the condition or medium of human cognition and aesthetic experience."[111]

Repetition implies movement and stasis, progress and regress.[112] The repetition of an image turns that image on itself as the same, as much as it points to an image changing, the comparison being the basis for change. In *Abduction of the Text: Total Eclipse* (1999), symmetry and seriality combine the various antagonistic senses of time. The passage of time in the serial *Artomic Passage 1, 2, 3, 4* and *5* (1999) is more straightforwardly calibrated in numbers and in the sense of the rising or setting sun or moon. This kind of simple numeracy, with the presentation of elementary forms in sequence, extends and intensifies the modular impulse that informs much of Zulu's work.

Considering elementary units as modules is perhaps too mechanistic for Zulu's constructions and all-over field works.[113] The former refers to multi-part works and installations: *Involution 1* and *2* (2002), *Camouflage 1* (1998), *Masquerade Shield* (1998), *Indluyengwe (Leopard's Lair)* (2000) and *Inyoni Yezulu, Izigubhu Zomoya (Spiritual Passage Through the Thunderbird Above the Land of the Gods)* (2001). The latter to single-part, less object-like, more field-like works, including *Sahara Sands* (1995), *Wavelength* (1997), *Study for Monumental Shield* (1998) and *Untitled Ivory Painting* (2002). Zulu's instinctive modular sensibilities include reference to natural or organic morphologies, the structures of living things, much like his 'grids' might refer to the patterns of land cultivation as much as the mapping of a pictorial surface. Modularity, system and series all point to the strong presence of the 'grid' and the spatialisation of design noted earlier.

The grid may also reference a specifically modernist attitude hostile to representation as conventionally understood. Certainly there is a deliberate patterned anonymity in much of Zulu's work, which aligns well with modernist abstraction and formalism. But this formalism is never mechanical, just as his representations are never instrumental. Something more humane and open is at work. Equating fire with life, we might see in Zulu's inflamed traces an almost post-expressive expressiveness.

Grids – and the all-over, poly-accented 'grids' of high-modernism – seem to be anthropomorphically inflected here, bearers of a very human energy. A good early example of this impulse is the aptly named *Baptism of Fire* (1995), baptism being associated with human name-giving, purification and regeneration under the aegis of

Detail, **Wavelength** (1997) | fire, water, air, earth and silk | 120 x 85 cm

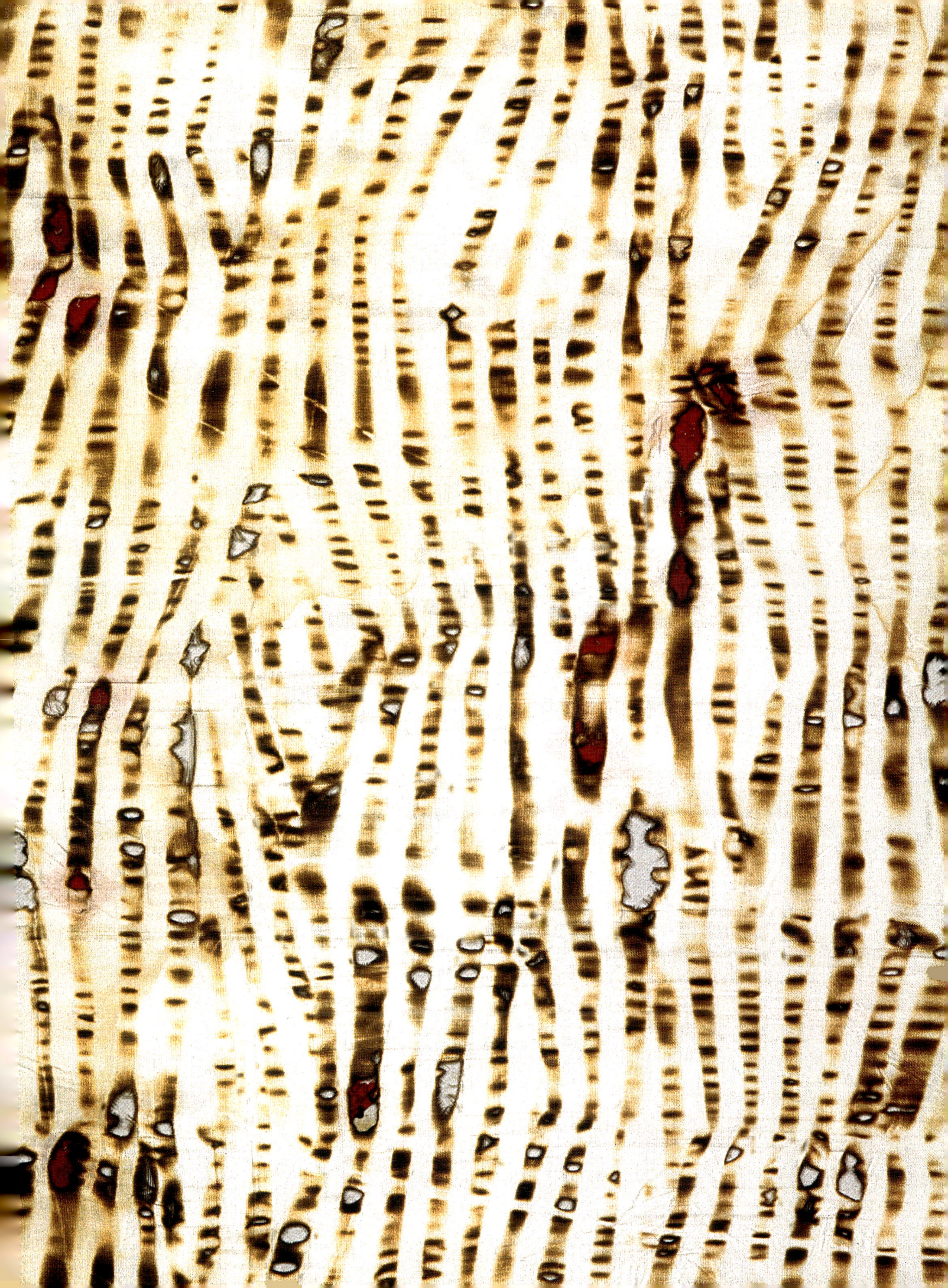

 Untitled Ivory Painting | (2002) | paint on board | 135 x 120 cm each

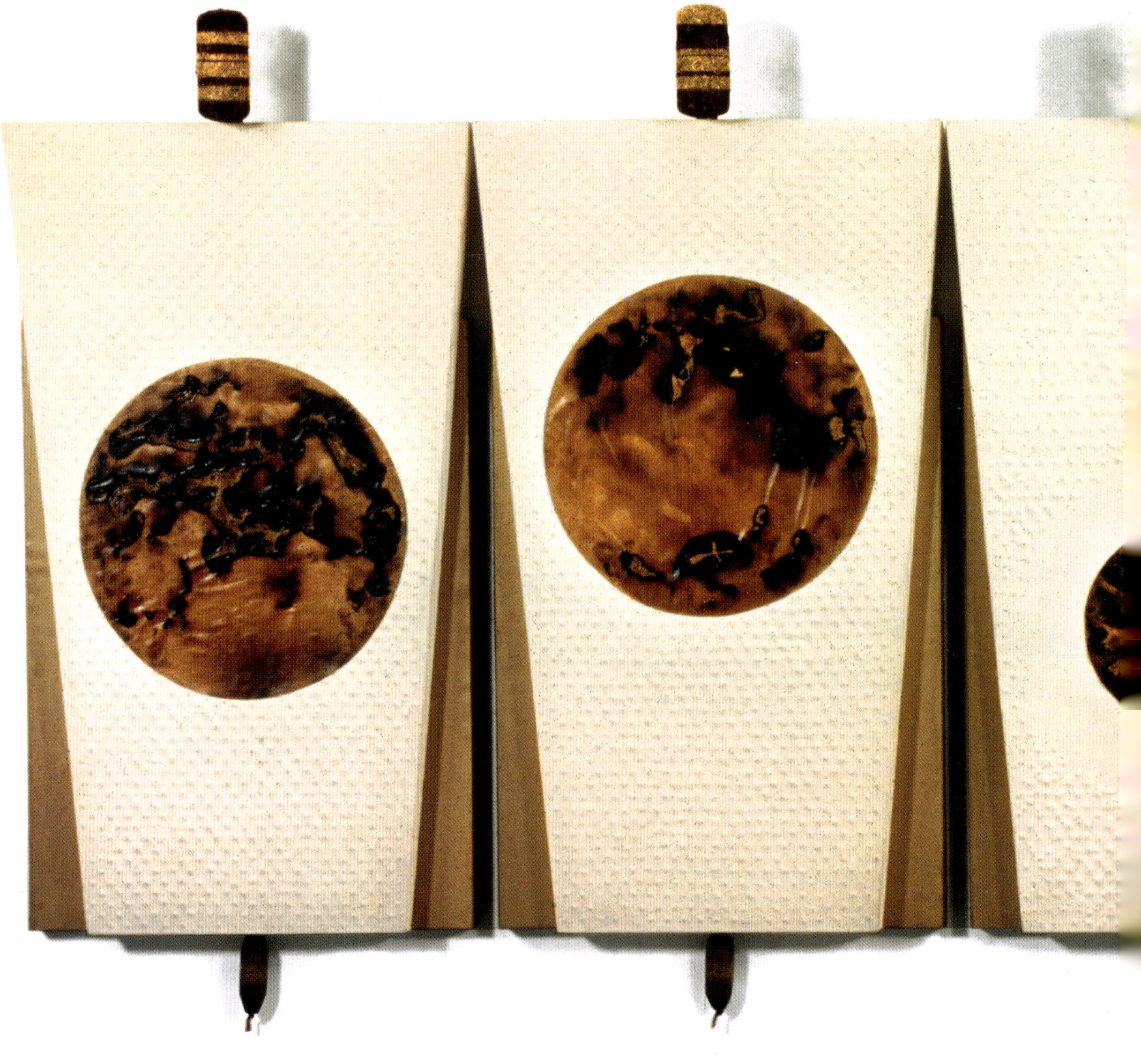

40 | **Artomic Passage** | (1999) | fire, water, air, earth, paper, canvas, metal and grass | 500 x 146 x 20 cm

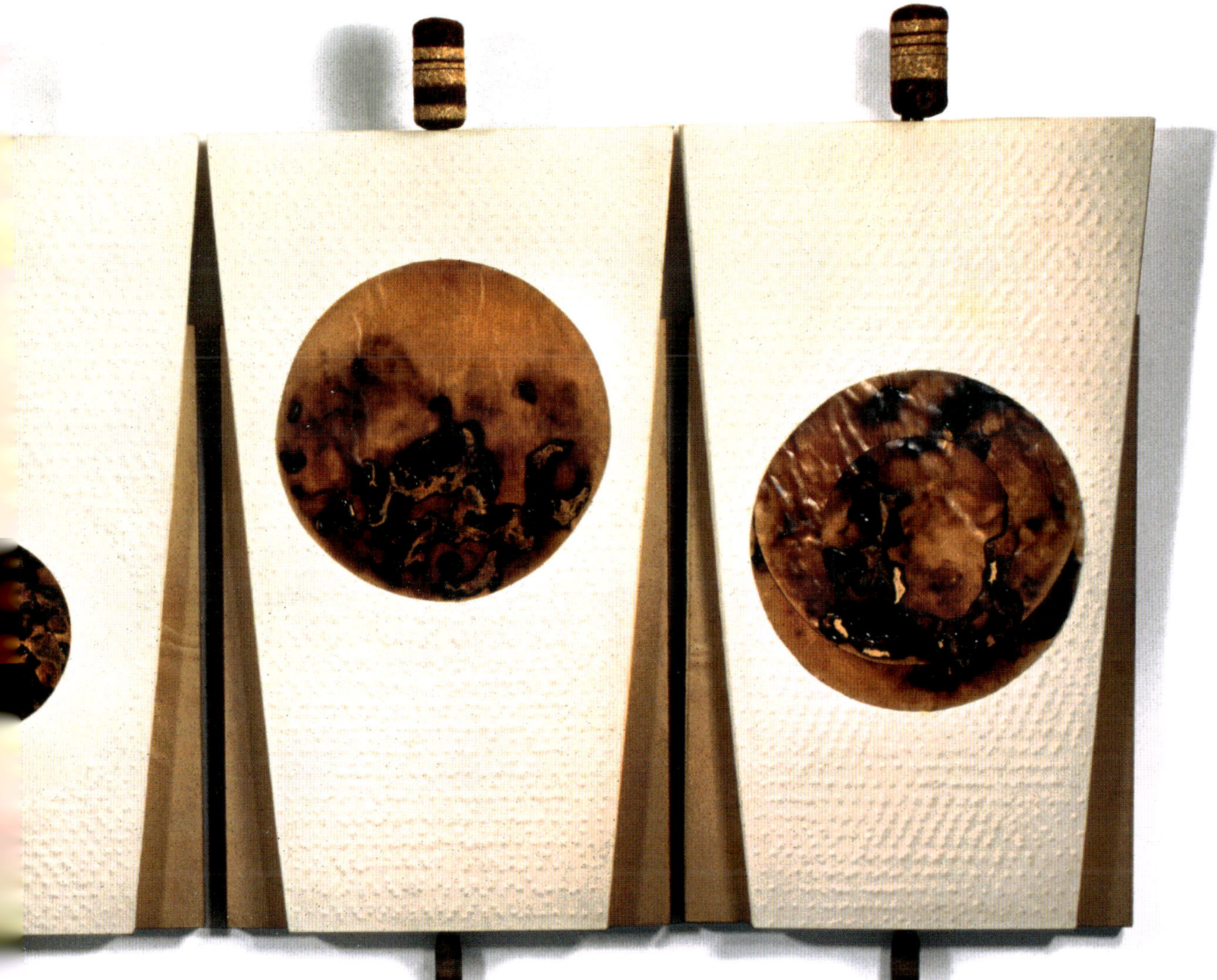

a divine force. The anthropocentricism in all this would see alienating mass-production as something not only of the industrial assembly line but also of soul-destroying agrarian labour. Zulu in some ways appropriates the systems of this production and allows us to meditate on the different but connected metropolitan and rural modalities of human labour. The artist's "Graft" floor installation is an excellent instance of this impulse.

Thus while the grid may be – using Rosalind Krauss's characterisation – "an emblem of modernity,"[114] in Zulu's work it cannot be a taken-for-granted metropolitan modernity. And while it might also be true, following Krauss, that "the bottom line of the grid is a naked and determined materialism," that materialism in Zulu's work is more generous and even dissident than allowed by modernist purism and means-to-end logic. Krauss is more to the point here when she acknowledges in her essay that

> by now we find it indescribably embarrassing to mention 'art' and 'spirit' in the same sentence... the peculiar power of the grid... arises from its potential to preside over this shame: to mask and reveal it at one and the same time. In the cultist space of modern art, the grid serves not only as emblem but also as myth.

Krauss could not have had anything like Zulu's work in mind when she penned these words in 1979, but her mention of 'spirit' and 'myth' makes them entirely appropriate.

Looking at specific works in greater detail will help us appreciate better the play of module and grid in his general creative project. Part of Zulu's modular impulse is captured in his use of particular natural forms. The accumulations of root and rhizome in *Endangered Roots* (1997) for example, which was part of the installations the artist created in the South African National Gallery in 1997 and at the Sandton Civic Gallery in 1998,[115] are good examples. In the first installation, the gridded, laterally and horizontally layered three-dimensional structures of precisely sectioned bamboo tubers interspersed by ranks of sweet potato make the point clear.

In these works the cut surface of each tuber is branded by a set of parallel lines. Impaled at one or both ends of the body of each potato and occasionally elsewhere are cut sections of weather-beaten barbed wire. In spite of being run through with the wire, the sweet potatoes all began shooting purple shoots during the exhibition in Cape Town. Zulu used this image of violence and growth on his invitation to *Camouflage* at the Millennium Gallery in Pretoria in 1998.

The artist's use of barbed wire – a key creative material for him – adds yet another symbolic dimension to his work. Barbed wire is ubiquitous in our social lives; it tops the high walls of suburbia, surrounds industrial sites, farms and the like. It defines and defends space. Thickets of barbed wire protect strategic installations and dangerous places, and barbed wire is as much part of urban topography as rural ecology.

As indicated when he spoke of his father's land, for Zulu barbed wire is strongly identified with boundaries. Speaking of the work *Landscape with Spheres: Study in Spaces and Structures* (1995), he says cryptically "that boundaries could be read as that which existed before... but they are made of a burnt mark which suggests the destruction of barriers" or "the bandages of a body after being hurt."[116] As with fire, an iconography of barbed wire is evident in South African visual art: Jillian Edelstein's photograph *Riot Provisions* (1998),[117] Kendell Geers's *T.W. (Deployed)* (1999),[118] Marco Cianfanelli's *Interference* (2002),[119] and Abrie Fourie's *Vyande/ Enemies* (2002) with Santu Mofokeng.[120]

Barbed wire has deep significance for Zulu, and understanding this is important for a reading of his work. Fleshing out the referential reach of barbed wire, historian Alan Krell writes:

> Barbed wire's simplicity of concept and ease of realisation belies the critical role it has played in the modern experience: territorial expansion and settlement, regional and international conflicts, incarceration and extermination. The most vicious tool of control, however, has other histories, constructed through image and text in the art, media and popular culture.[121]

Here the modernity of what Krauss suggests is 'shame' – the grid presiding over 'art' and 'spirit' – can be traced in a different way across different domains of social life. Zulu, in his poem "Silence Was Never Golden" writes "you wanted a pen to pen the history / of our beloved, but when I tried to give / I only touched the barbed wire barrier."

Krell also mentions the well-known global human rights 'brand,' the Amnesty International logo of a lit candle wrapped in a strand of barbed wire.[122] Conscientious objector Phillip Wilkinson who refused military conscription in South Africa in the 1980s was photographed lighting a candle wrapped in barbed wire prior to his trial.[123] Describing a photograph by Paul Harris in the *Sydney Morning Herald* in January 2002 of the wildfires in New South Wales, Australia, Krell invokes a scene which could just as well describe aspects of Zulu's art:

> There are tall blackened trees, many denuded of foliage and, in the immediate foreground, a strand of barbed wire, its knotted four-point barb verging on the grotesque. Impossible to identify its function, the wire stands defiant in the face of Nature's outrages.

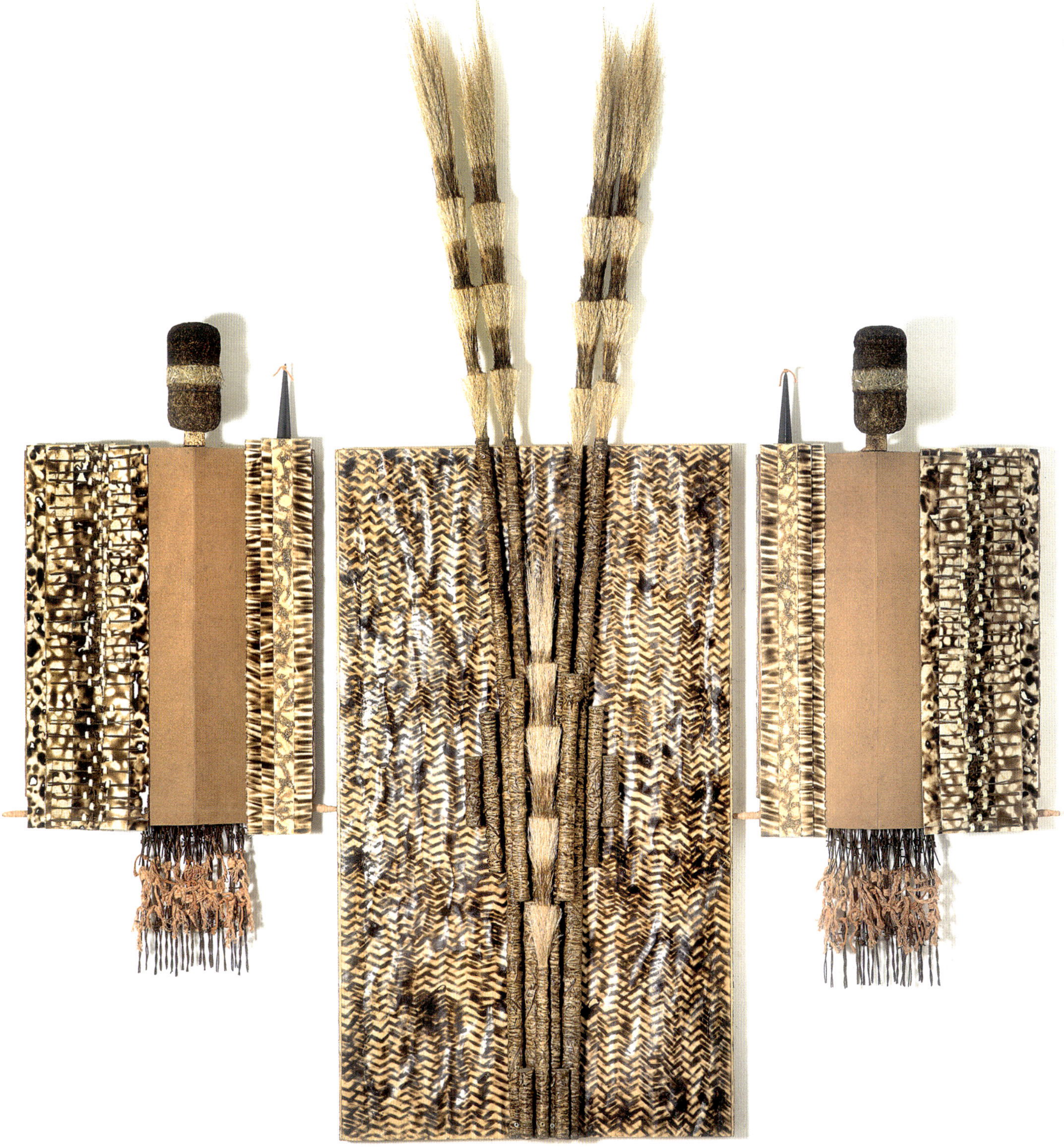

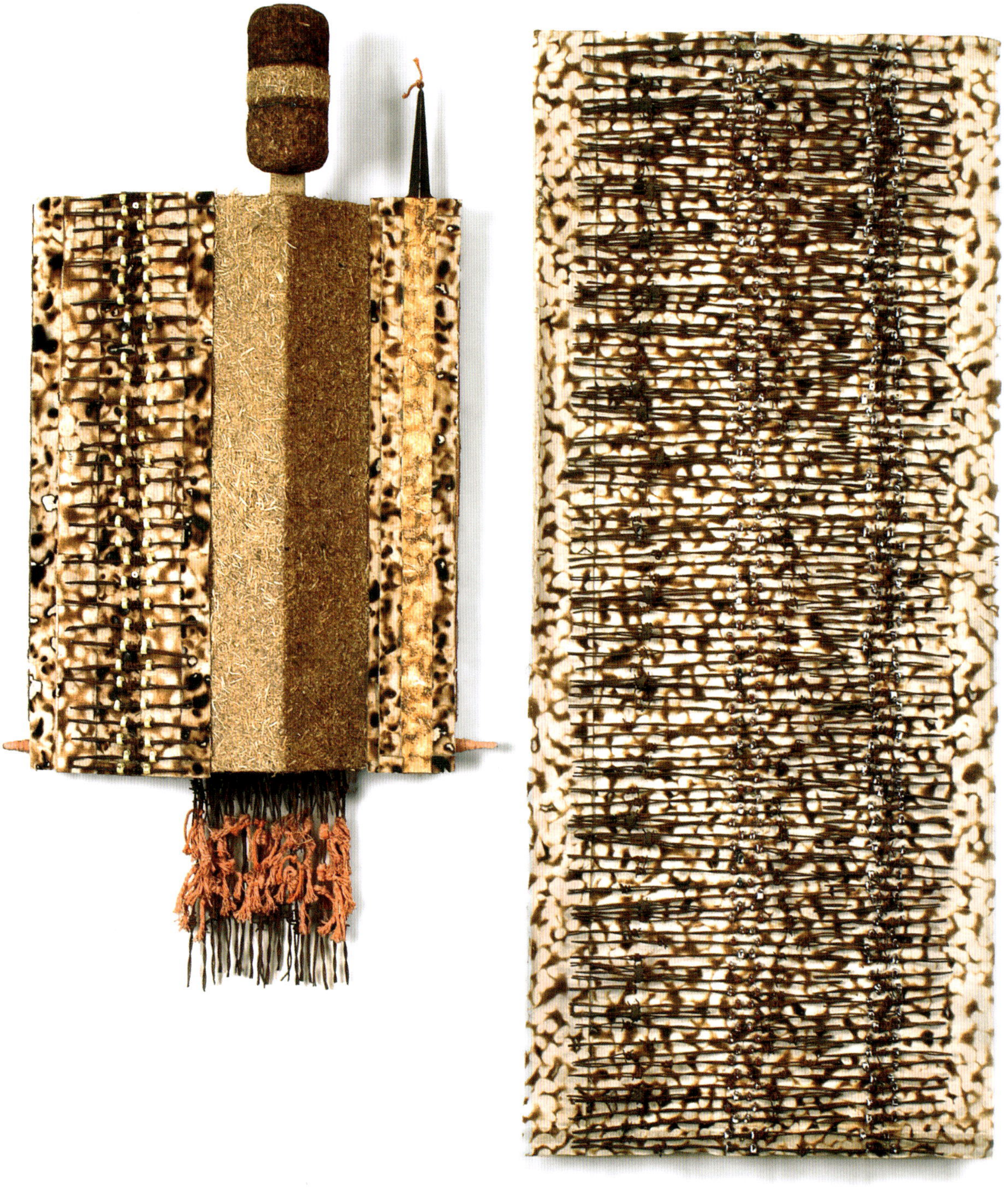

 Camouflage | (1998) | fire, water, air, earth and barbed wire | 114 x 60 x 20 cm

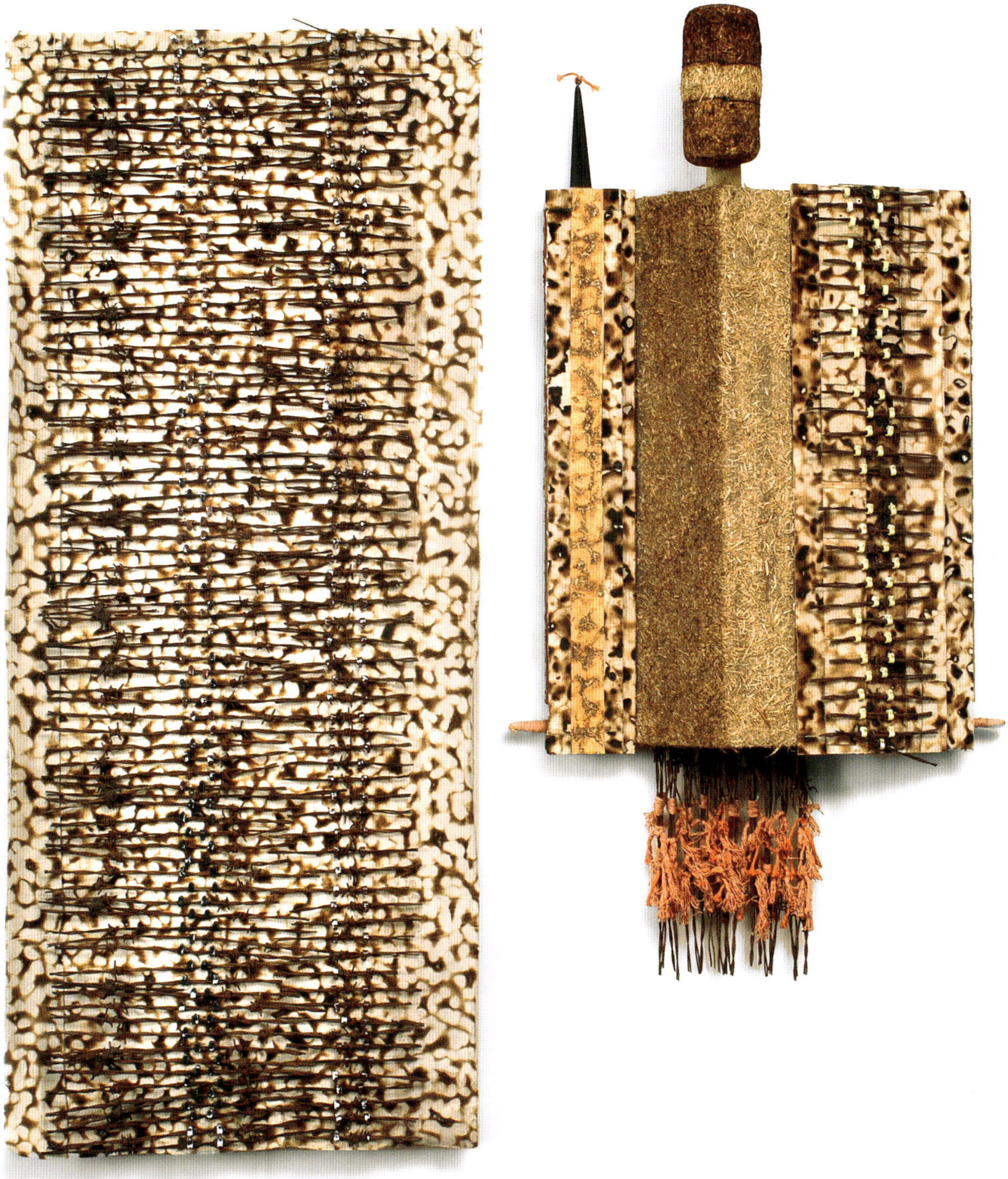

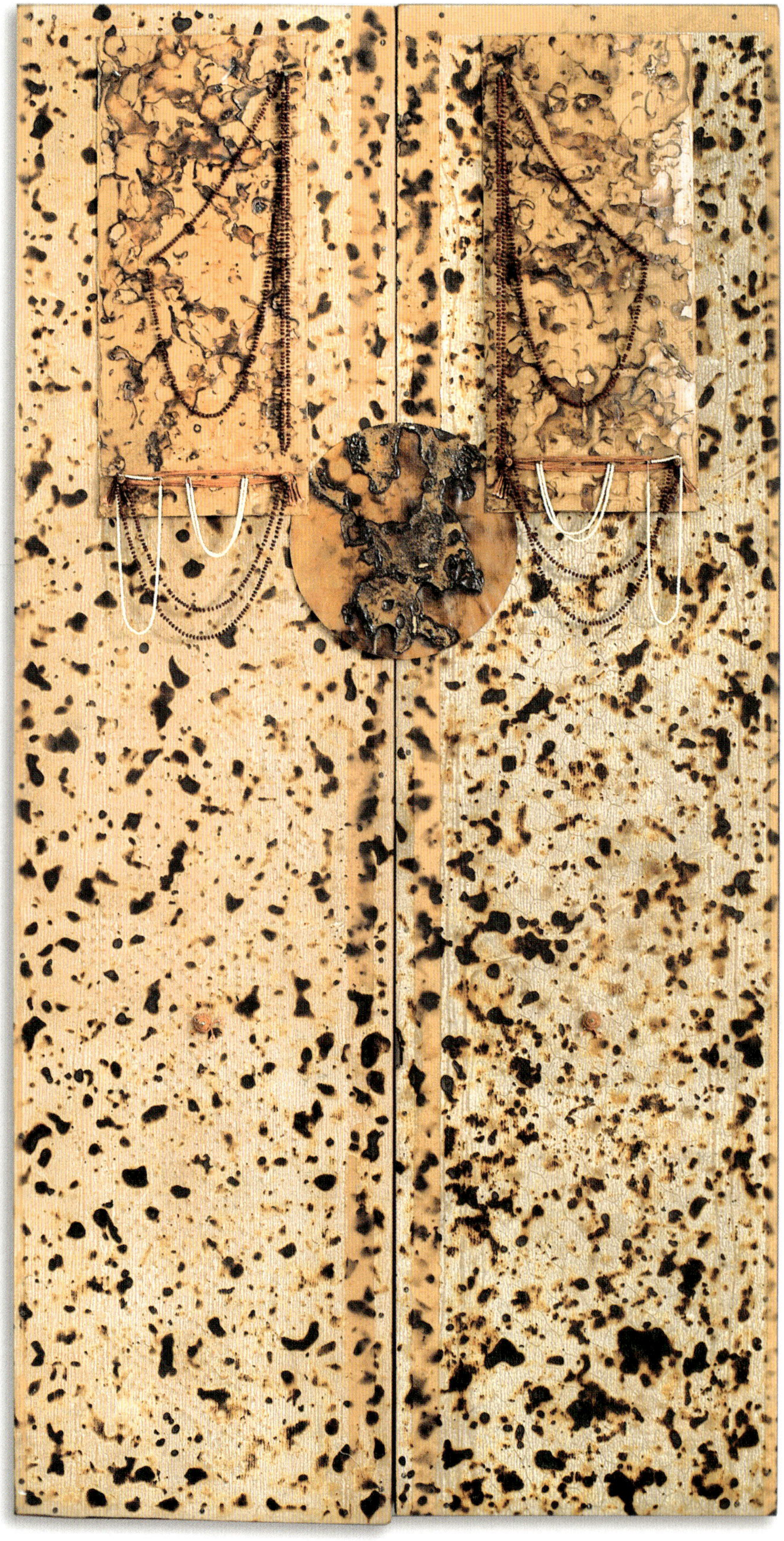

46 | **Baptism of Fire** | (1995) | fire, water, air, earth, board, paper, string, beads and seeds | 213 x 113 cm

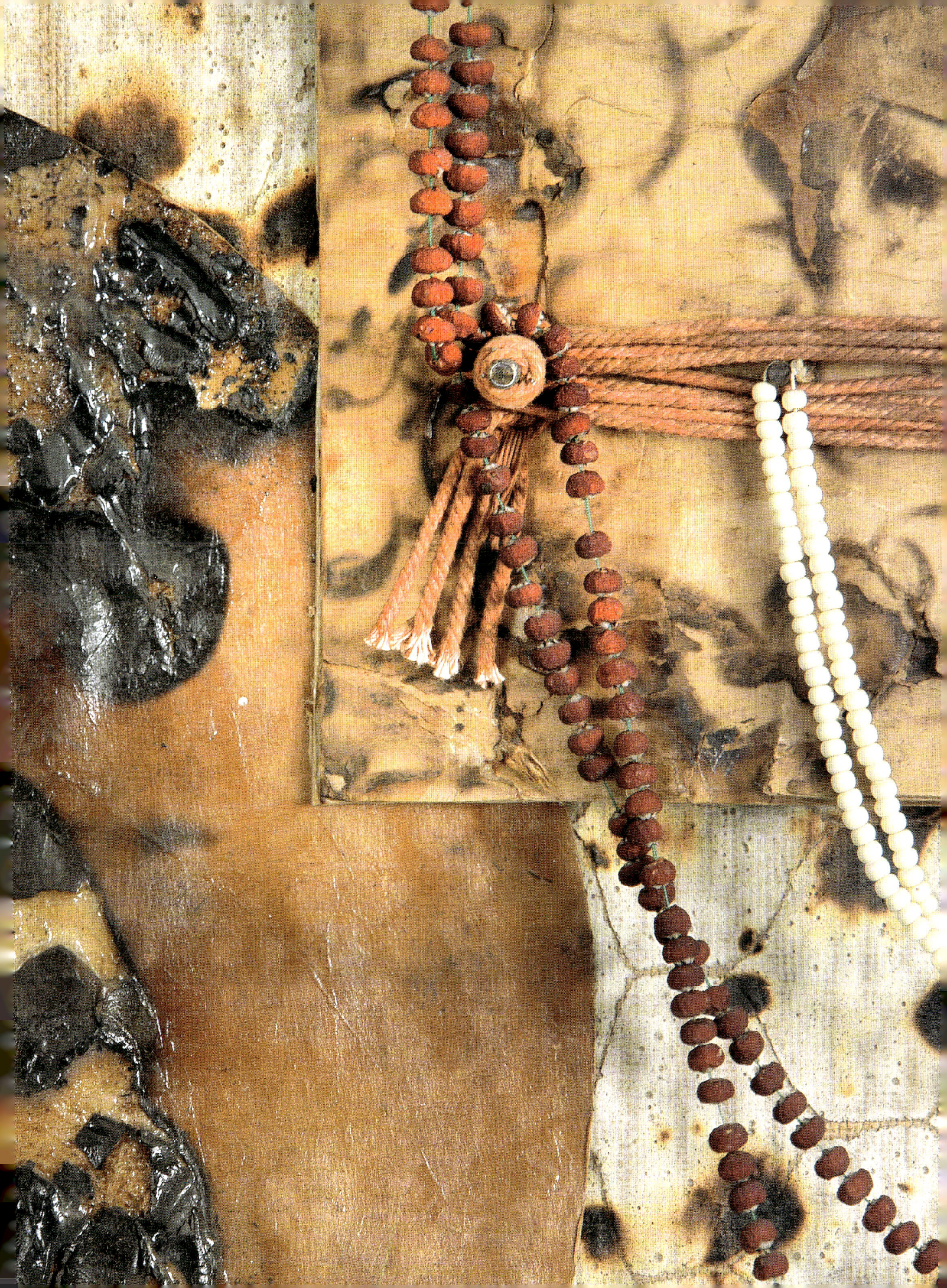

> A testament to human ingenuity, yes, but also, and more ominously, to its will to order, to control and, when required, to kill.[124]

In spite of the intrinsic drama of 'hot' materials like fire and barbed wire, Zulu remains resolutely dispassionate. The grid and the module serve this temperament like little else.

Zulu's work also often articulates an indeterminate space in which time is rendered as rhythm, a visual beat, a double, a sequence, a series. The tempo of time is a rhythm, a set of visual beats, which recall the features of music. Music is explicitly referenced in early works, such as *Passion Flute* (1995). Zulu's interest in music draws on a very rich tradition in South African art, exemplified in certain works by Dumile Feni, Jabulani Sam Nhlengethwa, Durant Sihlali, Nthubu David Koloane and Gerard Sekoto.

Zulu is also concerned with the play of language in the visual. His titles are narrative fragments – sometimes punning and cryptic – referring to military and social conflict over land, cultural terrain and historical narrativisation. He also uses newsprint from various newspapers in a number of works, and in doing so alludes to textuality and language in the construction of our everyday experience. Some of Zulu's titles are in his mother-tongue isiZulu, and therefore foreign to those not conversant in this language. The same applies to English. Readers of his work require translation, and the contestation of received historical narratives implicated at the outset.[125] His is the patient, uncompromising grassroots conservationist's critical response to disfiguring linguistic, narrative stresses of history. He is also sensitive to the language of oppression and liberation, as the triptych *Abduction of the Text: Total Eclipse* (1999) shows.

The deep ambiguity of the contending forces of creation and destruction – natural and cultural – can be seen in the lists of media the artist includes in the titles and labels accompanying his works on the wall, in space and in catalogues. His titles and other textual paraphernalia (including newsprint) are integral to our reading, and language – mother tongue or other tongue – is also a powerful part of his processes of mediation. His titles and accompanying texts anchor but do not limit the works in a specific affective and cultural world.

Zulu's work is clearly not in any strict sense 'abstract,' and to think so would be misleading. In fact he participates in an important tradition in South African art in which abstraction and figuration, form and reference, ornament and function interact. The referential reach of his work can explode in many directions, even with the sparest formal language. This quality is an intended consequence of the materials he uses. Martha Buskirk, in a recent study of contingency in art, makes an illuminating point in this regard about a recent generation of American artists:

> One striking feature in the work of several younger generations of artists who came to prominence in the 1980s and 1990s, and whose work incorporates allusions to art of the preceding decades, has been a careful attention to formal and material decisions not as an end in themselves, but as a means of addressing a wide range of cultural as well as personal references.[126]

Citing Janine Antoni's *Gnaw* (1992), Buskirk argues that "the cube was no abstract neutral form... but... a reference to minimalism." Yet "*Gnaw* also demonstrates how minimalism can be transformed into both a historical reference and, simultaneously, a model for a certain kind of objecthood."[127]

So, setting abstraction against reference goes against the synthesising spirit of Zulu's work. This critical point can be expressed in many ways. Generally, and importantly, it can be expressed in the terms of the public debate about art and politics initiated by Albie Sachs in 1989, a late version of a much older modernist debate about the relative autonomy of art in a socially fractured world.[128] A more recent incarnation of this train of thought is noticeable in these comments by Williamson and Jamal:

> In Sandile Zulu's burned works and collaged constructions, the township or the fight may not be visible and yet it is 'everywhere'. The struggle has shifted away from surface representations to the support itself. The medium – found objects and fire on paper and board – has become the message.[129]

The idea of a shift, as posited by Williamson and Jamal, in mediating the social and natural worlds we inhabit is an important marker of what political liberation has come to mean. Yet the distinctions and continuities between art and politics, between the cultural and the natural can be overstated. Zulu has stated that to him "the framework of addressing issues is metaphorical rather than direct or obvious... so you see in my work details which have reference to histories of religion, to revolutionary politics, art making, psychological relationships."[130]

Starkly stated, though, the idea of a radical shift occurring around 1994 skews our perspective on the past and we risk losing a real sense of the historical continuities which still shape and direct contemporary South African art. To think of rupture in this sense may not be helpful. Similarly, little in the unwritten history of South African art suggests that setting form against reference is a productive or accurate way of understanding the histories of art in this part of Africa.

 Sahara Sands | (1995) | fire, water, air, earth and canvas | 357 x 85 cm

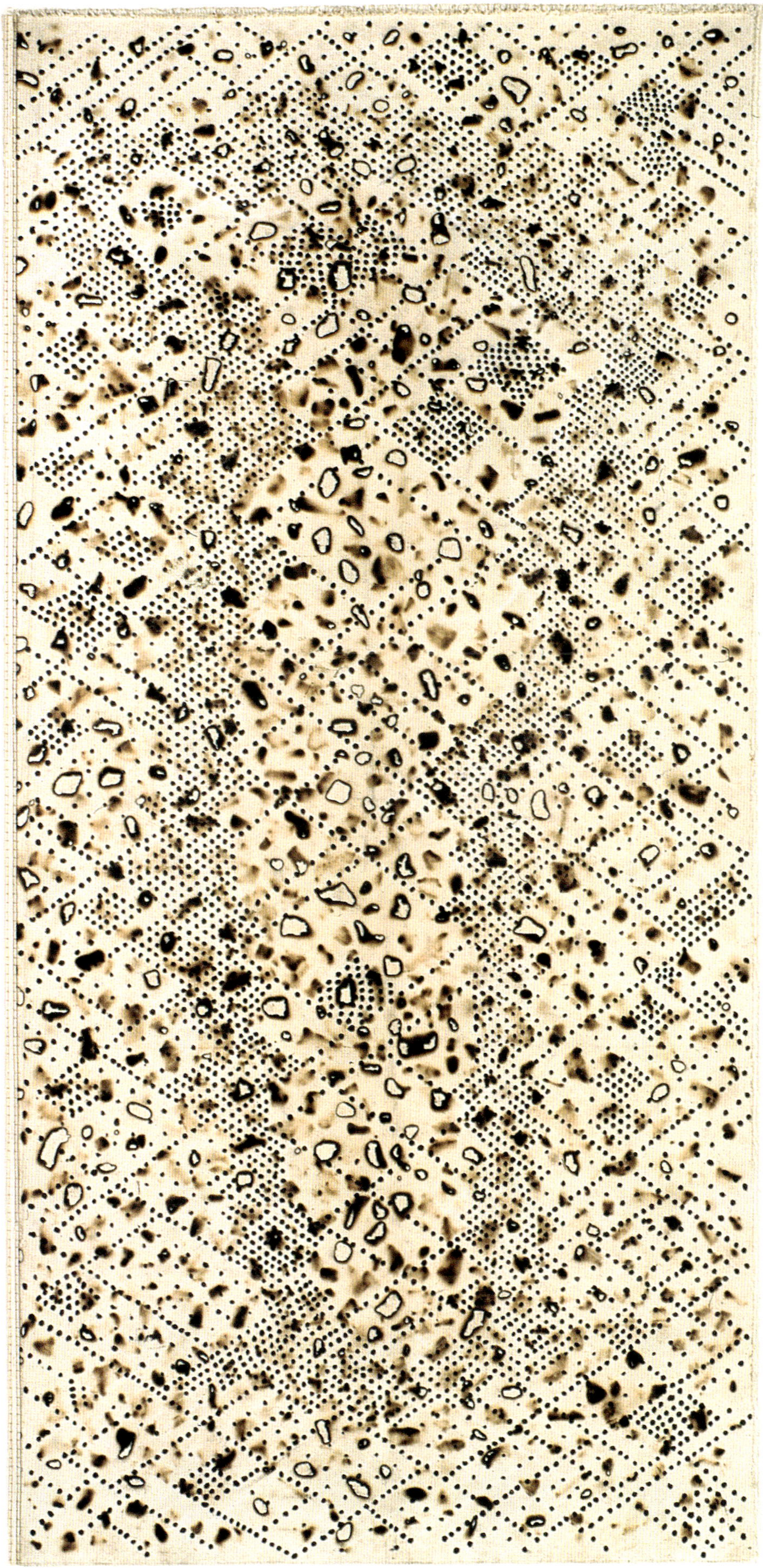

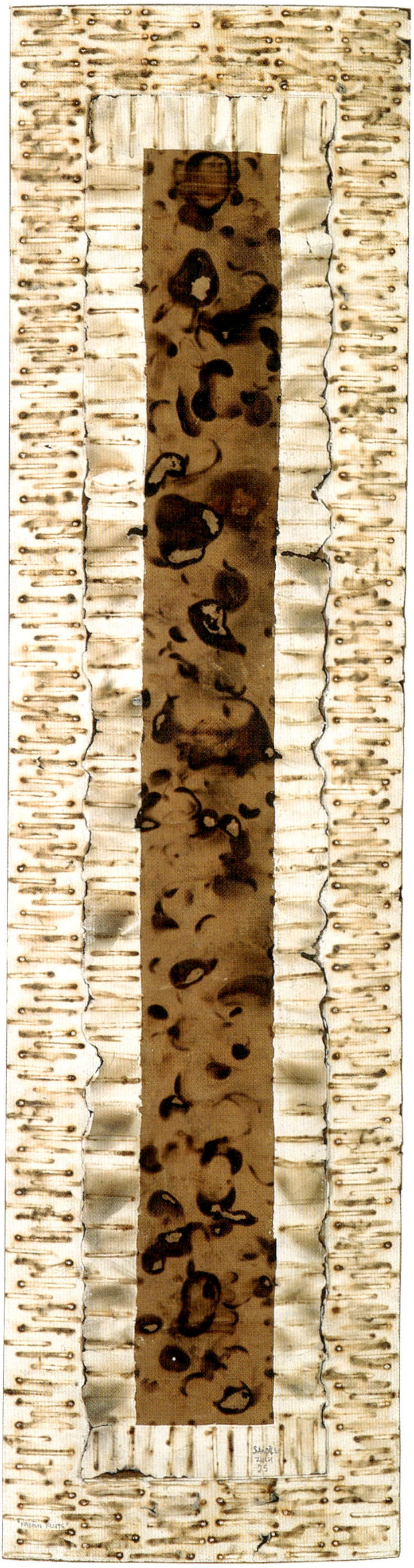

50 Passion Flute | (1995) | fire, water, air and earth | 150 x 50 cm

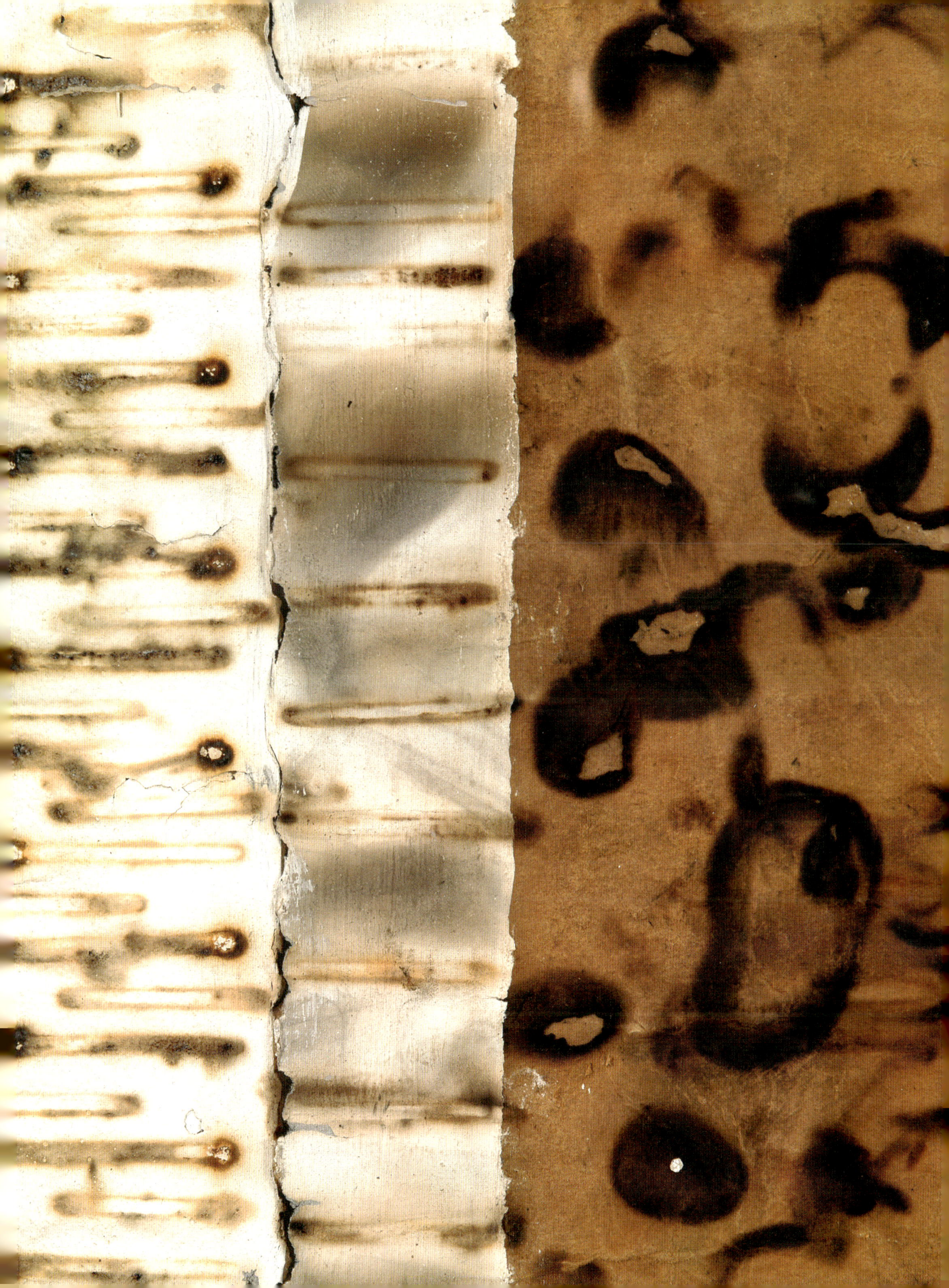

07. SIGN AND DESIGN

The referential dimension of Zulu's work warrants further exploration. The eclipse referred to in *Abduction of the Text: Total Eclipse* (1999) has already been linked with the battle of Isandhlwana. In some ways this link stretches interpretation to breaking point. It over-reads the image. But Zulu's intentions are broad and open. His minimal, sensuously formal work is not inimical to reference. The routes of reference are many; circumstantial evidence, free association, analogy, induction, deduction, serendipity and co-incidence, Zulu's own creative authority and his scattered statements of intention all infiltrate the networks of meaning he creates.

Writing in 1995, art critic Hazel Friedman identifies ambivalent critical responses to Zulu's work where the aesthetic and the symbolic – the form and reference – exist in uneasy, almost mutually exclusive relation. The risk of over-reading was clearly on her mind when she wrote,

> it's still early days for Zulu and in reading too much into these works there is the danger of romanticising them or imposing on them an arid intellectualism. Ultimately they reside in a formalist realm, serving as decorative surface displays. Depending on which stream of consciousness you choose to splash in, you can read them as such, or see them as worlds in a grain of sand.[131]

Time has passed since Friedman's words. Looking at his work now, these ostensibly opposed tendencies in reading – symbolic fertility on the one hand and formal sensuality on the other – are kept in sustained and vital creative tension. Neither eliminates the other, encouraging viewers to an active role in the experience of looking. Material and meaning interact, and it is from this intimate interaction that much of his aesthetic energy radiates. His art is open enough to spark a kind of directed reverie, a structured hermeneutic wandering neither arbitrary nor overly determined. This is an individual liberty of the eye and the mind, and part of what it currently means to make and view art.

But it is also true that the materials and processes he uses – his media and methods – draw us continually back to his *concrete* creations. His sensuous formalism thus animates and shapes – embodies – our interpretive adventures. The tension between the straightforwardly symbolic and the material stimulates new experiences as we tread the sometimes paper-thin line between our subjective projections and Zulu's own directed artistic purposes.

There is within Zulu's creative process a self-regulating and sometimes self-affirming/self-cancelling symmetry; the end is often a meditative state of suspension and ambivalence as in those works in two sections, such as the early *Twin Spirits* (1995) and *Baptism of Fire* (1995). We can read this ambivalence or ambiguity in a number of ways including as the quality precisely and powerfully expressed in this extract from *Age of Iron* by J. M. Coetzee:

> Groups of men were at work trying to rescue the contents of the burning shacks, going from one to the other, putting out the fires; or so I thought till with a shock it came to me that these were no rescuers but incendiaries, that the battle I saw them waging was not with the flames but with the rain.[132]

Perhaps the most obvious way of understanding this ambivalence is as a tension between form as an autonomous, wordless, self-referring interiority and as other-referential 'content.' Perhaps under pressure from the Sachs debate, Friedman writes, "if Zulu's recent output is anything to go by, the work emerging from this centre [Amakhono] suggests a refreshing post-apartheid sensibility, with the emphasis more on personal expression than reductive political statement."[133]

Sandile Zulu's project is thus relentlessly personal and political. It has both a *private* and a *public* dimension, a voice for the present seeking itself in disfigured history. But things, for all the elegance and balance of the form, are rarely stable. This kind of dynamic dialectical interplay between the personal and public, between intimate and social 'biography' has shaped much South African art since 27 April 1994.[134] It is within the distinctive space Zulu occupies in the cultural dynamic that he seeks renewal, a fresh start.

But there is an edge to this renewal. For Zulu's creative enterprise is almost perversely novel in that it obstinately follows a major tradition in South African art preceding April 1994.[135] Insofar as his artistic inclinations are of a piece with 'resistance art' of the pre-democratic period, his art may be considered anachronistic; a countertrend to the dominant 'liberated' art of the moment. 'Resistance Art,' the title of Sue Williamson's book published in 1989, has in many ways become a millstone for artists, even though the term covers a range of differentiated art practices. Art tagged as 'resistance' is at constant risk of caricature.

Williamson and Jamal confirm this; "'Stuck in the struggle' is a disparaging phrase used... by critics seemingly eager for an all-new, all-fresh artistic vision of the born-again land." They follow with the well-worn question; "if the resistance narratives of the past have lost their potency, what has taken their place?"[136] There is no simple answer to this, or as many answers as there have been responses to 1994. One would be a rejection of 'lost potency,' but however we answer, the 'if' poses difficult questions. The reflex by many artists, curators and critics to automatically resist resistance art is becoming a new orthodoxy. Whatever the gains, the cost of this new orthodoxy is high if it fails to appreciate the continuity of critical art with the resistance art of the past, and fails to recognize the forces that still

 Twin Spirits | (1995) | wood | 110 x 40 cm

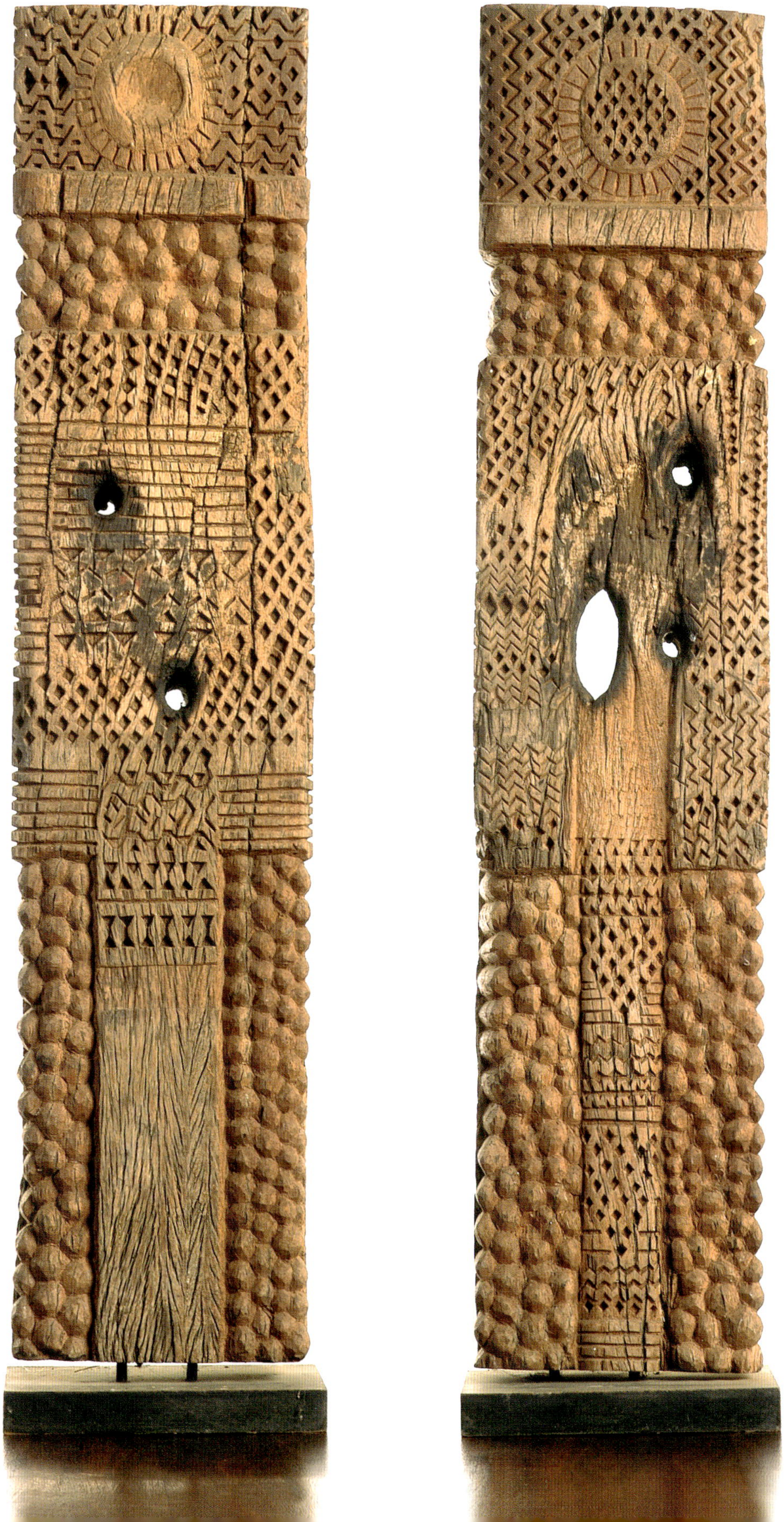

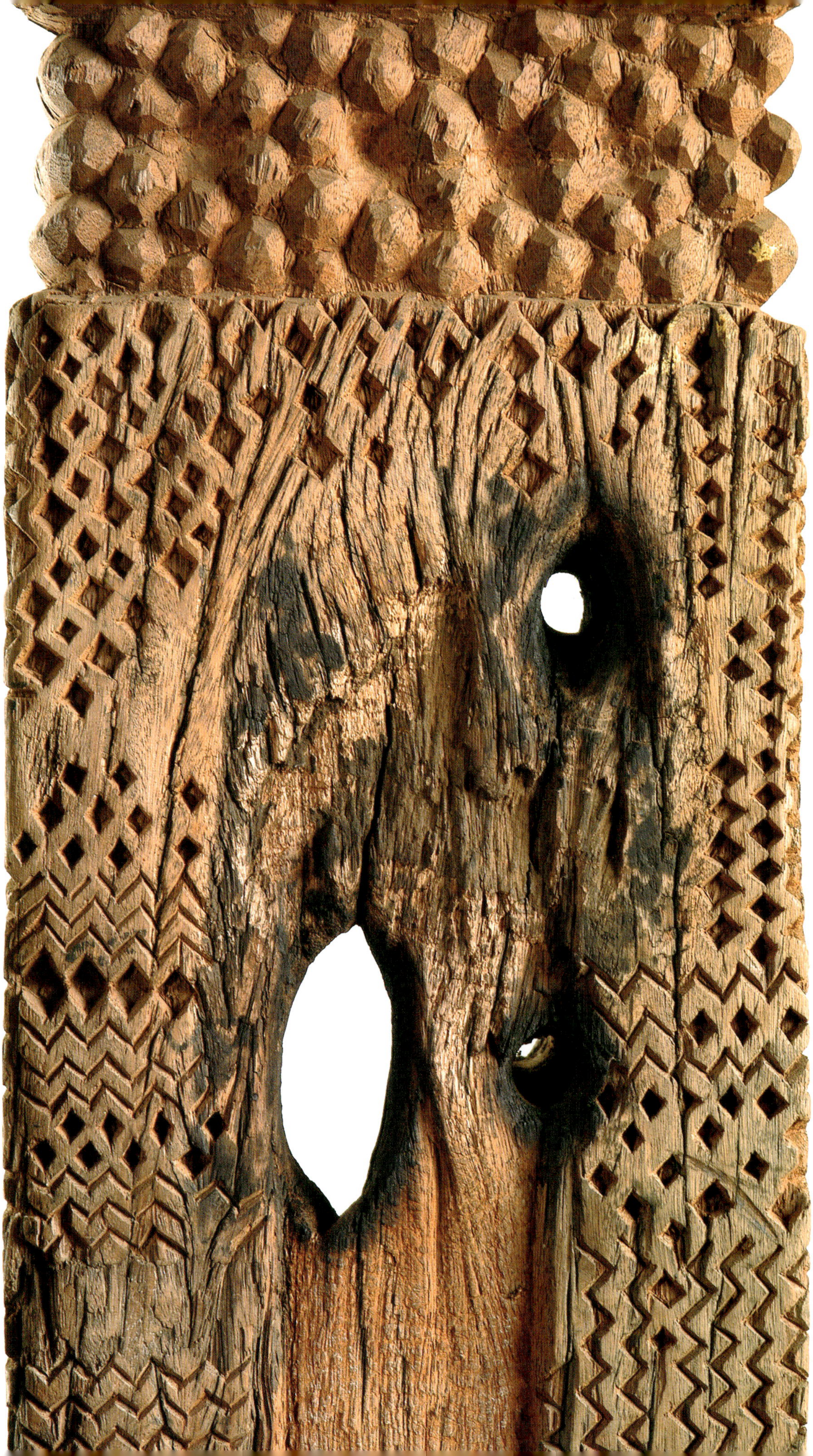

drive the power and point of critical art, in this case that of Sandile Zulu.[137]

Zulu still speaks the language of resistance whatever its currency now; of achieving a "critical mass," of aspiring to "critical, creative mass consciousness," of "revolution and liberation" through "purgation and cleansing... purification and renewal".[138] For all its apparent utopian eschatology, Zulu's ambition for the imagination should not simply be dismissed as rhetorically *passé* and aesthetically out of touch.[139] It engages, for one thing, a cultural politics resisting the critically overtraded local/global relationship, including the residual primitivism which still seems to inflect the reception of so much 'African' art abroad.[140]

Perhaps when the artist speaks of a "critical and theoretical framework for the analysis of my offerings,"[141] we should and should not take him at his word. The words "critical mass" cited earlier – with a hint of punning irony – unbalance our acts of reading and looking. This instability permeates many of his titles, which are readable on many levels. Writing some five years after Friedman, critic Ben Willcott restates the crucial relation. For him, Zulu's work "connects us to a distinct sense of culture and history through sensuous but ambiguous impression."[142]

> to deserve fire, men must cut open their chests /
> with obsidian daggers and surrender their hearts
> (Eduardo Galeano, "Fire")[143]

If we read in Zulu's work and words a more didactic and public aesthetic of 'struggle,' they might also be seen as a critical response to what writer Njabulo Ndebele once called the "hegemony of spectacle,"[144] which characterised so much of South African culture in the 1980s. For Ndebele, this hegemony obliterated intimacy, detail, contradiction and over-determination in matters of form, content and address. Zulu mobilises all of these qualities, if we spend the time to look and reflect.

The artist is sensitive to reductive readings of his work, whether in the direction of social reference (history) or form (materiality): "I am very aware that the question of self-identity is very much determined by one's cultural heritage," but, he continues, market pressure on local artists to represent and reflect their society and cultural history "robs the artist of his intention and conception of the work."[145]

These thoughts are important given the social pressures of the mid 1990s. Yet they are not only a corrective to the contending 'truths' of art, but part of an ongoing and open engagement between artist and audience.[146] Zulu's best work encourages us to a vital openness, a stimulus to emotionally strong symbolic speculation. As with much successful art, Zulu's work liberates imagination, feeling and thought.

It is clear by now that materiality is critically important in Zulu's work, and directly concerned with meaning. Something of what materiality might mean for us here, is captured in these words about 'modern materials' by Jeffrey Schnapp:

> instead of receding into passive role – as raw stuff to be worked, whose inherent value resides in their receptivity to human modification – modern materials... emerge as autonomous forces within an overarching modernist prosopopoeia. Beyond even their symbolic import, they become protagonists and heroes endowed with powers of agency and moral value, capable of sharing in the particular and universal attributes of human subjects and/or of serving as prosthetic extensions of humanity.[147]

To appreciate what this means fully can be daunting. But we could consider the straw-covered objects that actually became parts of an assemblage in *Frontline with Centurion Models* (1997) as an example. The basic form is a found object, a readymade industrial mould carefully covered in grass and partly singed by fire as illustrated in the "Graft" publication.[148] The whole installation is reminiscent of the serried rows of weapons in a defensive formation in a battle, or the static, formal display of weaponry in some colonial museum. Covered, camouflaged, burnt, innocuous industrial debris becomes imbued with dangerous incendiary purpose; the form looks like some sort of disguised explosive, a limpet mine, for example. Life-size plastic models of such mines were quite common in public places – police stations, post offices – in the last decade. They were meant to alert the public to the omnipresent danger of such 'terrorist' bombs. The objects and materials in Zulu's studio likewise resonate with fertile symbolic associations.

There is often a deep ambivalence in our attitude to such materials, especially the collateral junk of urban industrialism and the obsolete castoffs of technological progress. Zulu works with this ambivalence. Nature and culture, organicism and technology are often considered as somehow deeply antagonistic. One is pitted against the other, often violently. Such violence parallels the violence of the processes Zulu might use in burning, cutting, branding and so on.[149] Violence is everywhere present in Zulu's works; in slashes, burns, cuts, ties, nails, skewers and stitches. Edges and surfaces are scarred, sliced, scorched and singed. Titles tell of abduction, ambush, of frontlines, atomic births, conflagration and cremation.

Shields 1, 2, 3 and *4*, in the exhibition *Camouflage* (1998) suggest a more oblique relation to violence. But more decisive is the association between camouflage and survival, and the history of camouflage and modernist art.[150] Comprising defensive or aggressive mimicry, stealth and surprise, as in *Frontline With Target* (2003),

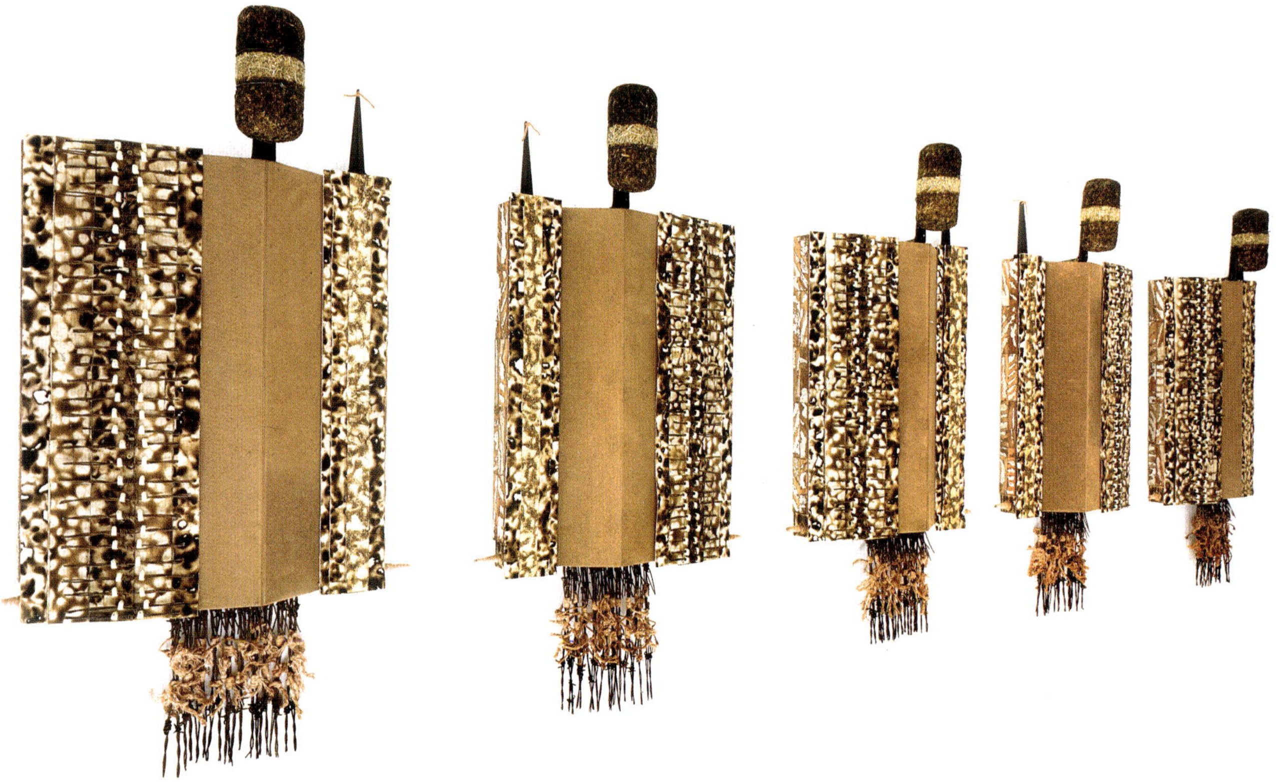

camouflage, according to Hillel Schwartz "has a compound paternity and a complex maternity." It is also part of faddish popular culture, as in branded global designer fashions. Schwartz goes on to ask an important question; "to what extent can we trust our eyes for the truth?" and makes the important observation that with "camouflage we broach our replication of the entire natural world."[151]

Replication, mimicry and copying are significant features of the contemporary art landscape.[152] Philosopher and cultural critic Elizabeth Grosz cites Roger Caillois, a French sociologist, as understanding camouflage in insects as a sort of excess, a "dangerous luxury" or "irrational residue."[153] For Caillois, an insect's

> ability to camouflage itself does not have survival value... Camouflage, the capacity to imitate one's habitat or surroundings, far from performing an adaptive function, witnesses the captivation of a creature by its representations of and as space, its displacement from the centre, for a 'consciousness' of its place (in its body, located in space) to the perspective of another. The mimicking insect lives its camouflaged existence as not quite itself, as another."[154]

Understanding camouflage in this way opens new vistas on the relationship between nature and culture. Replication – indeed visual representation – involves mimicry, as is clear in works like *Masquerade Shield* (1998) and similar works, all of which involve some kind of doubling or simulation. Mimicry, like camouflage, is part of both nature and human social life, asserting an unstable and shifting relation between what is natural and what cultural. This key aspect of Zulu's project also addresses what can be called a new 'humanism.'

Zulu's interest in camouflage thus points to a deep interest in our human ways of understanding 'nature' and 'culture.' This interest is part of a wider critical tendency among artists and intellectuals. For example, Stephen Harrison and colleagues argue that "new ways of thinking about 'nature' and 'culture'"

> have undoubtedly become one of the most important and exciting sites of interest in the social sciences and humanities because they bear the traces of three different debates: on the history and sociology of science; on nature and the environment; and, on the rapprochement between art and science. But they have also become an important part of thinking about... new ways of thinking about evolution, awareness, self-consciousness, emergence, information and, indeed, what science is.[155]

 Camouflage 2 | (1998) | fire, water, air, earth, barbed wire, grass and canvas | 114 x 60 x 20 cm

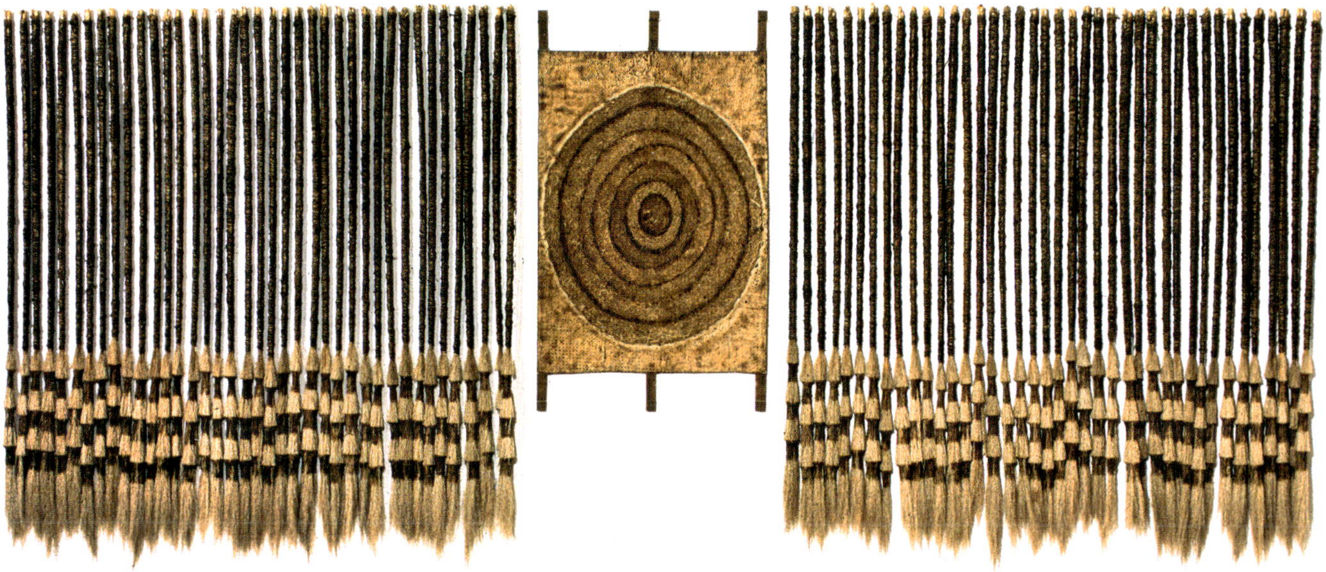

The relation between 'nature' and 'culture' is expressed in various ways in Zulu's work. In, for example, *Artomic Passage 1, 2, 3, 4* and *5* (1999) and *Untitled Ivory Painting* (2002), the surface of the field, or ground, is pocked by a pattern of small bumps. The form and geometry of these raised marks strongly suggests a pattern of lesions made on the skin of the human body or the depiction of warts on cow hides (*amasumpa*) on classical Zulu wooden objects such as milk pails.[156] What we have here is a form of writing on the body surface. Skin and canvas – or the surface of an object – correlate as fields for inscription. Inscriptions which must include body scarification, tattooing and other 'irreversible' forms of body modification common in many, perhaps all, cultures.[157] Zulu's early *Twin Spirits* (1995) and his more recent *Royal Court Art: Work 1* (2004) and works in-between express his interest in forms of body modification as they relate to identity.[158]

Skin thus equates with the surface of the canvas or object, all being image-fields.[159] Arnold Rubin, for example, speaks of the "artistic potency" of skin as "a vehicle for human expression."[160] Importantly for a reading of Zulu's work, Rubin goes on to observe that "irreversible modes of body art amount to a quintessential imposition of a conceptual – cultural – order upon nature."[161] Similarly, some writers argue that from a human evolutionary perspective, the universal impulse shaping writing on the body offers the prototype for visual art, for self-control and for the human control of nature.[162] A bit like taming fire.

Such body-work is incredibly diverse and has an ancient pedigree and a wide geographical distribution.[163] It was also implicated in the cultural dynamics of colonialism.[164] There are many examples of writing on the skin amongst the peoples of Africa, including the Yoruba (Nigeria), Ga'anda (Nigeria), Nuba (Southern Sudan), Tabwa (Democratic Republic of Congo), Baulé (Côte d'Ivoire) and Tiv (Nigeria).[165] Some of the earliest historical inhabitants of southern Africa also practised scarification.[166] Such scarification is a form of writing on the body, and part of what Marc Blanchard calls "a system of exoskeletal defences."[167]

Skin and non-human object surfaces thus constitute a kind of graphic geo-political ground for representation, a powerful idea for writers and artists. Zulu shares his interest in this idea with fellow artist Jeremy Wafer with whom he exhibited at the Michael Stevenson Gallery in 2003.[168] Sue Williamson, reviewing the exhibition, wrote that moving between the work of these two artists "gives the viewer a fine sense of what it can mean to be a contemporary artist committed to the African landscape."[169]

That landscape is somatic. In a strong sense Zulu (like Wafer) creates landscapes of the body, touching on a powerful sensibility in South African literature and art. We have a long indigenous history where boundaries between body and earth, skin and earthly surfaces, are fluid. Zulu's own words give us a stark sense of this exchange; "even though you bleed my blood / I love you / Land of the savannahs / Land of human kindness. I love you my land, you know?

Frontline with Target | (1997) | fire, water, air, earth, reed, grass and canvas | 500 x 200 cm

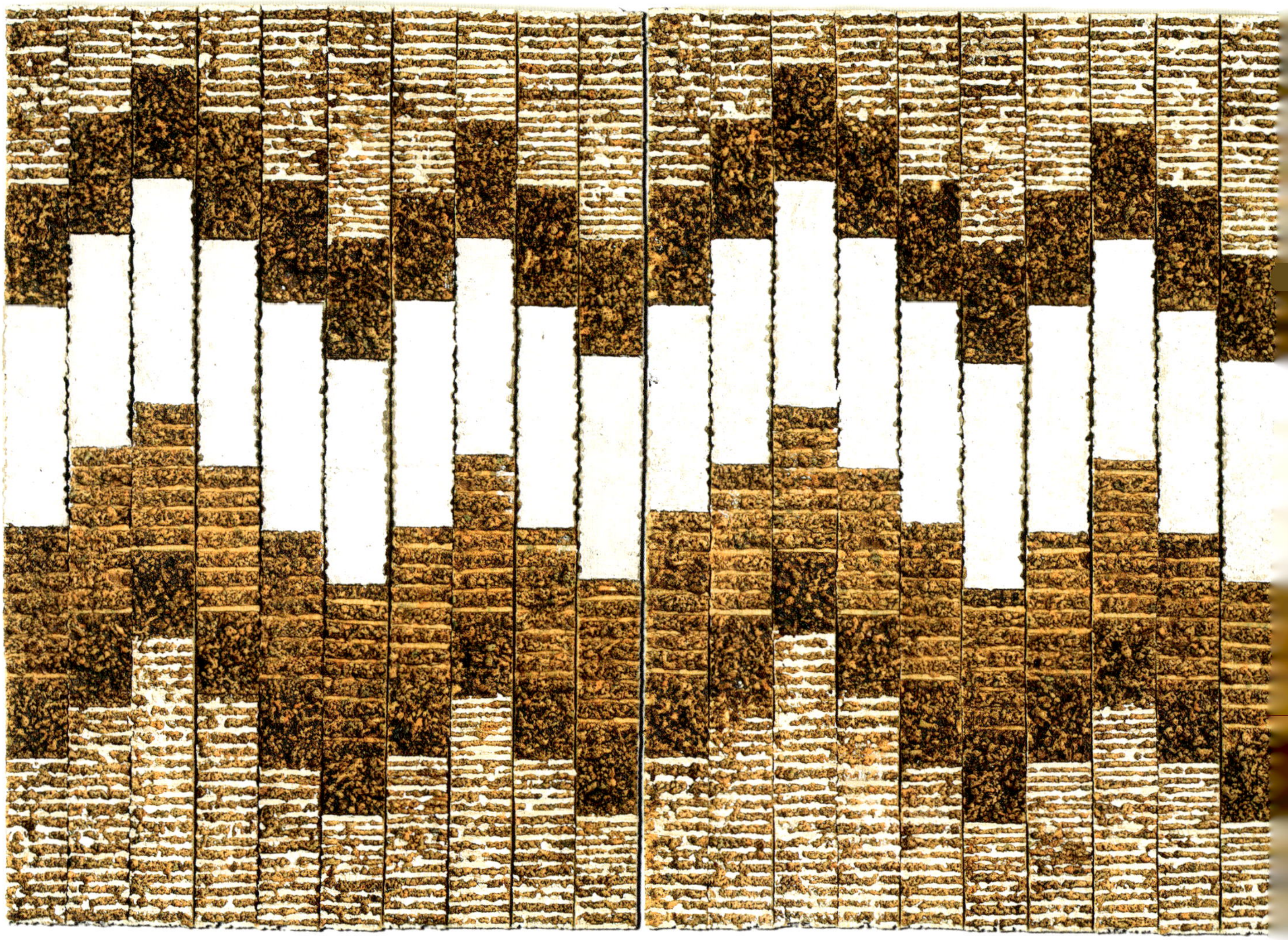

 Royal Court Art – Work 1 Image 1 | (2004) | fire, water, air, earth and foam | 332 x 114 cm

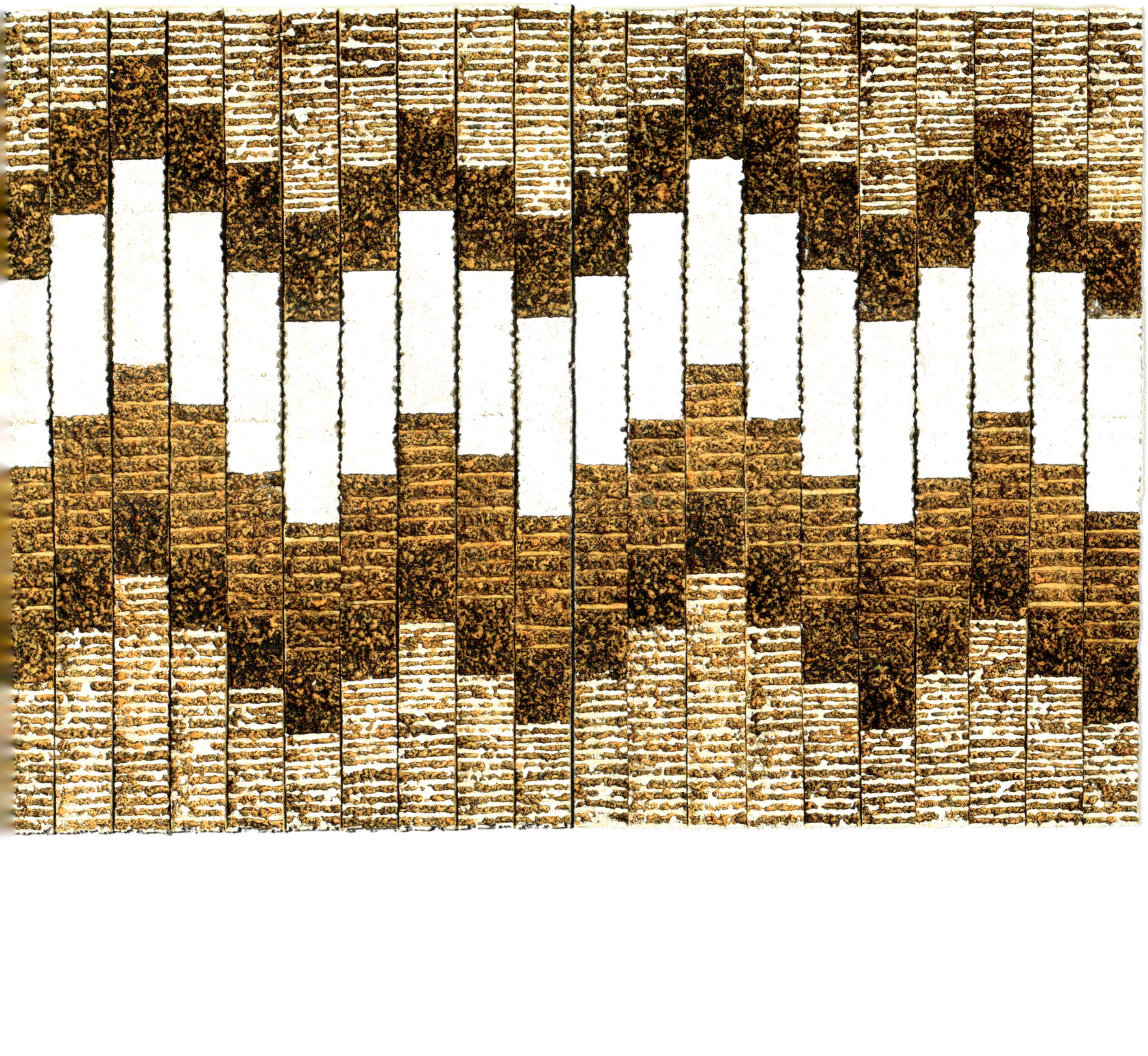

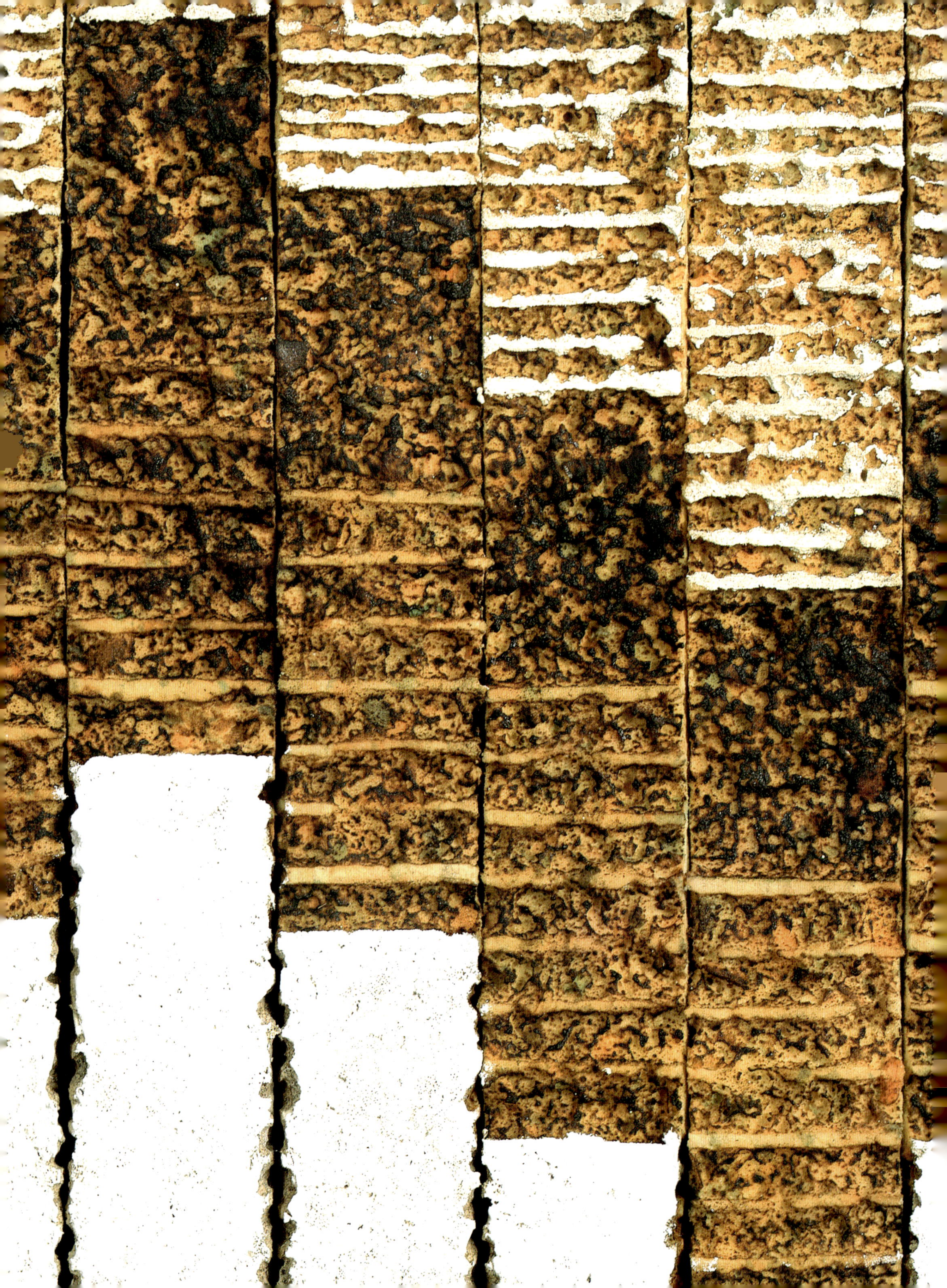

even though your body has grown soulless / I am your soul / even though you bleed my blood / I breathe your soil".[170] The language of a humanised land – be it metropolitan, settled, urban lots or wild and rural open veld – is present virtually everywhere in his work.

In his early *Landscapes with Spheres: Study in Spaces and Structures* (1995), for example, we find an image of parched earth, where the skin of the soil cracks for lack of water. Given relatively limited formal and material means it is remarkable how varied in form, intensity and intricacy his marking of surfaces is and remains, as is clear in his recent *Lines of Origin* (2004) and *Spinal* (2004). This variety of marking is repeated in his language of construction, which sometimes suggests weaving, plaiting or dappled light and shadow and other fugitive natural phenomena.

The striking connection between world and body, between the face of the earth and the human face may be considered as part of a larger humanist project. The humanisation of nature, an animation of the inert, the recognition of the spiritual in the terrestrial is powerfully linked to what it might currently mean to be an African, and why this meaning is important. As a strategy, or more problematically, as a kind of cultural fundamentalism, these questions are highly visible on the cultural and political agenda in post-Apartheid South Africa. The ideas embedded in such questions find dramatic public expression in President Thabo Mbeki's recent "I am an African" address:[171]

> I am an African. I owe my being to the hills and the valleys, the mountains and the glades, the rivers, the deserts, the flowers, the seas and the ever-changing seasons that define the face of our native land.
> My body has been frozen in our frosts and in our latter-day snows. It has thawed in the warmth of our sunshine and melted in the heat of midday sun. The crack and rumble of the summer thunders, lashed by startling lightning, have been a cause for both trembling and hope.[172]

The merging of land and body in this way is a major trope in South African art and literature. Writer Antjie Krog's notion of a 'country of my skull' is a recent and dramatic case in point.[173] Speaking of a river, of water in her *Change of Tongue* (2003), Krog writes, "Your body has become the catchment for an entire landscape of despondency... How can I talk to you? You with your surface as warm as skin and icy undertones? Do I need a special language? A new tongue? How?"[174]

Zulu implies more than depicts the body in his work, usually as a kind of humanised hieroglyph wrought from history and the earth. *Baptism of Fire* (1995) is an example, as are the central panel of *Frontline with Centurion Models* (1997) and *Camouflage 1* (1998). This implied body in Zulu's work – which is also a function of scale – is the locus of identity and its vicissitudes in this neo-colonial moment. As African intellectual Achille Mbembe summarises, colonialism was

> to a large extent, a way of disciplining bodies with the aim of making better use of them... But it would be wrong to reduce the meaning of colonial violence to economics. The whip and the cane also served to force upon the Africans a concocted identity...[175]

In Zulu's work the body and its surfaces inevitably query what it is to be human or indeed inhuman. The breaching of the intimate relation between the physical earth and the human body, the violence visited on both, speak to an (in)human existence. To redeem this violence, the artist's concern with certain 'indigenous' visual and oral forms and ways of being associated with Africa become significant. In this regard, anthropomorphism animates his work, whether by contiguity, as in the worker's trommel (metal trunk) filled with barbed wire in *Study for Abduction* (1997) or formal similarity, as in the implied figure in the central section of *Frontline with Centurion Models* (1997) or *Masquerade Shield* (1998). Fire itself is readily anthropomorphised; it is said to run, leap, crown and creep, escape, restore, smoulder and rage. It can also backfire.

In his *Abduction of the Text: Total Eclipse* (1999) scorching the paper surface creates a strong sense of larval flow, the cooling residue of the eruption of liquid fire in the core far below the surface of the world, seen from far above. Here the surface of the circle is wrinkled and seared in skin-like paper. The word 'tissue' comes most strongly to mind here, either as manufactured or as organic body material, parchment in which corporeal skin and terrestrial surface coincide.

Perhaps the general sensibility captured here is common in so-called postcolonial countries. Writer David Malouf, in an interview with cultural critic Nikos Papastergiadis, makes this pithy observation about settler and indigenous experiences of landscape. Malouf's text is relevant to South Africa, but especially to Zulu's particular forms of humanising and anthropomorphising the land:

> When those early European Settlers came to confront the Australian landscape, it wasn't the hostility of extreme drought and rain that was most frightening to them, rather it was the sense that the landscape reflected nothing back of their own humanity. They would look at it and it would remain as something quite separate. It has not been shaped by them and so they could not see their humanity in it... What the settlers in this book [*An Imaginary Life*] can't see is that the continent had already been completely humanised by the people who lived there.[176]

The same inclination to humanisation can also be expressed in other directions, for example, in non-human, animal skin. Zulu's Study for *Monumental Shield* (1998) and *Indluyengwe (Leopard's Lair)* (2000) express a powerful identification between the surfaces of the human body, the animal body, objects and the earth. Surfaces seem to co-mingle in a kind of pan-human animism in a process Zulu engages with quiet, almost ritual pleasure.[177] There is also, incidentally, a connection with fire here; an African myth from Sierra Leone links the leopard's spots with fire "Since then all the Leopards... have been marked all over their bodies with black spots where the fingers of Fire touched them."[178] For Zulu the leopard connotes royalty. Reading this work in terms of faunal camouflage, Zulu also references a nineteenth-century imperial Zulu regiment named after this graceful carnivore.[179] These works refer to the 'lair' of both animal and army, but also, beyond this, through the image of a rolled up reed mat above the camouflaged field in *Study for Monumental Shield* (1998), to the more homely place of hearth and hut.

In another, more recent exhibition, "Tremor" (2004), travelling in Europe, the earth seems subject to wider seismic stellar and subterranean forces. The specific works on this exhibition, *Procession of Stones* (2004), *Procession of Ambers 1* and *2* (2004), *Labyrinth of Genes and Elements 1* and *2* (2004) all suggest an expansion of his work into more abstract microcosmic and macrocosmic topographies. One commentator suggests that these later works "exist in a world of their own," which underlines the move to a greater simplicity, spirituality and abstraction.[180] Zulu's *Points of the Delta* (2003), for example, refers to a triangular sedimented landmass at the mouth of a river, where the single flow of water disperses into tributaries before emptying into the ocean. Great civilizations – the Indus, the Nile, the Tigris-Euphrates, the Huang – have developed in the fertile, arable ground of deltas. The shards of history often found in delta archaeological digs become his *Shards of the Delta* (2003). But Zulu's vision is celestial and terrestrial. Both the terrestrial triangle and the five-pointed star *Delta Cephei* – in the core and halo of the Milky Way – make up the works for *Points of the Delta* (2003).[181] In the "Parliamentary Millennium Project" exhibition of November 2002, the Milky Way is depicted as smoke from an earthly, human fire.[182] The five-pointed star is present in the artist's studio arrangement described in Section 02 above. The star is made from the link fencing and already industrially shaped to morph easily into the celestial figure.

Yet another way of seeing the interaction of opposing tensions that Zulu mines so creatively involves forms of knowing and experience which are commonly considered antagonistic. Here I am referring to art and science, spirit and materiality. Art historian Sandra Klopper, writing of Zulu's *Untitled* (2003), suggests that in this work the artist explores

> the psychosocial mapping of the human brain... This relationship between science and art is historicised, in Zulu's case, through an evocative approximation of scientific drawings of the human brain that serve to underline the delicate fragility of human existence.[183]

A number of works have titles which suggest the detachment, rationality and objectivity we often associate with scientific knowledge: *Study in Genetics* (2004), *Agitated Artom* (1997), *Elementary Units and Relationships 1* and *2* (2003), *Amatshehlathi (Stones of the Forest)* (2004), *Labyrinth of Genes and Elements* (2004), *Procession of Stones* (2004), *Procession of Ambers 1* and *2* (2004), *Birth of a New World* (1996) and *Abduction of the Text: Total Eclipse* (1999). Zulu's word 'involution' – *Involution 1* and *2* (2002) – puts one in mind of evolution, and the highly variable, systemic process the term suggests. But, at a remove to be sure, it also intimates revolution, an entirely more convulsive social force in which yearnings both spiritual and material coalesce.

Recently Zulu installed a site-specific work in the Cathedral of St. John the Divine in New York.[184] St. John is of a scale only second to St. Peter's in Rome. The cathedral was a fitting venue, as it allowed the artist to work with an almost literal 'spirit' of place, and develop further the more metaphysical aspects of earlier works. The space within the church "has spiritual, symbolic and political power."[185] Five human-scale canvas panels flanked the nave of the St. Boniface Chapel. These panels mediated the soaring scale of the cathedral chapel, transforming intimidation into intimacy.

Four of these canvases are marked by a serpentine, sometimes broken line. This line puts one in mind of the meandering fossilised trail of some ancient microcosmic creature writ large. The pattern is also an extension and expansion of Zulu's interest in the morphology of brain and entrails, metaphorically cerebral thought and gut feeling.[186] Zulu was conscious of referencing surrealist automatic drawing in this work, specifically that of Andre Masson.[187] Here, however, the traces are the product of water, string and fire. The fifth panel is, unusually, not marked in this way, bearing rather a tracery of white chalk gestures on an off-white ground.

On the floor, small groups of rounded rocks collected from the precincts of the Church were arranged. Each pair – one large, one small – was organised in a way which referred to grain grinding stones still quite common in rural areas in this country. Zulu also placed a stone at the lower extremity of the inverted spear of an eleven foot bronze military angel, St. Michael the Archangel. This and other stones, "the stone on the top of the sword, the stone on the altar, activate the space."[188] The artist was also sensitive to the earthy tones of the stone used in the cathedral building and the stones he brought from the outside. He sought to dramatise the interconnectedness between nature and culture within a spiritual

Lines of Origin | (2004) | installation at Cathedral of St. John the Divine, New York

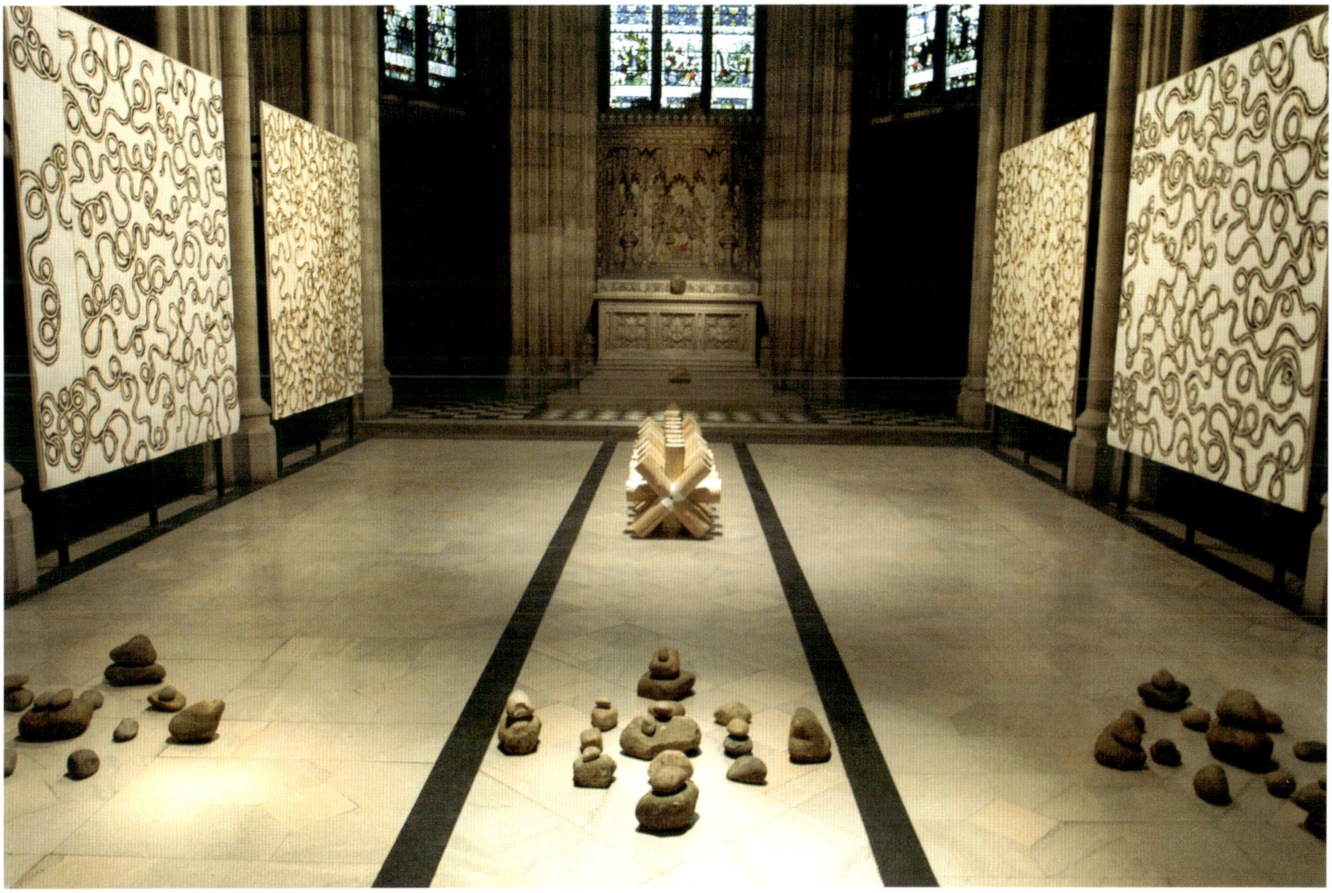

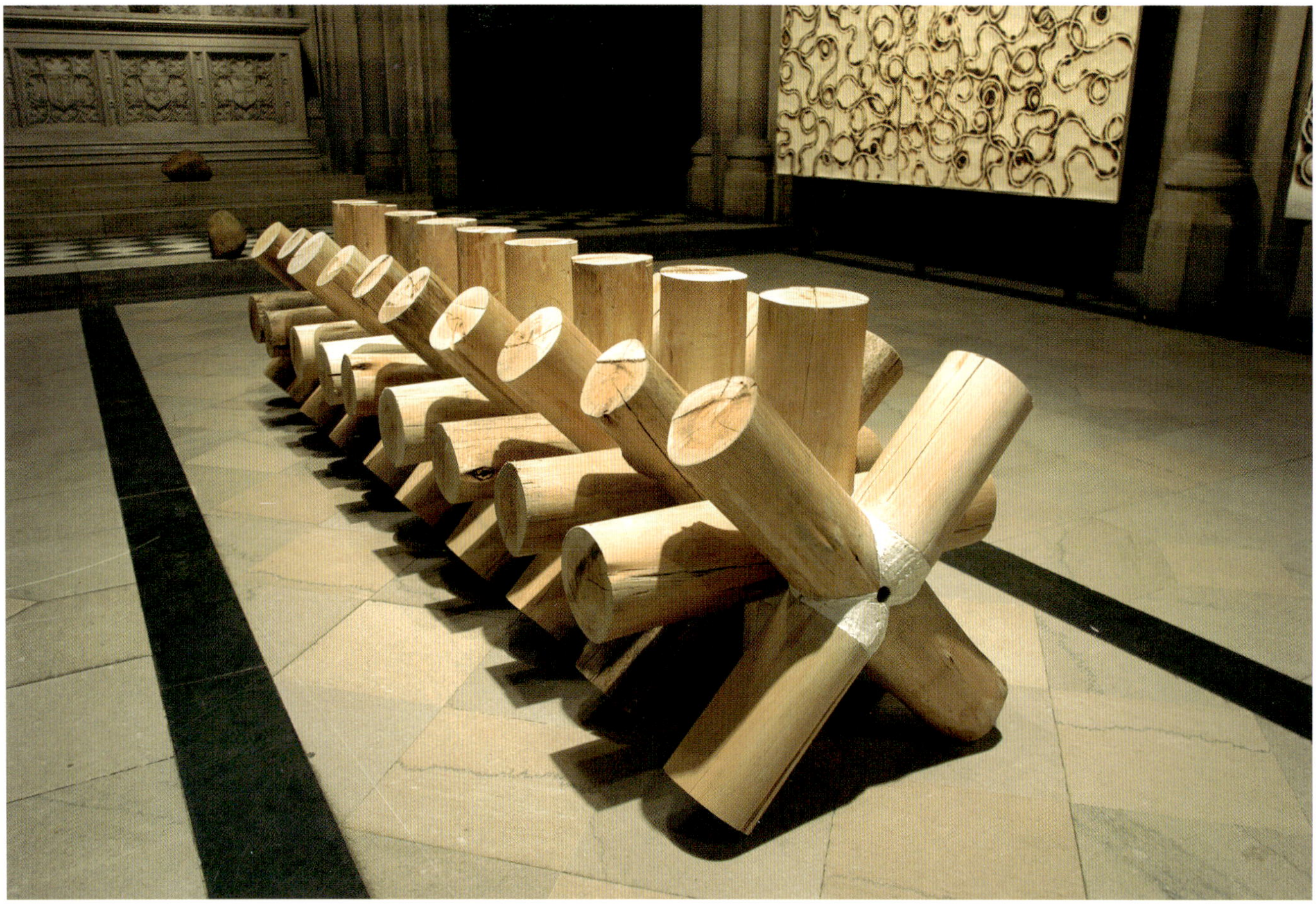

 Spinal | (2004) | wood | 230 x 58 x 54 cm

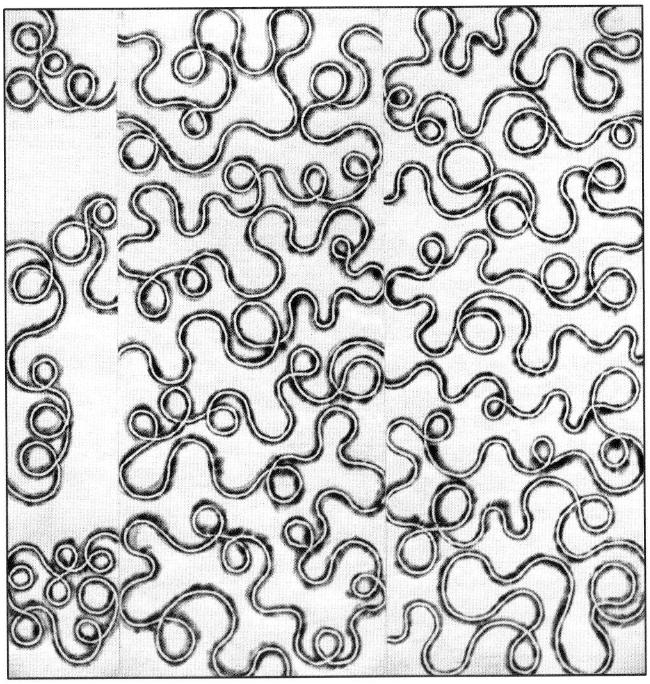

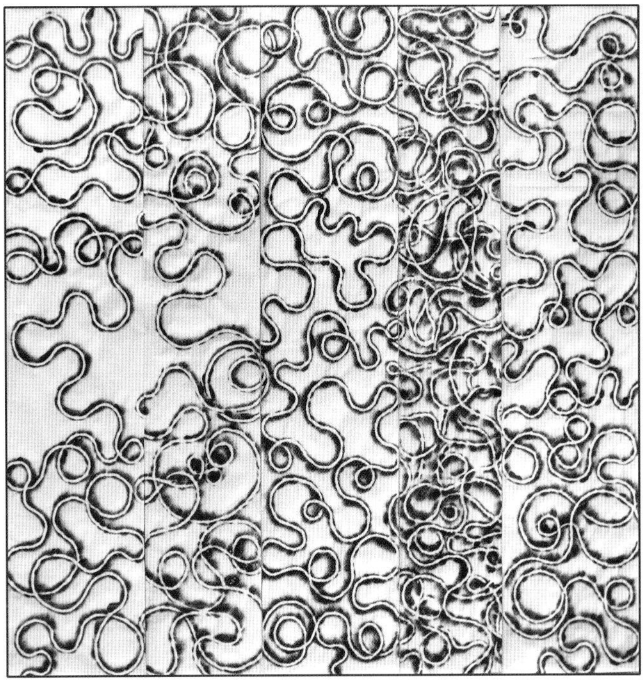

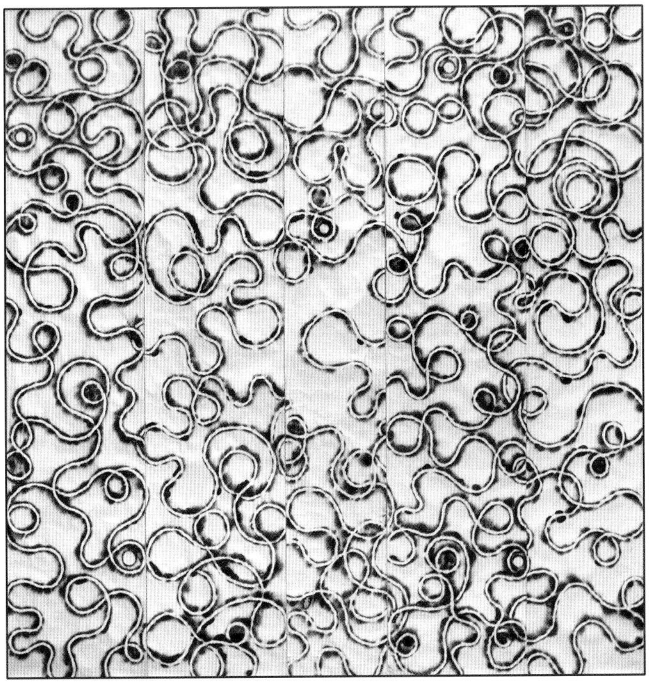

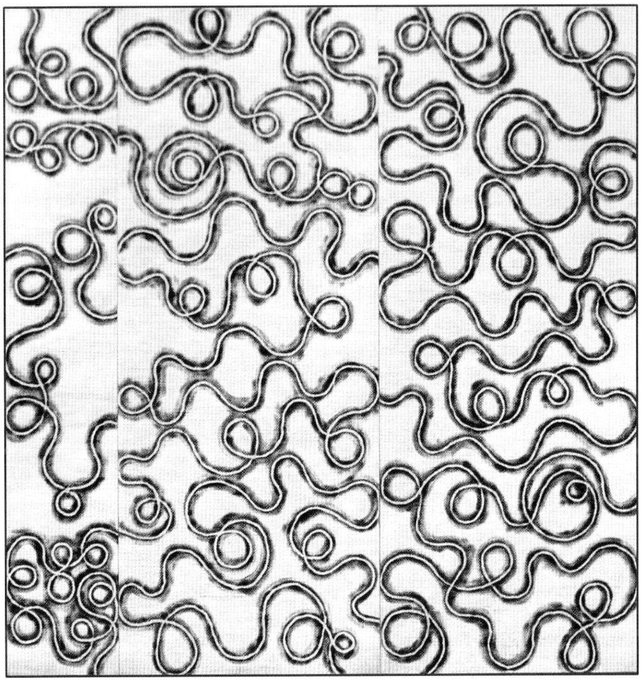

Lines of Origin | (2004) | fire, water, air, earth and fibreglass paper | 243 x 243 cm each

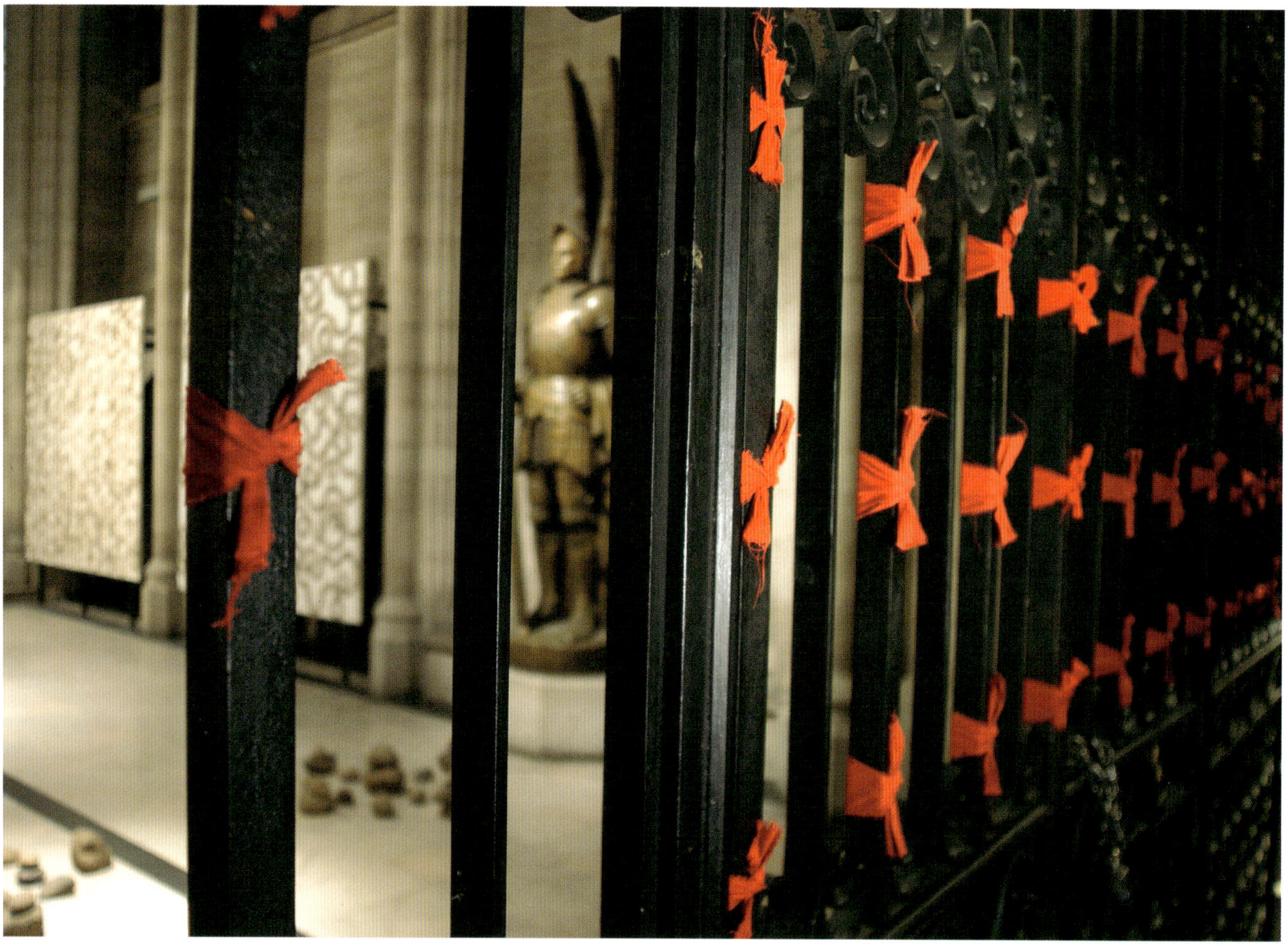

wholeness by emphasising these links. Red cotton cloths were knotted on the entrance grid of the Chapel, and at strategic places within the space. Red is one of the most richly symbolic and embodied of colours, associated with blood, consecration and a sanguine disposition. This last underscores a reading of the rock as a metaphor for a steadfast, resolute selfhood.

Along the main axis of the chapel lay what looked most like a tank-trap. Zulu speaks of this as a 'spine,' something emphasised by being lined up along the central axis of the space. The structure is also articulated in that it comprises alternating kinds of modular crosses ('x' and '+').

Three works, *Artomic 1* (1997), *Artomic 2* (1997) and *Artomic Passage 1, 2, 3, 4* and *5* (1999) refer us to a pamphlet from June 1997, in which Zulu introduces two words that articulate his artistic interests and relate to this aspect of his work; 'artomism' and 'artomic'. Through 'artomism' the artist seeks to address the "psychological struggle of imagining and desire." According to him, 'artomic' – identified with fire, burn marks and "pyrotechnic effect" – derives from the words 'art' and 'atomic.' Atomic energy is the most powerful currently harnessed by human society and, like fire, is a potent force for good and ill, for creation and destruction.

Zulu relates his ideas to an early psychophysical theory of atomism which held that all states, mental and material, interrelate. All comprise elementary units and space, and, as far as fire goes, the Pythagoreans believed that "fire is characterised by a pyramidal shape, while the Atomists thought fire atoms were spherical."[189] The idea sketched by Zulu in his 'artomic' series, can usefully be thought of as engaging what science writer Richard Feynman identifies in the following passage:

> If, in some cataclysm, all of scientific knowledge was destroyed, and only one sentence passed onto the next generation of creatures, what statement would contain the most information in the fewest words? I believe it is the atomic hypothesis – that all things are made of atoms... and that everything animals do, atoms do. There is nothing that living things do that cannot be understood from the point of view that they are made of atoms, acting according to the laws of physics.[190]

Part of what Zulu is trying to capture in his ideas of 'artomic' and 'artomism' is what philosopher Gaston Bachelard characterises as the 'dialectic' of fire, that is, the relation between inner and outer world, between subjective feeling and objective knowledge. It is also a searching for the almost transcendentally elemental in both materials and relations.[191] In conjoining 'art' and 'atomism' Zulu seems to desire, through the choreography of primary, elemental forms and processes, a new start.

But in what direction? Zulu speaks quite explicitly of "socio-historical issues," of "colonisation and decolonisation."[192] From our reading of Zulu's work, and the link between the first democratic elections and renewal, the artist would not want the history that hurts,[193] or the violence that structures that history to be put aside and forgotten. But then he would also presumably not want to petrify that history into a static and unchangeable obstacle to our moving forward.

His response to renewal is in the direction of a new humanism. This intellectual and spiritual turn is also expressed by Zulu's deep interest in a pan-African cultural impulse, or a rooted sense of 'Africanness.' Like other contemporary artists from the continent, Zulu has a powerful feel for the continental value-systems and forms of knowledge crucial for identity and conduct that colonialism sought to sunder or appropriate to its own ends.[194]

The geo-history of the continent is a strong creative motivation for many artists. More specifically, an important dimension of time, a dimension that shapes the beginning of modernity in Africa lies in the relation between permanence and transience, eternal and ephemeral.[195] In other words, what lasts, and what is lost. What stays the same, what changes. Zulu has expressed this dynamic in the language of recuperation – time as simultaneously a kind of redemptive return to origins and a forward movement – directly in his earliest independent works.

In the early multi-panelled, figurative work *Annunciation* (1993), his parched, intense and measured pictorial style anticipates his more mature work. What he depicts iconographically also prefigures in a more literal symbolic register what was to come. Zulu drew ruins, and speaks of these in a tone of provocative, even militant nostalgia.[196] Pictographs (hieroglyphs), static, symmetrical and hieratic figuration in a pictorial space speak of time immemorial. This early work marks Zulu as a romantic, a view both supported and complicated by the mixed spiritual and intellectual traditions of his formal faith.[197]

Zulu's Afromanticism addresses the redemptive power of ruins and ruination, the possibly ancient African roots of world cultures, animism and humanism, history and ancestral myth, scarification and spirituality, the place of individual and collective human agency in an unknowable, magical and mysterious cosmos.[198] Referring to *Annunciation,* Zulu insists on our understanding of, for example, the place of Egyptian culture in Africa, and Africa in the development of civilization and varieties of humanism.[199]

But Zulu is also interested in Africa in another way. Using fire and form he draws on powerful if controversial ideas of distinctively 'African' experience. This impulse to indigenous or native being manifests in many ways, but most obviously in the reparative desire for pre-lapsarian, which here would mean pre-colonial, origins and a usable past for the present. In South Africa recently

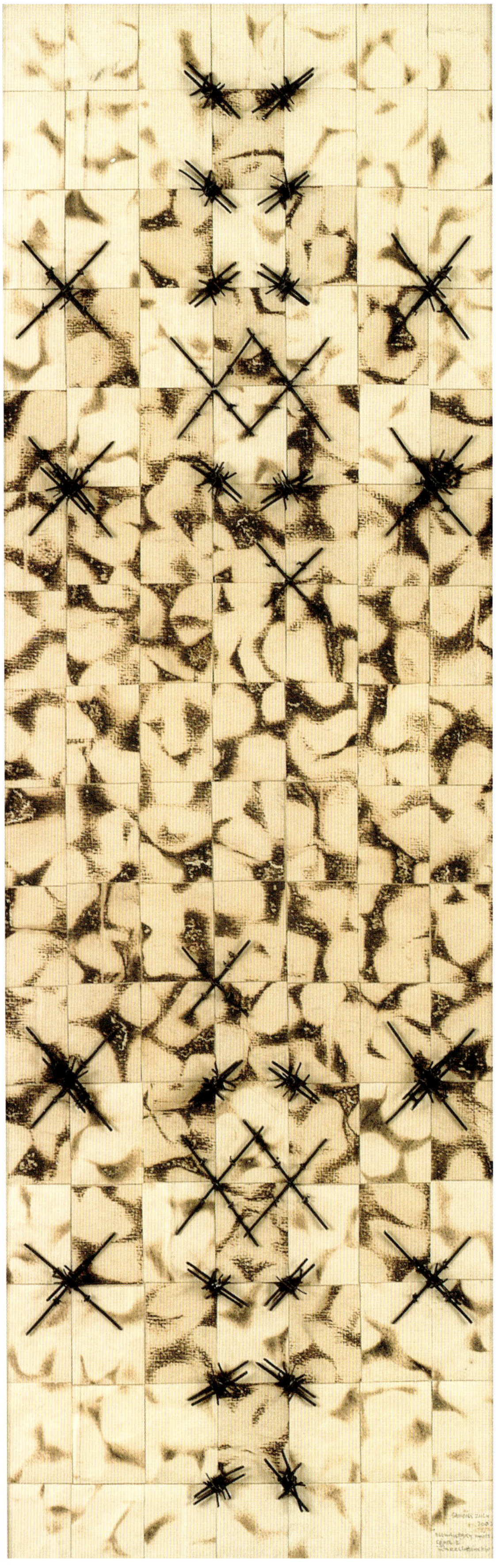

such thinking finds expression in the idea and possibility of an African Renaissance.[200]

Ideas of origin, Africanity, indigenous genius, the authority of identity are controversial, but here productively so. Zulu's work urges us to recognise this productivity, however much it risks being a kind of cultural fundamentalism. As Salah Hassan rightly observes,

> 'return-to-sources' movements in the realm of art... or the intellectual reaction to the colonial situation in general, do not reflect a unified and even process. This process ranges from total rejection of and resistance to the Western 'colonial' culture or rule, to advocacy of a synthesis of the native culture and 'Western' elements.[201]

There is of course a spectrum of responses possible to the quandary of rootedness and origins, and the ideas of authenticity based on these, especially given the traumatic uprooting of the past in a present effected by colonialism and its contemporary offshoots. Another way of looking at the recuperative impulse within a synthesising creative attitude invokes something we might call an 'African' humanism, a slightly contradictory usage, as humanism implies more a global than a continental humanity. Notwithstanding this, K. Geyekye, for example, argues that if we

> were to look for a pervasive and fundamental concept in African socioethical thought generally – a concept that animates other intellectual activities and forms of behaviour, including religious behaviour, and provides continuity, resilience, nourishment, and meaning of life – that concept would most probably be humanism.[202]

Considered in the light of Zulu's iconography of fire, the search for such a humanism summons the voice of Frantz Fanon. Speaking of the sterility of inflammatory fervour, Fanon writes,

> These truths were a fire in me then [three years ago]. Now I can tell them without being burned. These truths do not have to be hurled in men's faces. They are not intended to ignite fervour. Every time [fervour] has burst out somewhere, it has brought fire, famine and misery.... And contempt for man. Fervour is the weapon of choice for the impotent. Of those who heat the iron in order to shape it at once. I should prefer to warm man's body and leave him. We might reach this result; Mankind retaining this fire through self-

 Elementary Units and Relationships 1 | (2003) | fire, water, air, earth, vinyl and wire | 120 x 50 cm

> combustion. Mankind set free from the trampoline that is the resistance of others, and digging into his own flesh to find a meaning.[203]

Zulu, the cool "hardworking arsonist,"[204] draws on the kind of composed self-sufficiency, self-reliance and sovereignty which Fanon so powerfully describes here. Fanon's fervour is in some ways present in Njabulo Ndebele's ideas of exorbitant spectacle which dominated the years of vicious racial oppression.[205] It also resonates with Achille Mbembe's conceptualisation of the "aesthetics of vulgarity."[206]

The dramaturgy of spectacle both continued and terminated in the Truth and Reconciliation Commission (TRC) in the late 1990s.[207] The TRC has arguably provided an important anchor and beacon for much critical post-1994 art in South Africa,[208] stimulating diverse responses from intellectuals, writers and artists within the country and beyond.[209] Material poverty, spiritual destruction, land-hunger, the contending norms of cultural conduct across power-inflected difference, the dignity and sanctity of the body, social equity and justice, an entire moral landscape of emotion and desire, self- and other consciousness became conspicuous in the TRC.[210] As, indeed, did those forms of historical desire and denial constitutive of our moral and affective universe. The varied creative and intellectual responses to the TRC bear testimony to what a fundamentally generative, creative phenomenon it was. These sometimes match the intensity of the varied modes of communication – oral, written, photographic and performative – which shaped the TRC process itself.[211]

Apartheid was a crime against humanity, separating us from ourselves and the wider world. This crime and the image of humanity it tried to destroy provide the experience and energy present in much of Zulu's creative effort. The cultural antidote to Apartheid inhumanity and its tenacious traces in the present is perhaps best captured by the idea of *ubuntu*.[212] This idea provided the TRC's ethical compass, and that of the new constitution, and the idea may be considered a spring and container for cultural creativity.[213]

Moeketsi Letseka makes the links explicit, arguing that humanisms of Africa find expression in *ubuntu, umuntu ngumuntu ngabantu* (Nguni), or *motho ke motho ka batho* (Sotho).[214] The TRC reports spell out the idea in this way:

> As far as traditional African values are concerned, the fundamental importance of *ubuntu* might be highlighted. *Ubuntu*, generally translated as 'humanness', expresses itself metaphorically in *umuntu ngumuntu ngabantu* – people are people through other people.[215]

For Constitutional Court Justice Makgoro the spirit of *ubuntu* "emphasises respect for human dignity, making a shift from confrontation to conciliation,"[216] while Mfuniselwa Bhengu links *ubuntu* explicitly to democracy.[217] Constitutional Court Justice Pius Langa speaks of its absence as part of a crisis in civil society.[218] Scholar Mark Sanders also refers to the loss of *ubuntu* during apartheid.

> In the most basic sense, ethics is a relation to the other. Ubuntu is an ethics of human reciprocity that shows that there is no ethics that is not also against apartheid. To identify a loss of ubuntu is thus to identify the evil, the untruth even, of apartheid in all its forms...Ubuntu operates a certain dispropriation. If set out... as the ethics of responsibility, ubuntu captures how the relation to the other is prior to the selfhood of the self, how the relation is a condition of possibility for the self-hood of the self...[219]

Importantly, Sanders also refers to the mutability of the concept as a communitarian alternative to human rights. For Sanders, *ubuntu* "has within it the ability to alter itself," and with this the stabilisation it offers is "powerful but provisional." *Ubuntu* takes place between members of a community, but also, critically, between strangers:

> The other is prior to the self, and the self comes into being in a response to and for the other. Formalizing ubuntu as a communitarian alternative to human rights brings a provisional stability during a transitional phase. However, it is ubuntu's essential dispropriation – of *umuntu* and *abantu* – that works against any *single* formalization of human-being acquiring permanence as the basis for ethics and politics.[220]

The evil associated with witchcraft, for example, is also "the very opposite of *ubuntu*, of hospitality and sharing and of those virtues that make one human and good and life worth living."[221]

Arguably *ubuntu* seems yet to attract the hyperbolic hubris of, for example, the idea of an African Renaissance[222] and the earlier 'Rainbowism,'[223] both of which surfaced during the first years of our democracy. Like any ideal it is also a romance which can be appropriated and overused, by artists as much as politicians, in a facile and superficial way. Artists are often uncomfortable with social orthodoxies implied by notions of African humanism.[224]
And it may be that, uncomfortably, humanism in Africa as elsewhere exists in the breach more than the observance, in inhumanity.

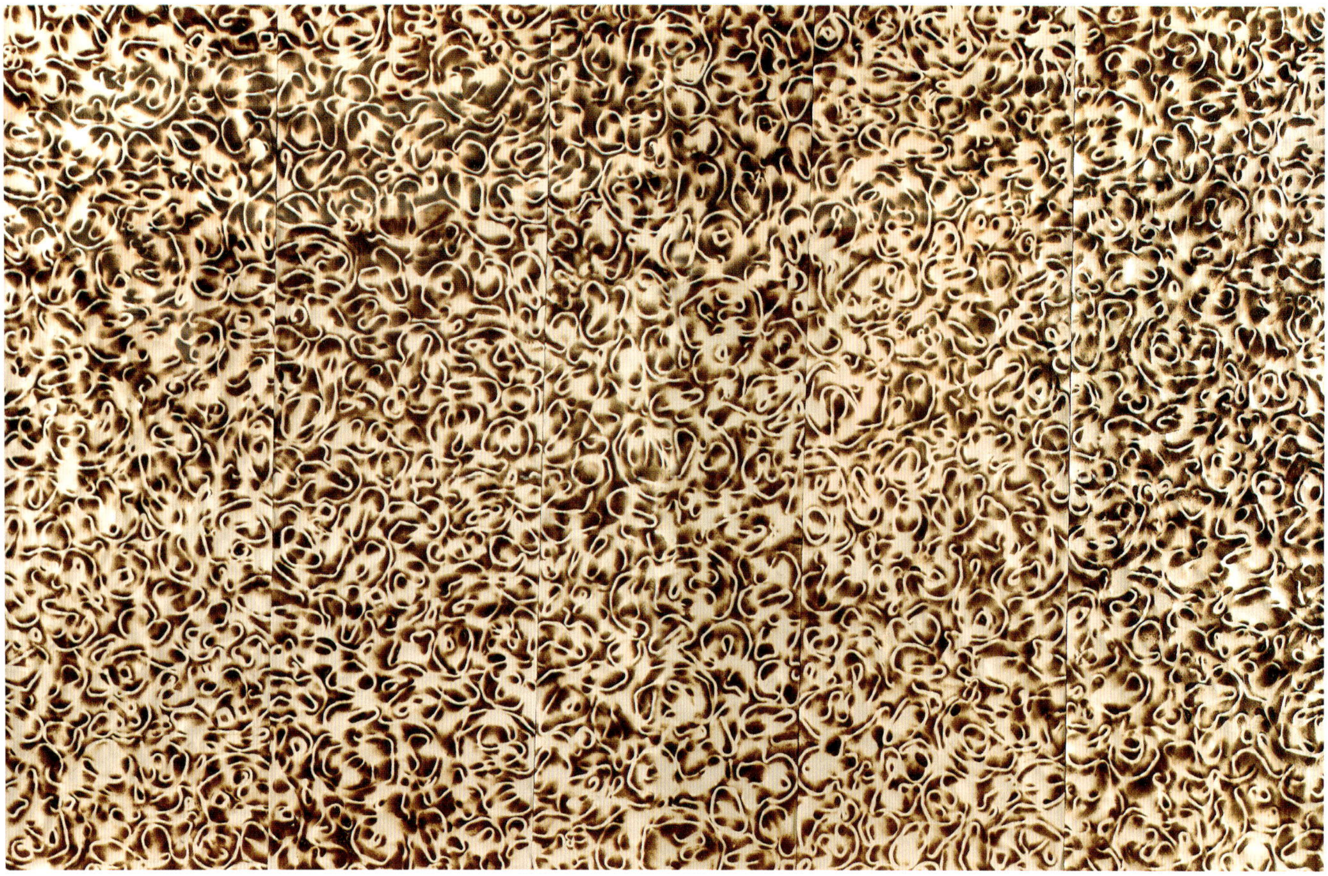

 Labyrinth of Genes and Elements 2 | (2004) | fire, water, air, earth, canvas and wire | 300 x 200 cm

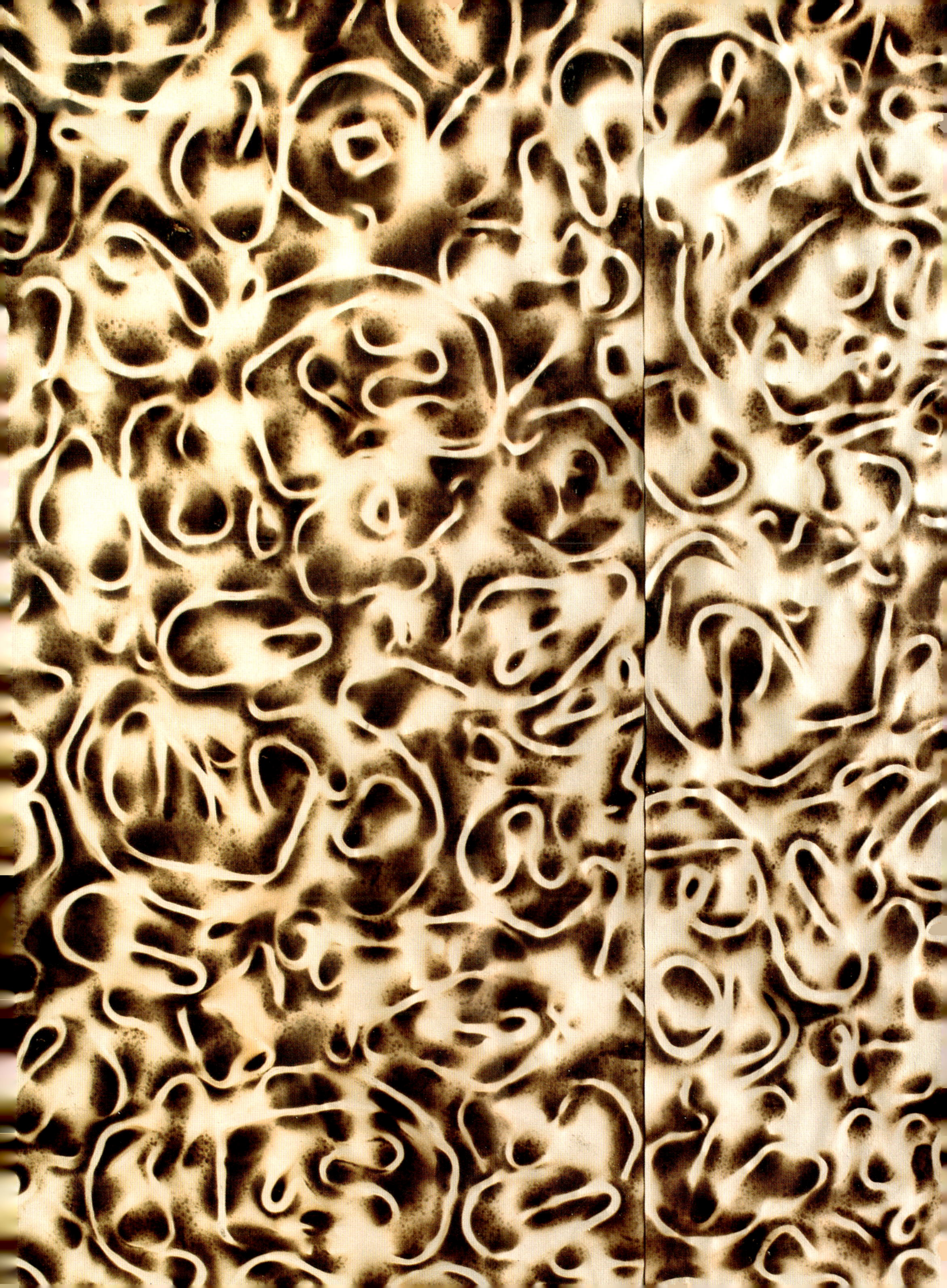

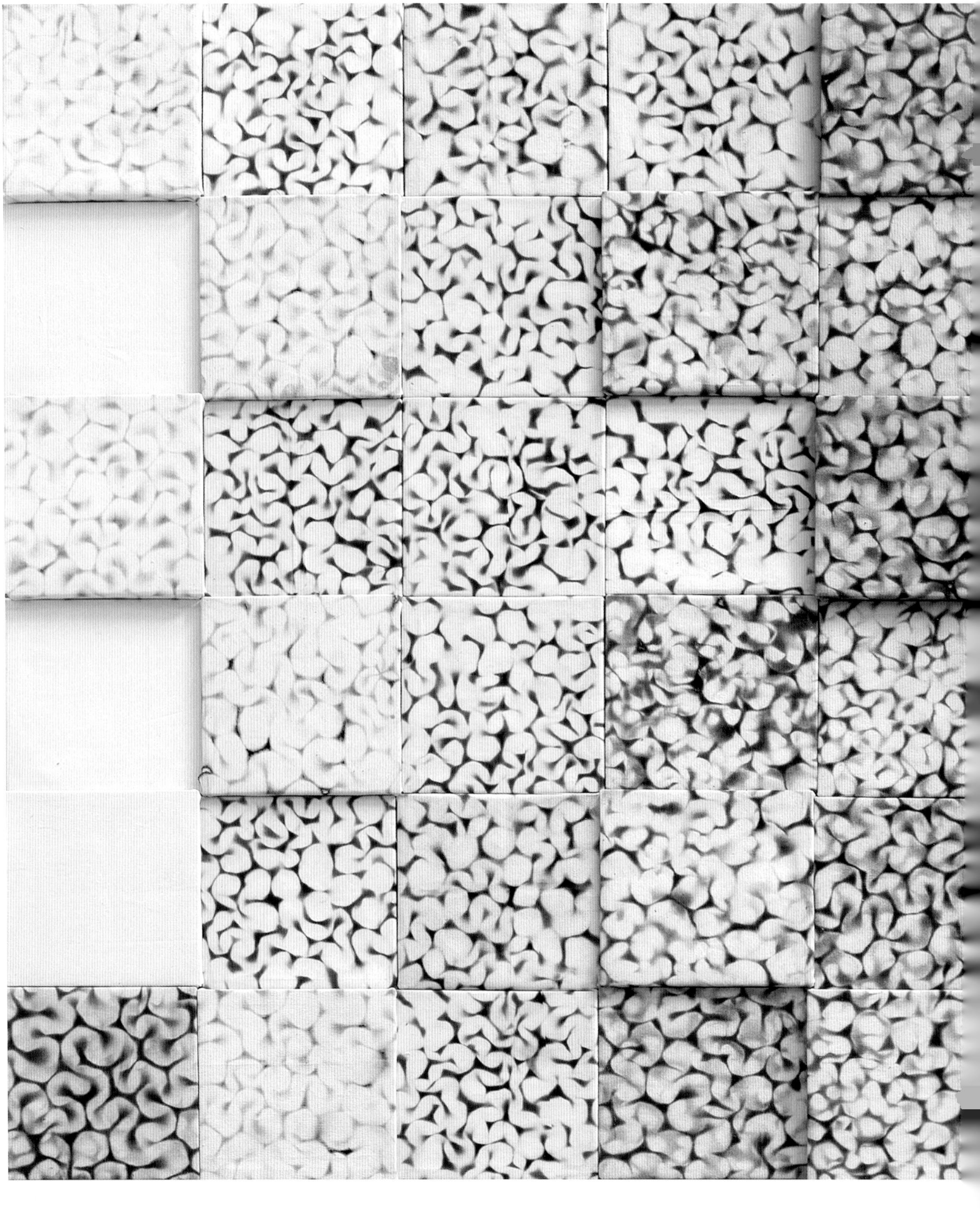

 Labyrinth of Genes and Elements 1 | (2004) | fire, water, air, earth, canvas and stones | 300 x 180 cm

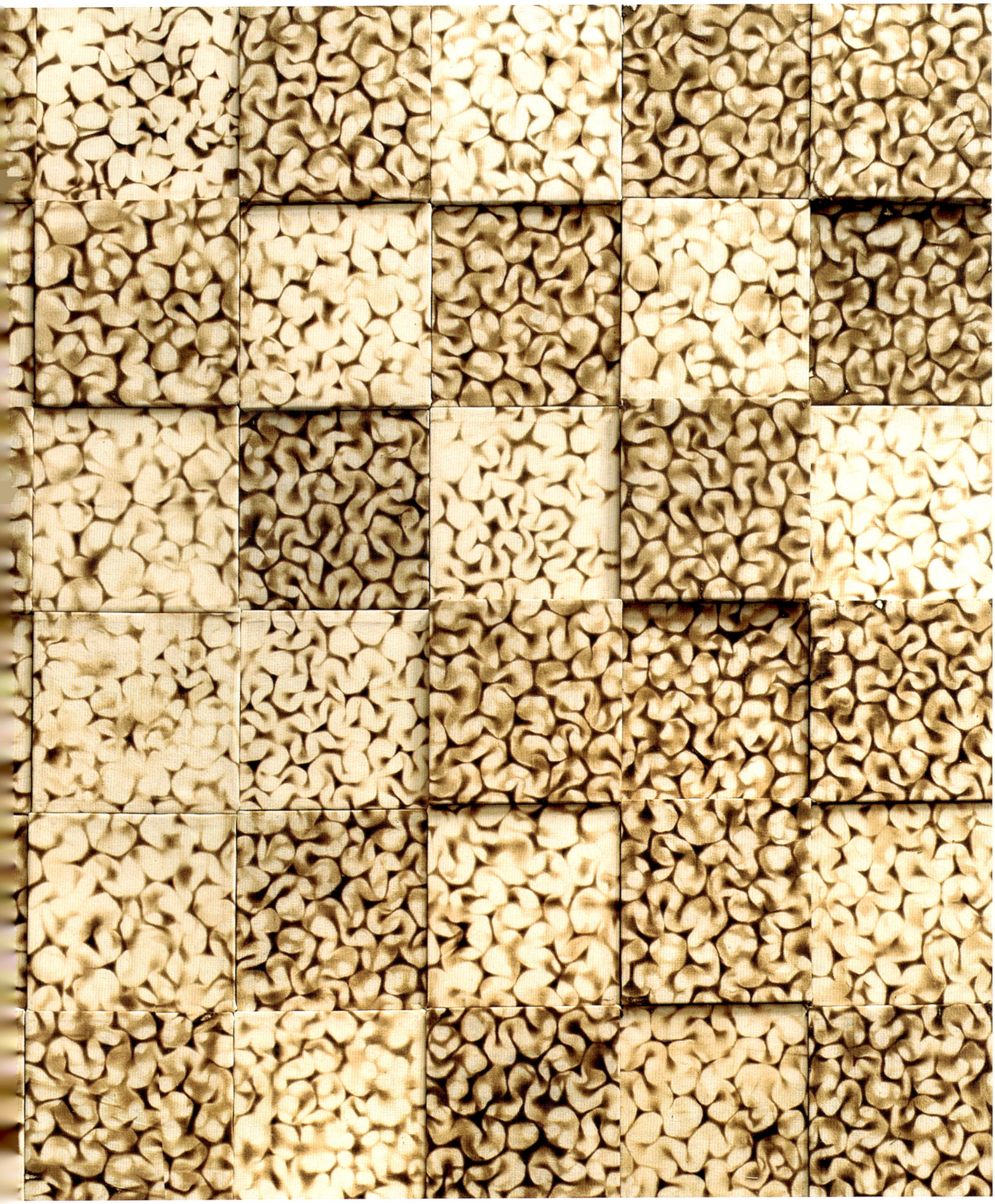

08. STARS LOOK LIKE FIRE (COMING FULL CIRCLE)

At any rate its invocation here, and perhaps in the critical literature on the sentimental subject of humanism, is strategic and not fundamentalist. The word 'humanism' recalls Chinua Achebe's comments about the tag 'African' used by different speakers: "Each of these tags has a meaning... a penalty and a responsibility."[225]

There is thus no prophylactic against sentimental or opportunistic appropriation of *ubuntu*. Like other ideas of humanism *ubuntu* cannot be inoculated against hubris, and the risk increases if we lose sight of the violence embedded within our social relations, our senses of community, our history. Consciousness of violence, be it internal or external in source, is creatively necessary. Violence is part of Zulu's choice of fire as a medium. Metropolitan cynicism and the sophistry of ideas of humanness by artists and writers are also part of this violence.[226] If we retain a consciousness of violence whatever its source, and the conflicts and contradictions this consciousness provokes, sentimental appropriation seems less likely. It is a matter of the strategic articulation of violence of conflicting experiences and the ideas that represent them. This is a hard point to make when violence and its effects are everywhere present, often traumatically so. It is also hard to make, given the tainted humanism that underpinned so much colonial expansionism.

Externally, violence is deeply implicated in the dark underside of the historical humanism of the Enlightenment. It propelled the genocidal inhumanity of colonialism, its complicity being something of which Zulu is clearly aware. As Frantz Fanon and our own Steve Biko remind us, enlightenment humanism went hand in hand with rapacious European imperialism, signalling not humane emancipation but enslavement and "an avalanche of murders."[227] African humanism seeks something different, a search which takes as it backdrop the continent's own complex background of persistent internal violence and social strife.[228] For Zulu, in his "Song of the Spirit," "in the end / I shall walk away triumphant / my blackness more beautiful than in lifetime / in my white skull / shall grow the mast of liberation."

Drawing on the humanism in *ubuntu* opens insights into those intricate but decisive social forces which condition our art making. It can focus our creative responses to the actual historical challenges we face. The TRC and the African humanism that guided it produced an aesthetic and ethical eco-system, a powerful symbolic and affective cultural atmosphere. It allowed us to draw breath.[229] Zulu's creativity does indeed breathe, air and wind (nature's breath) being so central to his project. This artist's engagement of the 'nature/ culture' dynamic, his humanising of nature, his humane appropriation of urban discards, his anthropocentricism, can all be considered part of the practice of *ubuntu*. In the poem "Unveiling a Tombstone," Zulu writes, "he rejected static art /a futurist a master earth artist he was / deeper than trails and scars / of inhuman forces..."

Zulu recalls a memorable moment, when he was about ten, in which his artistic ambitions were acknowledged. After formal study at school, he and his fellow pupils were meant to practise reading and writing. Zulu often did neither, preferring to draw with whatever material came to hand including charcoal on pieces of scrap paper he collected. Drawing absorbed him, and broke the numbing tedium of academic work. But more than this, drawing was a pleasure. Zulu's teachers, as teachers often do, took a dim view of his straying from the prescribed path, and the boy was routinely scolded and punished. Eventually the headmaster came to hear of this obstinate pupil's odd behaviour after class. Asked why he insisted on drawing instead of academic work, the youngster answered, "Because it gives me a rest.... Because I enjoy it. It helps me do the other work better."[230] The surprised headmaster was impressed by his strength of will, his passion and his insight into what he was about and from then on, the teachers left the boy alone to continue his creative meditations. What we see now are the fruits of such tolerance by those with the power to make or break a creative process before it starts. The fruit is nourishing, if bittersweet.

Fed by edgy experiences from rural and urban living, the temporal present in his work is animated by the desire for a partly lost past, a struggle for recovery stained by violence. A sharp sense of the conflicts that make up our history gives his work an intense depth and a quiet vitality. In the 'natural' world of agriculture and the wild veld, the artist harvests and processes material close to him, free and ecologically non-invasive: reeds, roots, grass. Yet he also manipulates more malignant, toxic, aggressive materials: barbed wire and industrial debris belonging to a world of human waste, enclosure and fear. His interest is in militaristic culture, in nature and history as competition. His major medium is fire, his temperament cool. It is through such a temperament that the artist annexes a long history of "decay, destruction, renewal and purification,"[231] ceaselessly searching for an affective, aesthetic alchemy of a very material kind. His devotional distance allows him to manage the messy, mutable and ancient archives of creative life in, as he puts it, "the social and psychological struggle for freedom of creative desire and imagining." Poet and writer Eduardo Galeano writes that the "sword of fire opens up an avenue..."[232] Zulu's work opens just such an avenue, humane, vivid and bold, never pacifying the pulse of life.

Zulu's art offers us a meditation on our resources of life and creativity as well as death and destructiveness. In this artist's hands, in his imagination, searching becomes a generous energy, an expressive communication, a form of recovery, of creative restitution, a romance. Playing with fire enchants us all, much like the night sky. In a poem by one Diä!kwain (ca. 1873), Dorothea Bleek's "favourite murderer" and part of the Bleek household until her death, speaks of hamerkop, staring into water and "sees everything / even that the stars look like fire.[233]

Detail, **Royal Court Art – Work 2 Image 2** | (2005) | fire, water, air, earth and plastic pipes | 610 x 130 cm

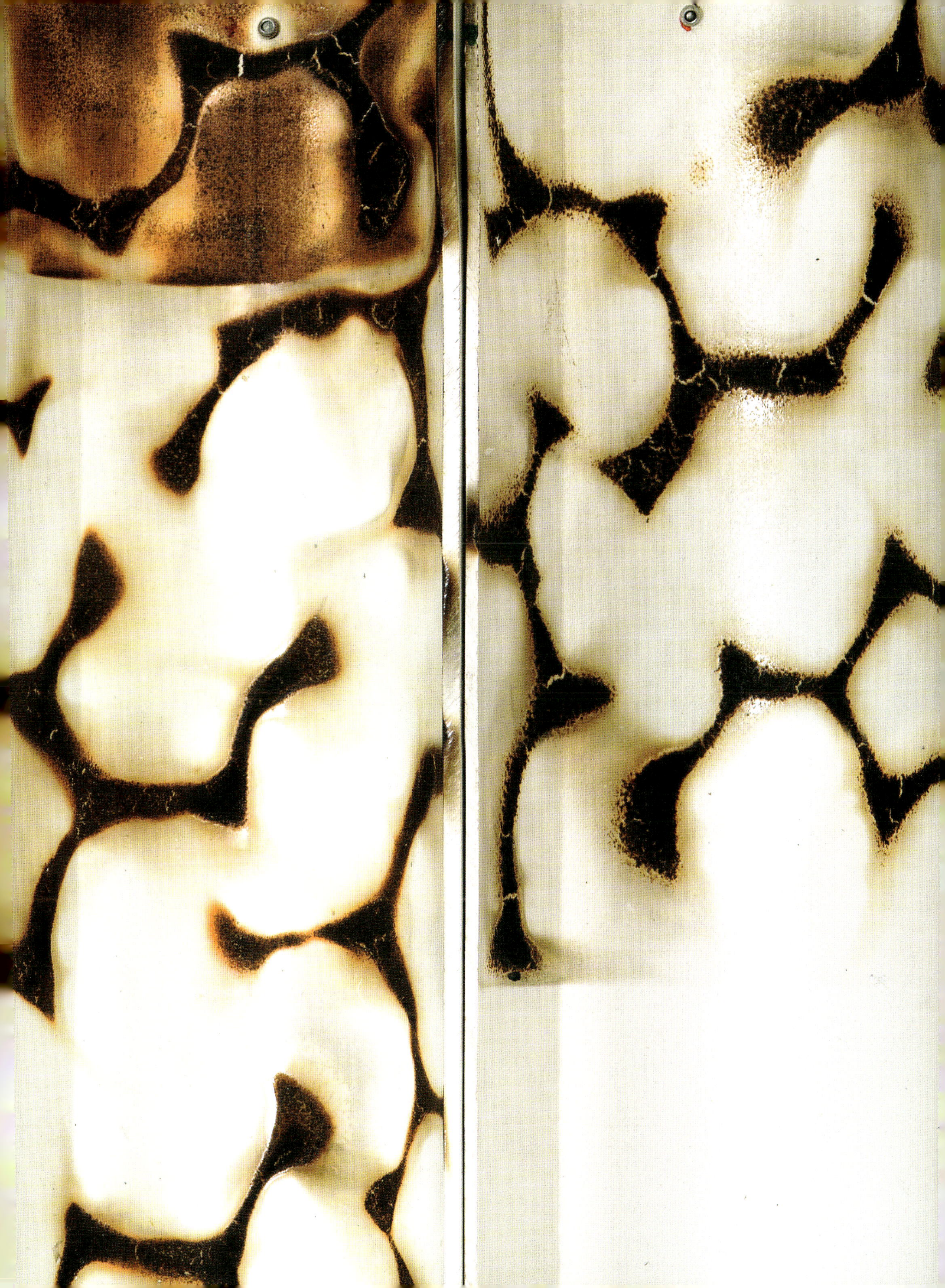

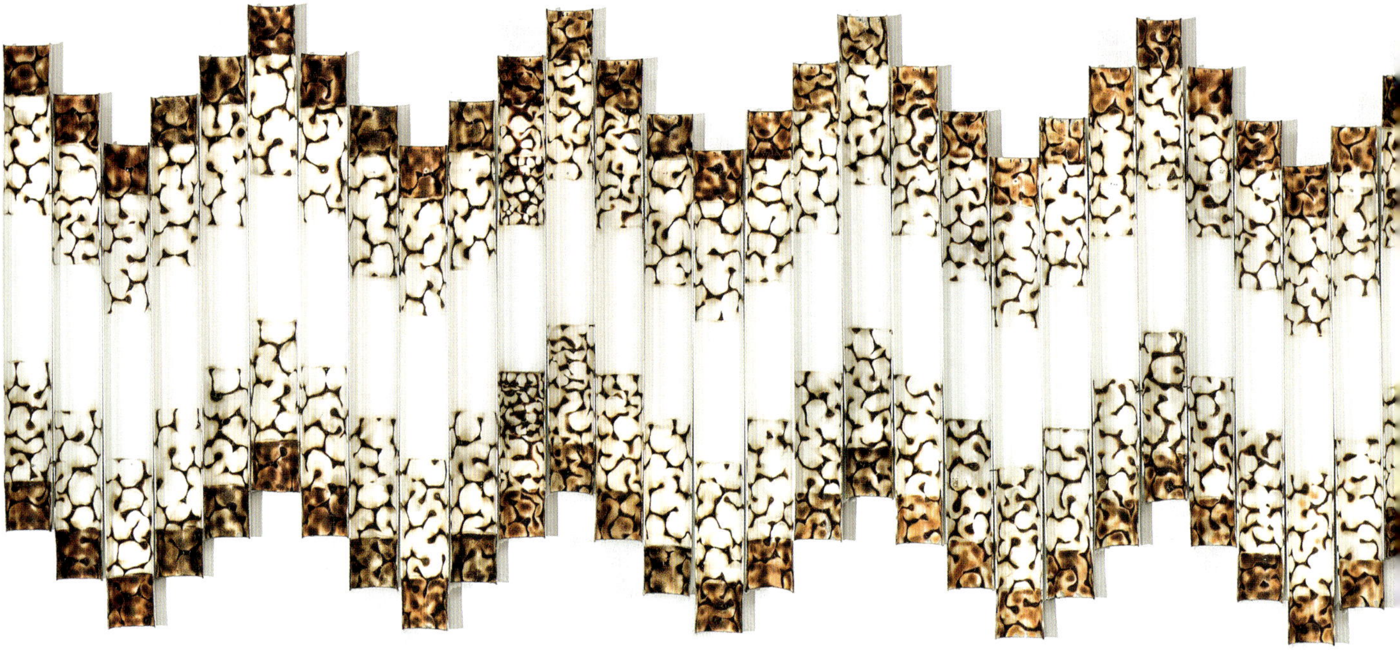

NOTES

1 The sources of these words are Ndebele (2003) 110-111 and Coetzee (1988) 50-51. The original poem Coetzee cites, "Nuus Uit Die Binneland" [News from the Interior] reads "*droogte en brand, en gerug / van sprinkaan, aardbewing en oproer / of daardie skroeiende binnelandse lug / – dan, dan / weet ons op watter vasteland ons boer.*" The third extract is from a selection of unpublished poems made available to me by the artist. All references to Zulu's words, unless otherwise stated, refer to these unpublished poems written in the late eighties.

2 These are the four elements in Greek natural philosophy; for an account of these and the fire-centred 'phlogiston' theory see Elkins, 60.

3 See Richards (1999) 146-163. All other references are in the notes.

4 A word on my use of 'our' or 'we' in this text. While in common conversation this collective pronoun is mostly unproblematic, in more formal discourse it can assume an imaginary collectivity which does not exist, or is internally inconsistent, contradictory, and conflicted. Like many of my compatriots, I recognise myself well enough in Thabo Mbeki's "I am an African" speech (Maharaj, 11-15), and also recognise key elements of, amongst others, Max du Preez's various comments on African identity. This recognition challenges me to refer to some kind of collectivity which, however disputed, provides a reference point for what I write.

5 Unpublished discussion/interview, May 2004.

6 For example, the shield and military tunic in Laband and Thompson, 14,16, and Mangon, 68-69. Aspects of Zulu's work directly reference the shield. The wall elements in his installation for "Graft" include metal rods sharpened at the bottom and with a grass-covered shape near the top. Shields as cultural weapons became part of our visual culture in the violent 1990s. Anthea Jeffrey writes "In Mid-October, [1992] thousands of members of the IFP, led by Chief Buthelezi, and armed with axes, knobkerries, sharpened metal sticks and spears marched through the streets of Johannesburg in protest against provisions in the *Record of Understanding* [1992] mandating the banning of traditional weapons and the fencing in of hostels" (373). 'Cultural weapons' became the subject of an intense public debate at the time. What had been largely ornamental and historical for many city-dwellers transformed into something quite different. Rob Nixon notes that it "was decreed that their (Inkatha supporters') spears, clubs, knives, battle-axes... did not constitute instruments of war, but were to be respected as 'traditional cultural weapons'... Inkatha effectively claims not just the right to display specific weapons – the *de rigueur* knobkerries, shields, and sticks – but more sinisterly, to go about armed as an expression of a putatively warrior temperament that enjoys the imprimatur of history" (198-199). The display and possession of dangerous weapons, which included 'traditional cultural weapons', was eventually banned by the South African Government in 1996.

7 See, for example, Arnoldi and Kreamer, and Sieber and Herreman. For critical reflections on hair, see Mercer, 115-139, Lang, Delaney, and Levine in Eilberg-Schwartz and Doniger, 32-76, and Erasmus, 380-392.

8 Pyne (2004) 107-108.

9 Cited in Mbiti, 212.

10 Unpublished interview/conversation, July 2004.

11 For a memorable image of stoning, see Peter Schütz's three-dimensional *The First Martyr III* in *KKNK*, 34.

12 Gandhi Malungane speaking about June 16 in Brink, Malungane, Lebelo, Ntshangase and Krige, 28-29.

13 Unpublished interview/conversation, July 2004.

14 Pyne (2004) 109.

15 Unpublished interview/conversation, July 2004.

16 Crais, 130. Crais writes, "Fire... has continued to be a basic way of dealing with witchcraft, a strategy of doing away with evil, ultimately also a temporal marker separating past and present. But whereas fire had earlier been used to cleanse the locale of witchcraft, the body itself has increasingly come to be seen as a central locus of evil. Importantly, to destroy the body by fire was also to destroy the soul and thus prevent it from returning to haunt the living." There is a link by fire between classical African ways of dealing with evil, and contemporary forms of immolation like necklacing.

17 In *Auto da Fé* Elias Canetti refers to the burning of a library. Book burning suggests censorship and violent destruction of the human right to knowledge. Perhaps the most notorious occasion of book burning occurred at many German Universities on 10 May 1933, anticipating the later picture burning on 20 March 1939 by the Nazis. If we consider that orality transforms

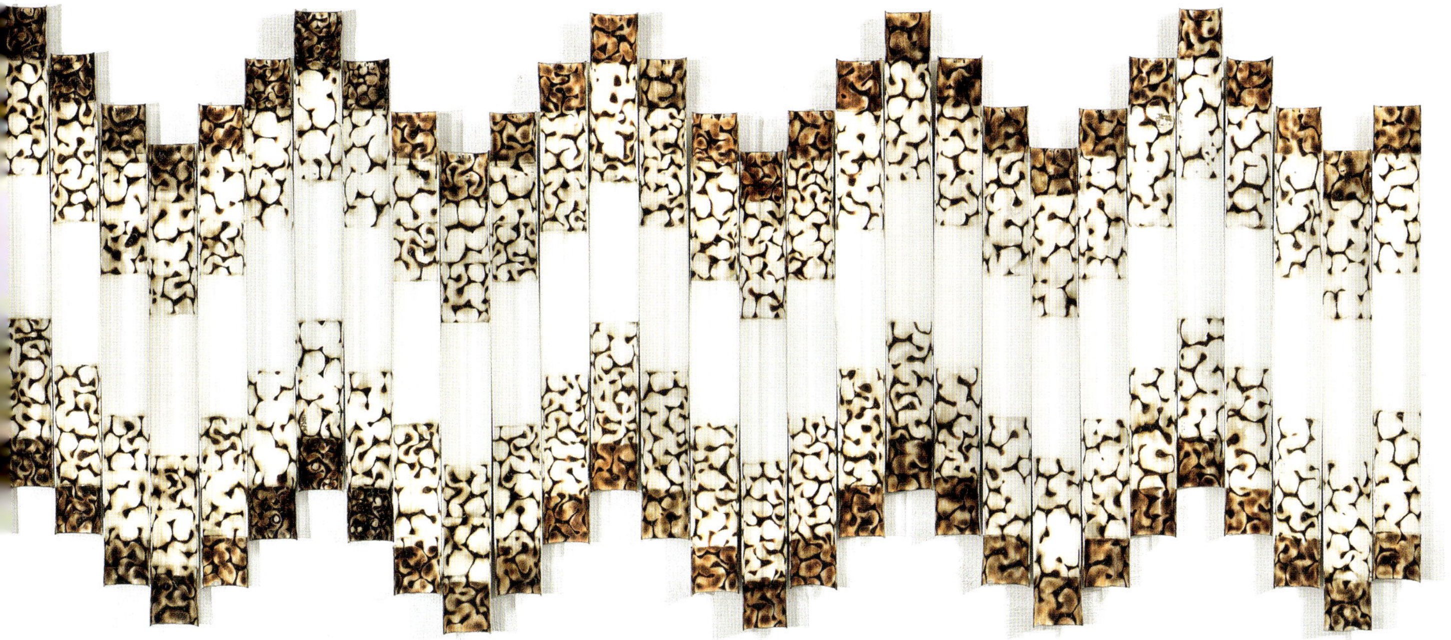

bodies into books, pyromantic book burning would turn on the bodies of such bearers of knowledge. This violent turn is expressed in a different way by the illustration in Connor of a book made of human skin (43). Susan Stewart writes that one of the great *topoi* of Western literature is "the face as book," (127).

18 Coetzee (1980) 110-112. In *Digging Through Darkness: Chronicles of an Archeologist,* Carmel Schrire mentions Coetzee's use of fiction and archival 'fact' in a way that shows how fine is the line "that separates assumed reality from imagination" (6).

19 See Homi Bhabha's "Sly Civility," 93-101.

20 Breytenbach, 12.

21 Steinberg, 258. Steinberg describes a moment when he "imbibed the landscape as a native does; everything marked by a thousand particulars; the history of power and people engraved in every mutation." Earlier in the book a farmer utters these words about his unwanted neighbours, "You lose control. They take down your fences and their cattle start wandering onto your property. A bull with venereal disease gets among your cows, and soon your whole herd starts dying off. These cattle have not been dipped; they have picked up hundreds of diseases. They urinate on the grass and your cattle eat the grass. So when the blacks' cattle wander onto your land you have to seal it off for months until the disease is gone. You get to a point where you cannot farm" (19).

22 J. M. Coetzee (1992) characterises Paton's novel as religious tragedy; "the dispensation under which man suffers is unshakeable, but... our pity for the hero-victim and our terror at his fate can be purged by ritual reenactment" (348).

23 Paton, 7.

24 Paton, 112.

25 Abrahams, 259-260. In this long poem, Lionel Abrahams writes, "I half forget what poetry we read (our own? Newfound Mtshali's? Plath's?)" (260). The mine dumps in and around Johannesburg have found their way into the work of various visual artists, including David Koloane, Durant Sihlali, William Kentridge and Clive van den Berg.

26 This is rhetorical, but unhappily it also has a literal dimension. There are many, many unmarked graves across the landscape dating from the last thirty years and before; see 'exhumations' in Edelstein, 210-225 and 550-569 in *The Truth and Reconciliation Commission of South Africa Report.* Recently, the remains of migrant workers from the diamond mines in Kimberly were discovered in unmarked graves in that area. Zulu's unpublished poem "Ezulwini" bespeaks these unmarked deaths; "in a gaping wound of the limping earth / in a pit of stinking darkness / they dig a flint / moistened by streaming sweat / and buried alive without coffins / without a funeral service / Ezulwini / in a pit of stinking mortality..."

27 Zulu's poem is in English and Zulu. The Zulu verse reads *"mvelinqangi osemazulwini / yiba nathi kulensunguzi / Sisikelele / usiphateh ngetaru / ungasidanisi / Bawo sikhalela izinsapho / ezilambileyo."*

28 Quoted in Williamson and Jamal, 72.

29 Quoted in Williamson and Jamal, 72-73.

30 Edmunds, n.p..

31 Quoted in Bachelard, 22.

32 Pyne (1997) 20.

33 Goldhammer and de Ronde, 1.

34 Khan, 128.

35 For this purifying and cleansing aspect in classical African cultures, see Mbiti, 55-56.

36 Unpublished interview/conversation, July 2004.

37 An interpenetration of socio-political and spiritual violence in immolation by fire is noted by Clifton Crais. Of the Eastern Cape, Crais writes, "At night different conflicts unfold... In a hidden place men suspend a suspected robber over a fire and demand confession. The man screams, flesh burns, the suspect dies. The night is filled with mysterious, dangerous movement, the motion of witches and the terrible, seemingly relentless violence of men" (2, 116).

38 Crais, 4.

39 Unpublished discussion/interview, May 2004.

40 The concept of violence is surprisingly difficult to articulate. Paul Crowther offers a useful account of violence in painting (54-59).

41 Pranger, 44.

42 Gottlieb (1976) 307. Critic Willoughby Sharp touches on the connection between Euro-American minimalism, luminism and kineticism in an early article: "While fire has long been recognised as an indispensable and mysterious force, the modern artist has been the first to isolate it as an aesthetic element" (326-327). Sharp names artists Yves Klein, Takis, Jean Tinguely and Bernard Aubertin.

43 Other works are Dennis Oppenheim's *Polarities* (1972), *Radicality* (1974) and *Pretty Ideas* (1974), and Susan Hiller's *Monument* (1980-81). From a literary perspective Susan Stewart speaks of fire in relation to Swift's Gulliver (87).

44 Figs 16a and 16b in Lippard, 176-177. In "Ritual" Lippard inventories a number of works involving fire contemporary to that time of romantic atavism in art: "Fire is a boundary – between health/luck/fecundity and illness/bad fortune/barrenness; between light and dark, or between life and death. It is the universal symbol of transformation, of soul escaping from the body, and it has always been associated with sacrifice – human and animal. The victim was often the most beloved, since it was an honour to be chosen as a means of ensuring the community's continuing life in these macrocosmic death and rebirth rituals" (175). Lippard's pop-primitivism (or more accurately neo-pop-primitivism) is excessively romantic, but does give us a wider context for Zulu's fireworks.

45 For reproductions of Beuys see Tisdall, 236-241, and for Bill Viola see Rush, 142.

46 See Nettleton, Charlton and Rankin-Smith, 90-91. For an early example see Tivenyanga Qwabe's "Untitled" (ca. 1939) reproduced in Rankin, and "Mziwakhe Mbatha" in Thorpe. Jo Thorpe writes, "[Mziwakhe Mbatha] generally carves in *mhlambamanzi* white wood and uses the traditional burnt wood method for emphasising certain aspects" (84). For a brief discussion on the history of this mode, see van Robbroeck, 128.

47 See Peires (first paperback edition), the cover of which reproduces this work.

48 For Nthubu David Koloane see Hug and Vogel, 72, Kim Berman in Perryer, 48-49 and Bernie Searle in Golinski and Hiekisch-Picard, 106-107 and her catalogue *Vapour*. Other 'fireworks' include Randy Hartzenberg's *Domestic Baggage: Unearthed* (1992), William Kentridge and Doris Bloom's *Fire Drawing* (1994), Brett Murray's *Language and Land* (1996), Benny Gool's *Death of Rashaad Staggie* (1996) and Andrew Tshabangu's *Joubert Park* (1997). These are reproduced in Williamson and Jamal, Waller and Bedford.

49 See Williamson and Jamal, 52-55 and Taylor, 274-276.

50 Oliphant, 17-18. The brazier is also central in Mautloa's *Progress Wall* (1995). For Williamson and Jamal the brazier, "represents in the life of the townships – an instant fire, a point of warmth where passersby can gather for a moment to talk and laugh…." (40).

51 From a rather dismissive source: Park, 52.

52 Pesci, 16.

53 Unpublished discussion/interview, May 2004.

54 Quoted in Mazibuko, 9.

55 Guthrie, 205-206 and Kahn, 132-155 and 197-213.

56 Philosopher Iris Murdoch's account of Plato's narrative is as follows: "The pilgrimage which restores our knowledge of this real world is explained in the *Republic* by the images of the Sun and the quadripartite divided Line, and by the myth of the Cave. The prisoners of the Cave are at first chained to face the back wall where all they can see are shadows, cast by the fire which is behind them… Later they manage to turn round and see the fire and the objects which cast the shadows. Later still they escape from the Cave, see the outside world in the light of the sun, and finally the sun itself. The sun represents the Form of the Good in whose light the truth we see; it reveals the world, hitherto invisible, and also a source of life. Art and the artist are condemned by Plato to exhibit the lowest and most irrational kind of awareness, *eikasia*, a state of vague image-ridden illusion; in terms of the Cave myth this is the condition of the prisoners who face the back wall and see only shadows cast by the fire" (4-5).

57 See Graves, 143-149. The account Graves gives is of a dispute about the gods' portion of a sacrificial bull. Prometheus was arbiter, and he tricked Zeus, upon which Zeus punished him "by withholding fire from mankind." Prometheus gained access to Olympia (through Athene). "On his arrival, he lighted a torch at the fiery chariot of the Sun and presently broke from it a fragment of glowing charcoal, which he thrust into the pithy hollow of a giant fennel-stalk. Then, extinguishing his torch, he stole away undiscovered and gave fire to mankind." Zeus avenged himself by having Prometheus chained naked to a pillar in the Caucasian mountains, where a greedy vulture tore at his liver all day, year in and year out; and there was no end to the pain, because every night [exposed to the harsh elements]… his liver grew whole again" (144-145). Hercules eventually set Prometheus free. *Tityus* (1548-1549) by Titian and *Prometheus Bound* (1611-1612) by Peter Paul Rubens and Frans Snyders are amongst the better-known sixteenth- and seventeenth-century European paintings on this theme.

58 Credo Mutwa, 6.

59 Stewart, 87 and da Vinci, 421.

60 In poetry it is a strong theme. For individual poems see Mogale, 121, Mnyaka, 89-90, Mtshali, 42-43, Ndlazi, 109 and Papane, 110; and collections, Mtshali (1980) and Mzamani.

61 The Zulu combatants called the killing field the "Plain of Bones"; see Laband, 101.

62 Laband, 96.

63 "For weeks three impressive processions had been winding their way through the country to the monument… the boys of the Voortrekker Youth Movement… who were to make an indelible impression upon the thousands of spectators as they carried three thousand flaming torches through the night towards the amphitheatre…" E. G. Jansen, in a piece titled "The Growth of an Idea" wrote, "A remarkable event [was] the arrival of the torch bearers on Wednesday evening. One of the torches was carried from the statue of Jan van Riebeeck in Cape Town, a distance of over a thousand miles – symbolic of the spread of civilization from the Cape to the far north. Others came from Dingaanstat, where Piet Retief and his followers were massacred in 1838. The torch-bearers along both routes were boys and girls belonging to the Voortrekker scouts, who had organised the event. Each bearer carried the torch for a certain distance and then handed it over to the next bearer; the last two were to hand over the torches to the Centenary Committee near the monument. The torch-bearers were met some distance away and accompanied to the scene by their comrades from the Voortrekker camp, who were all carrying torches of their own. It was a wonderful sight when the torch-bearers came down the hillside, like a river of fire…" (68).

64 Cited in Kertzer, 36-37. A provocative historical moment with tables turned can be drawn from something David Harrison recounts in his book on the 'white tribe' of Africa. Harrison writes of the alleged turning of the national anthem by Afrikaans schoolchildren in the rural Eastern Cape around 1915: "Koot Vorster recalls that the boys made [the anthem] tolerable by altering the words; God save our noble King / Wash him in paraffin / And put fire on him" (54).

65 Haymans, 31-32. The bipolar language of the barbaric and the civilized wracks these accounts of conflict. In the symbolic résumé of the tapestries at the Monument, lightning and fire were prominent. Nellie Kruger writes; "The thunder and the flash of lightning in the background symbolises the massacres perpetrated by the barbarians on the Voortrekkers and the silver lining in a cloud signifies the deliverance after all the disasters… The iron tyre (of the wheel) is blood-red, indicating that it has rolled through blood… Below the Drakensberg are the mists of uncertainty from which emerges a string of small Voortrekker wagons accompanied by women with torches to signify the coming of civilization" (19-20).

66 By naming *Australopithecus prometheus*, Professor Dart, working at Makapansgat, "was commemorating the discovery of carbon in the breccia from this same site twenty-two years before. It seemed likely in view of the carbon that *Australopithecus* had discovered the secret of fire but this is an angle I have never been able to confirm satisfactorily despite subsequent investigations of bones for carbon" (quoted in Wheelhouse, 67-69).

67 See Hofmeyr, Ch. 6 and 7. For another account and assessment see Naidoo.

68 Brain, 262.

69 Mitchell, 68.

70 Penn, 13.

71 The scorched earth policy involved the deliberate destruction by burning of Boer homesteads, farmlands and cattle by the British Army during the Second Boer War. In her "Introduction" to a memoir of her time in England (ca. 1899) Emily Hobhouse writes that "holiday-making was spoilt that year. There could be no freedom of mind for enjoyment with that terrible war going on and each morning's news of battles, farm burnings and devastation cast a shadow over the usual picnics and pleasures" (24).

72 Plaatje, 133. The film was based on a book titled *The Clansman*, "notorious… for its glorification of the activities of the Ku Klux Klan" (Willan, 193).

73 Ridgeway, 51-53. For a remarkable account

of representation, language, hate speech and performativity referencing flag and cross burning see Butler.

74 Plaatje, 134.

75 See Saunders and Southey, 170.

76 See Harker, 58-59 and Weinberg, 182-187.

77 Ndlazi, 109. Good texts on the uprising are Brink, Malungane, Lebelo, Ntshangase, Krige and Mokadi.

78 Mtshali (1986) 43. Fire seems to have inspired many of the poems in Mtshali's collection *Fireflames* (1980).

79 Mzamani, 72.

80 Nolizwe Mnyaka, "I have had enough of the fire / Its warmth brings memories of bodies / Tortured, killed, maimed and burnt" (89).

81 See Goldberg and Malik.

82 See Elliott, 82 and the contribution by the Imvaba Artists' Group based in Port Elizabeth, 81.

83 See Richards (2001).

84 Ndebele (2003) 74.

85 Necklace: A car tyre filled with petrol used to burn political opponents, especially those regarded as collaborators and informers. The tyre was usually forced over the head and shoulders of the victim's head and shoulders, immobilising them, doused with petrol or paraffin and then lit. For further information, see Schärf and Ngcokoto, 360-1 and note 43. According to Manganyi and du Toit necklacing became a norm of execution in the townships from 1984 onwards and was used by both pro and anti-government groups (371). Straker, Moosa, Becker and Nkwale give the following account: "The incidents of necklacing were so horrifying and numerous... that the origins and roots of the practice in common social processes have been all but obscured. They were not confined to the urban areas. While in the towns the usual rationale was that the victim was an informer or *impimpi*, in the rural areas witchcraft accusations were common. Wherever burnings took place, however, similar social processes were involved. The burnings of putative witches and *impimpis* (informers) all occurred in contexts of massive social upheaval and catastrophic community disruption, after traumatic and violent events had threatened the entire community and led to the injury and death of some of it members" (114). Death by fire of witches and the necklacing of *impimpi* are linked, as indicated by a 1980s liberation song transcribed by Krog (1998): "Informers, we will kill you. Hayi! Hayi! / Witches, we will burn you. Hayi! Hayi!" (188). On necklacings and burnings narrated at the TRC, see *Truth and Reconciliation Commission of South Africa Report,* Vol. 3, 108-112.

86 Williamson, 123.

87 See also Mandla Sibanda's *Life in Flames.* Artist Billy Mandindi also made two other images relevant here, *Homage to Township Art* (1989) and *Lifebuoy* (1995). For these and the other images cited see Younge, 17, Elliott, 63, fig. 2 and Hug and Vogel, 142.

88 See Richards (2004) 122 and *Art South Africa* Vol. 1, No 3 (Autumn 2003).

89 Pauw, 153.

90 Pauw, 154. Death-squad operatives Dirk Coetzee and, amongst others, Almond Nofomela and Joe Mamasela were notorious participants in the activities of Vlakplaas, a farm near Pretoria used as a base for hit-squad activities. Coetzee was handpicked in August 1980 to establish Vlakplaas, ostensibly as a base for askaris. An askari is a "former guerrilla recruited by the security forces" (Krog 1998, 282) to identify and arrest trained Umkhonto we Sizwe infiltrators. "Because of the unit's secret nature," according to Pauw, "and the fact that the askaris were already trained soldiers and were at the mercy of their captors, the unit became the ideal base from which operations against the enemy could be launched" (151). The quote in the main text refers to two men, Vuyani Mavuso and Nkosinathi Dlamini, who were earmarked to 'disappear.' The two were unsuccessfully poisoned and then executed by gunshots to the head; "one of the policemen stepped forward, placed his foot against the neck of one of the captives, pressed the barrel of the Makarov against his head and pulled the trigger... Seconds later, the other man was executed in the same manner" (154).

91 Figure 2 in *Johannes Mashego Segogela: 'Devils, Angels and Other Things'*

92 Morris, 8.

93 See Pyne (199) 19-34. The relationship between fire, creativity and civilization in deeper forms of human mythologising is rich but often double-edged. Speaking of the denigration and heroization of the 'mythological artist' Ernst Kris and Otto Kurz refer to the punishment meted out by the gods for those who harbour "the ability to make images." This punishment should "be seen in a wider and more sublime context: it appears to be intimately linked with the symbolic significance of fire, as a sign of creative potency, and the harnessing of fire as one of the earliest cultural accomplishments in the history of mankind" (87).

94 Morris, 5.

95 Bachelard, 7.

96 Zulu's account involves a story of his family forbears and splits in the family that distanced his direct ancestral kin from its royal lineage.

97 It is noteworthy that a work of this title by Jeremy Wafer was included in the show he and Sandile Zulu shared in 2003. Wafer's mixed-media *Isandhlwana* (1995) is reproduced in *Panoramas of Passage: Changing Landscapes of South Africa*, 96, plate 105.

98 Laband: "Both Zulu and British were blinded by the smoke and dust and, pressed together in the mêlée, struck out wildly on every side. The horror was increased by a partial eclipse of the sun, which was at its greatest extent at 2.29 p.m." (226).

99 Laband, 226.

100 Laband and Thompson, 102. According to these authors, "[t]he Zulus believed in a mystical force, *umnyama* which was darkness or evil influence. It reduced resistance to disease and created misfortune. A person polluted by *umnyama* could only be purified by symbolic medicines and rituals. In its worst form it could be contagious, people being treated withdrew from society and all pleasurable experiences, as if they were in mourning. Warriors about to go to war were in particular danger of pollution since taking a human life caused an especially virulent form of *umnyama*. On the first day of essential rituals, the *amabutho* collected great heaps of firewood and green mimosa. A black bull, which represented all the evil influences in the land, was caught on the second day and killed bare-handed by an *imbutho*. War-doctors, or *izinyanga* cut strips of meat... treated them with black medicines and then roasted them on a fire of the wood collected the previous day. The *izinyanga* then threw the strips of meat into the air and the *amabutho*, who were drawn in a great circle, caught and sucked them. Meanwhile, the *izinyanga* burnt further medicines and the soldiers breathed in the smoke and were sprinkled with cinders from the fire. Then, finally, to expel dangerous influences, each warrior drank a mouthful from a pot of medicine, and a few at a time vomited the contents into a specially dug hole" (15).

101 Laband, 226.

102 For a compelling account of the battle, see Laband and Thompson, 109-113. The victory of the British over the Zulus in this battle which followed Isandhlwana, according to Laband and Thompson, diverted public attention from the British disaster at Isandhlwana. On the Rorke's Drift art community, see Hobbs and Rankin.

103 See Hobbs and Rankin, 130, and also Williamson, 16.

104 Quoted in Laband and Thompson, 104.

105 Quoted in Laband and Thompson, 100.

106 From an unpublished poem by Sandile Zulu.

107 From an unpublished poem by Sandile Zulu.

108 For an account of syntax/system in American art of the sixties, see Alloway. Alloway makes a point which seems to have influenced the local reception of Zulu's work. "What is missing from the formalist approach to painting is a serious desire to study meanings beyond the purely visual configuration" (51). The wholesale transfer of comments from Alloway's context to ours requires qualification but is nevertheless useful to a wider understanding of this aesthetic phenomenon. Such a transfer also raises important questions regarding 'Afro-centric' and 'Euro-centric' systems of knowledge. My own sense is that different knowledge systems do have their integrity and autonomy, but these cannot be reified as the exclusive and fixed possession of any particular culture.

109 On time in art see Colpitt's discussion of Michael Fried's criticism of minimalism, 93-99.

110 Goldhammer and de Ronde, 1.

111 Quoted in Colpitt, 94. Morris also made a *Burning Planet Series* (1985) that resonates with aspects of Zulu's aesthetic orientation in its reference to fire and celestial bodies.

112 For an excellent contemporary exploration of time and the image, see Gill.

113 Especially if we consider the literalism and facticity of Anglo-American minimalism, characterised as it is by mechanistic materialism and transparent methods, decreased emphasis on self-expression and radical self-containment which allegedly admits "no veiled allusions,

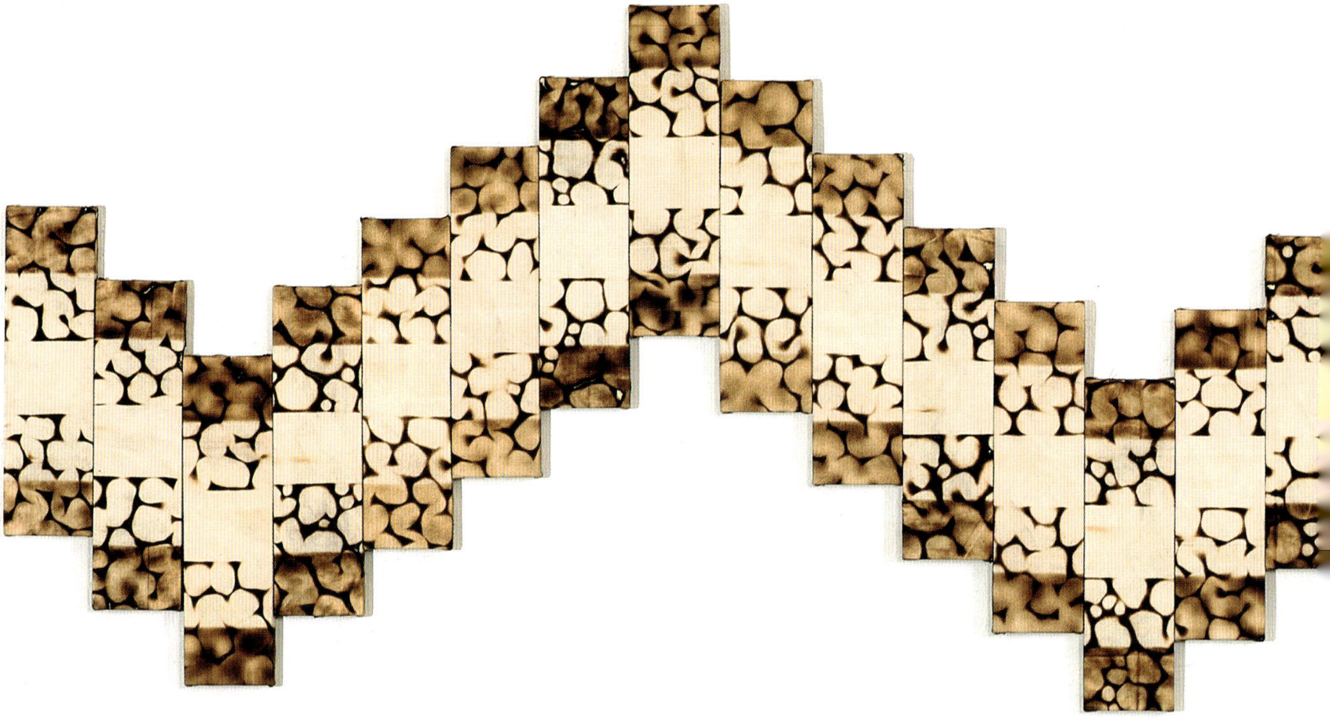

covert references or subjective content... within the strict confines of the logical system" (Colpitt, 59).

114 Krauss, n.p.

115 This was for the show "Graft." See Richards (1997) 234-267.

116 Zulu quoted in Williamson and Jamal, 30.

117 Edelstein, 181.

118 Krell, 173; Geers mentions that the razor mesh fence he used is a South African patent (Cochrane Steel). See also Razac.

119 Stevenson and Rosholt, 94 and Marco Cianfanelli in *KKNK*, 14.

120 See Abrie Fourie and Santu Mofokeng in *KKNK*, 18-20.

121 Krell, 7. Krell devotes a considerable part of his discussion to Lord Kitchener's incarceration of Boer women and children in concentration camps.

122 The logo was designed by British artist Diana Redhouse on request by AI founder, Peter Benenson. Benenson thought of the image of the candle and barbed wire which recalled a favourite proverb: "Better to light a candle than curse the darkness."

123 *Out of Step: War Resistance in South Africa,* 104.

124 Krell, 184. One of the many controversial Benetton ads of the mid-1990s "shows a gray sky with strands of barbed wire in the foreground. The poster tells us that the barbed wire comes from far-flung places: Johannesburg, Belgrade, Tokyo, Dublin, Beirut, Jerusalem, Budapest and Hamburg." See Salvemini, 126.

125 For comment on 'indigenous' language, see Makoni, 242-248 and Ndebele (2000) 191-196.

126 Buskirk, 137.

127 Buskirk, 137.

128 See de Kok and Press, and Sachs, 73-81. The older debates to which I refer in this case would include those in Europe before the Second World War, published as *Aesthetics & Politics.*

129 Williamson and Jamal, 70.

130 Williamson and Jamal, 70.

131 Friedman, 32.

132 Coetzee (1990) 88.

133 Friedman, 32.

134 This is the date of the first democratic elections held in South Africa. Much has been written on the elections as event and symbol; see Brink (1994) and (1995), Reynolds and Bell and de Villiers. For the second election, see Lodge.

135 The term 'South African art,' at least since 1994, strongly signals a relation of art to nationalism, part of 'democratic' nation-building.

136 Williamson and Jamal, 7.

137 There are many complex questions here. The common rhetoric of radical rupture, a critical break with the past, is itself hardly new in art contemporary practices. While Williamson and Jamal's introduction is valuable, posing this question in the way they do risks glossing over a contradictory cultural moment. There is a tendency among artists claiming specifically avant-gardist credentials to relegate 'resistance art' to the past and to reduce it to caricature. This tendency continues the process that began with a debate on culture, change and freedom initiated in 1989 by Albie Sachs. See de Kok and Press, and Brown and van Dyk. Many international events since 1990 have energised local art and had a marked impact on South African art. A good starting event is David Elliott's "Art from South Africa" held in 1990 in Oxford, England, and from there the first and second Johannesburg Biennials and the participation of South African artists in the Biennials of Istanbul, Sao Paulo, Havana and Kwang Ju. The spate of 'decade' shows is also instructive. In the process of developing practices and critical languages that actively articulate local/global relations, much of hitherto 'political' (resistance) art's capacity to create a credible relationship with orthodox social power has been seriously misunderstood. In my estimation Zulu's art makes little room for this kind of misunderstanding.

138 Zulu, 15.

139 I cite Geers's criticism of Zulu in note 226 below. Geers's view of Zulu's work is partly captured in the words "decorative clone," and expresses a wider critical attitude to 'serious' art. Friedman, for example, uses the phrase "decorative surface displays," which diminishes the iconographic reach and material multiplicity of Zulu's creative enterprise. This is, in one view, something of a replay of the primarily American debates about 'pattern painting' and the decorative in the 1960s and 1970s.

140 Certainly it would resist reading a regressive, primitivised innocence into African visual cultures by metropolitan, and largely Western, audiences. This mystifying attitude disguised as appreciation invokes the kind of deeply conservative 'primordial,' generic Africa which afflicts the reading of art from this region. Zulu's

 Royal Court Art – Work 3 Image 3 | (2005) | fire, water, air, earth and canvas | 440 x 104 cm

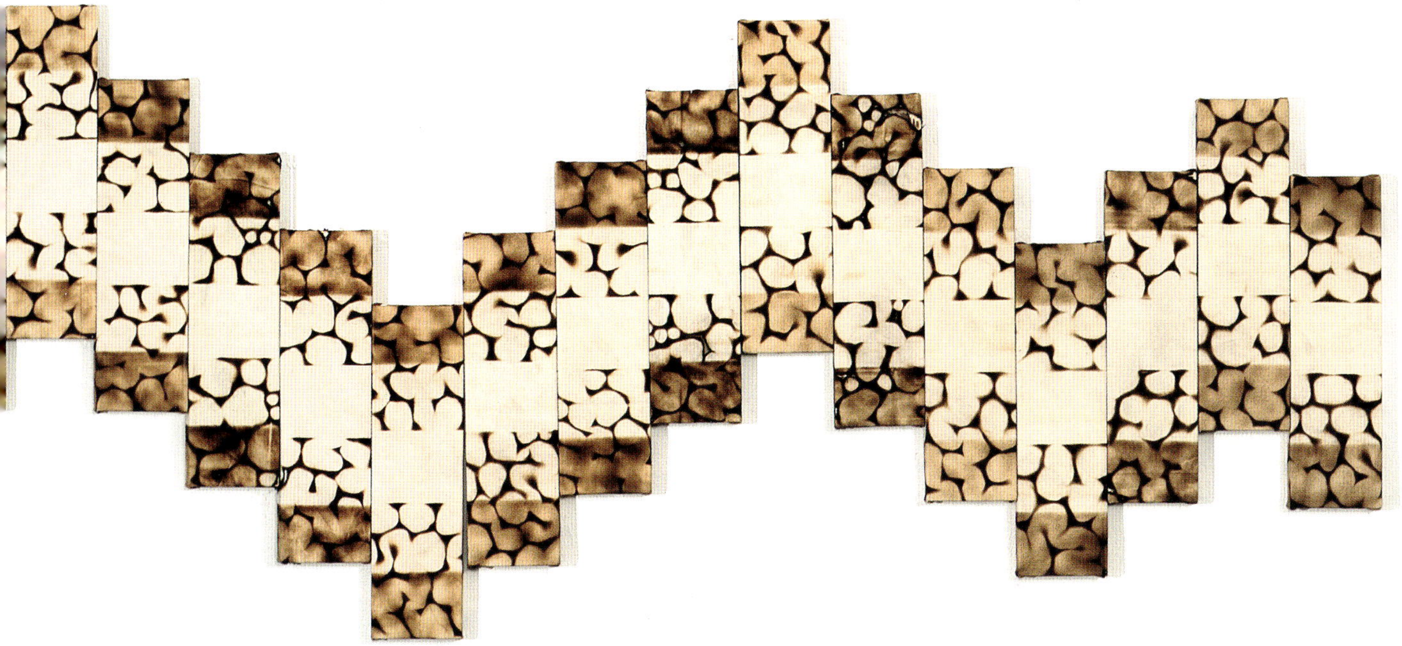

works insist on a strong, even romantic sense of locality, but without parochialism. They also discourage various forms of theatrical cynicism of an over-commodified, globalised artworld. For some idea of what this might mean in America, see Foster (1996), and on Western cynicism more generally, see Bewes (1997). Bewes's short discussion of violence is also illuminating.

141 Zulu, 15.

142 Willcott, 42.

143 Galeano, 11-12.

144 Ndebele (1991) 47.

145 Williamson and Jamal, 70.

146 Materiality as structure and medium has meaning and value in and of itself, as demonstrated by Zulu's use of fire. For some our ideas of the political and the currency of conceptualism constitute a new orthodoxy, almost a new formalism, but now without the logic of history and emphatic materialism that characterised previously hegemonic modernist formalism, however that modernism was mediated in the post-colonial world.

147 Jeffrey Schnapp speaks of "how certain materials...the clean, agitated, intensified materiality befitting a new age of electricity and steel – became identified with modern forms of embodiment.... Like tempered glass, reinforced concrete, aluminium, stainless steel, and plastics, artificial textiles belong to a privileged family of modern materials" (191-192). Michael Carter also captures the basic points in suggesting that all art "rests upon a set of *material substrates*, each of which has their own distinctive histories... these histories... would lie at the very deepest [temporal] levels. That these dimensions are so often overlooked or ignored in contemporary art histories is due... to the fact that the most frequent way in which we encounter art objects today is in the form of reproductions. This tends both to evaporate the distinct material properties of the things and render them into a set of equivalences via the dominant visual technology, the photographic image. This rendering down of objects to the common coinage of the photograph makes it easier for us Moderns to treat the material and symbolic dimensions of an art work as absolutely separate. This was not always so and in the past the particular stuff out of which the symbolic object was made tended to migrate across the material/symbolic dividing line and have important repercussions for what the object meant " (64-65).

148 De Bord and Bester, 266.

149 It is important here to recognise that the use of 'natural' processes and materials may encourage thoughts of the 'primitive' intuitive artist labouring under the Western delusion of the noble savage. Speaking of Survival International, Aidan Campbell mentions that the British establishments traditionally acclaimed the so-called martial races, that is such tribes as the Zulu in South Africa... For the elite, these tribes can be distinguished from other Third World Peoples because they typify the Western image of the 'noble savage.' Campbell goes on to argue that "radical critics of the establishment are highly suspicious of top people's support for tribal peoples. In particular they are hostile to the traditional conception of the 'Noble Savage' which they consider paternalistic. They are much more sympathetic to the Modern Primitive approach to technology which is steadily replacing the old-fashioned anti-technology of 'noble savagery'" (34-25).

150 See Behrens and website http://mitpress2.mitedu/ejournals/Leonardo/isast/spec.projects/camouflagebib.html

151 Schwartz, 176.

152 See Schwartz.

153 Grosz, 189-190.

154 Grosz, 190.

155 Pyne (2004) 107-109.

156 My thanks to Julia Charlton for bringing this to my attention.

157 See Favazza, 153-156. For a populist, 'new age' account see Camphausen and for comment on these so-called 'new primitives' see Torgovnick, especially her discussion of "committed piercers" (195-203). In rather more apocalyptic fashion, critic Paul Virilio seems to see the "infatuation with scarring and piercing" as continuous with extreme "expressionist acts" (citing the Thousand Hills Radio in Rwanda calling for acts of genocide) and a coming "officially terrorist art" (57-58).

158 Unpublished discussion/interview, May 2004.

159 Discussing the material culture and language of the Igbo household, Chike Aniokor makes the important observation that the "the decorative rendering of female household objects reproduces and amplifies those that are painted on the body, known as *uli*... The relationship between material object and the human body

occurs in the male domain as well. The chip-carving style and pervasive geometric designs that appear on carved stools, palm wine ceremonial pot, and ivory tusks are also worn on the forehead as *ichi* scarification marks as a protective envelope" (234).

160 Rubin, 17.

161 Rubin, 16.

162 Ellen Dissanayake, 108-109, 112.

163 See Rubin. The matter of bodily pain and creativity also has a long history, and may be linked to our cherished metaphors of creativity as fire. Kay Redfield Jamison (1993) in her study of art and madness, titles her book *Touched with Fire: Manic Depressive Illness and the Artistic Temperament* and includes various examples of this metaphor from a largely Western cultural canon.

164 Eric Gable considers the "ways in which Africans and Portuguese in late-colonial era Guinea Bissau copied each others' bodies to visualise themselves" (294).

165 For European awareness of the "relatively extreme forms of body art practised by the peoples of Africa, Asia and the Americas early in the 'Age of Explorations' see Rubin, 14-15.

166 Ronald Singer writes, "Bodily mutilations are recognised in populations throughout the world... Throughout Africa numerous practises were, and still are, known. Artificial deformation, such as the filing or chipping of the teeth, the removal of teeth and body scarification is well known. Bushmen still practice the latter..." (129). This is an old text, and we would question some of the terminology now.

167 Blanchard, 287-300. There is a negative and a positive dimension to what Blanchard calls "exoskeletal defences." Mark Gustafson notes that "marking the body with a permanent sign in a compulsory situation is a clear means of exercising... a 'microphysics of power' over that individual." But, Gustafson also notes that together with this "advertisement of constraint and affirmation of control, there is the effort to alter an individual's mind-set, one's notion of selfhood and personal empowerment." Gustafson quotes this revealing comment about social inscriptions of power and internal subjectivisation attributed to Alfred Gell; "The inside-facing and outside-facing skins are... one indivisible structure, and hence the skin continually communicates the external world to the internal one, and the internal world to the external one. This traffic, mediated by the skin, is the formative principle of the ego's basic sense of selfhood in the world" (24-25). For an interesting discussion of ornament, decoration and European art history see Rampley, 138-163.

168 For a discussion of the reference to scarification and the body in Wafer's work see Frost, 34.

169 Williamson, 72. Jeremy Wafer quotes Mangema Fuzi's early description of the battle in *Panoramas of Passage: Changing Landscapes of South Africa*, 97

170 From an unpublished poem by Sandile Zulu.

171 Mbeki, 31-32. See also "Interviews: African Renaissance" in Nuttall and Michael, *Senses of Culture*, 107-121, and also Ramose, 600-610 and Bester, 10-11.

172 In another poem of Sandile Zulu's titled "Sun of Africa," we read "We know not the day we first saw you... / when you blaze, you burn relentlessly / like burning zeal in shrouded hearts / like burning land / forests of white dry landscape / like boiling tears of a force I know... We cannot abandon our convictions / to burn to ashes"

173 Antjie Krog's "long white shudder of ash" (1998: 264) also resonates in this context; see also 210. For an interesting account of new 'animal' geographies in which the relationships between human society and the non-human, living world are central, see Wolch and Emel.

174 Krog (2003) 281-282. For a remarkable discussion of Krog's "the Beloved Country" see Wicomb, 159-181.

175 Mbembe, 113. Mbembe's book in part tackles the question of post-coloniality directly; "have we really entered another period, or do we find the same theatre, the same mimetic acting, with different actors and spectators, but with the same convulsions and the same insult? Can we really talk of moving beyond colonialism?" (237).

176 Papastergiadis, 78-79.

177 For an interesting discussion of the relations between animals and humans, see Fudge, Wolch, 119-138 and Lynn, 280-297.

178 See Parrinder, 126 and Tembo, 29.

179 For a brief account of the significance of the leopard and leopard skin pattern in various forms, see Klopper, 20-22. Dan Rakgoathe speaks of the leopard in one work about initiation. Durant Sihlali also painted a number of watercolours which included leopard skin patterns (ca. 1986), *The King's Crown, The King's Kaross* and *The Queen's Kaross*. Mashego Johannes Segogela made a work of Nelson Mandela riding a leopard in the late 1990s, while Peter Schütz made a sculpture of the head of a leopard-skin, and Claudette Schreuders's *The Hero* shows a man riding a leopard.

180 Willcott, 40 and 42.

181 These notes are from a press release from Michael Stevenson Contemporary for the exhibition 23 July – 16 August 2003.

182 The picture was sourced from the South African Astronomical Observatory and the project "an intervention, illustrating a range of 'perspectives on and of Africa'" (project pamphlet).

183 Klopper (2003) 60. Zulu's 'artomic' thoughts are important here and his simplified forms echo the conceptual graphics one finds in abundance in scientific illustration.

184 See Perryer (2004). The show, "Personal Affects: Power and Poetics in Contemporary South African Art" was curated by David Brodie, Laurie Ann Farrell, Churchill Madikida, Sophie Perryer and Liese van der Watt, and held at the Cathedral of St. John the Divine and the Museum for African Art in New York, 21 September 2004 – 3 January 2005.

185 Unpublished interview/conversation, October 2004.

186 See Zulu, 167.

187 See Lomas, 28-30.

188 Unpublished interview/conversation, October 2004.

189 While not the explicit source of his thinking, the origins of one 'theory' of atomism are illuminating here. This 'theory' seems to have survived mainly through the writings of the Roman poet Lucretius (98-55BC), the pre-Socratic Greek philosophers Leucippus and Democritus (ca. fifth century BC) and others. Atomism, put simply, appears to hold that matter exists as four elements; air, earth, fire and water. Substance and void characterize the 'atomic' economy. Without void, space for dynamic interaction, for changing relations would not be available. For Lucretius, at least, "creation out of nothing is nonsense. So is destruction of things to nothingness" (22). Lucretius' mode is poetic, and he addresses 'matter' in all its multidimensionality, including animus (mind) and anima (soul) (11). This resonates deeply with Zulu's creative enterprise.

190 Quoted in Bright, 121.

191 As Bachelard concludes, "inner fire is dialectical in all its properties, a replica, as it were, of this fundamental dialectic of subject and object – so much so that it only has to flame up to contradict itself. As soon as a sentiment rises to the tonality of fire, as soon as it becomes exposed in its violence to the metaphysics of fire, one can be sure that it will become charged with its opposite" (111).

192 Zulu, 15.

193 Jameson, 102.

194 This is a controversial area and attracts wide comment. For an introduction see Teffo, 103-117 and also the other essays collected in Higgs, Vakalisa, Mda and Assie-Lumumba. On 'africanisation' see Makgoba.

195 For a comprehensive, subtle treatment of 'modern' time, see Osborne. On time and art, see Bal, 79-99.

196 Unpublished discussion, May 2004. For a general discussion of the cult and culture of ruins, see Woodward.

197 Unpublished discussion/interview, May 2004.

198 The literature here is immense, but a useful entry point remains Mudimbe's, "The Power of the Greek Paradigm." The key text is Bernal. For a sustained critical discussion framed in terms of Afrocentricity, see Walker. The essays by Appiah, Gates and Garlake in Phillips, for all their difficulty in defining a critical contemporaneity, are useful here.

199 Thabo Mbeki stakes a claim in his speech: "As a human presence among all of these, a feature on the face of our native land as it has just been defined, I know that none dare challenge me when I say I am an African... My mind and my knowledge of myself are formed by the victories that are the jewels in our African crown, the victories we earned from Isandhlwana to Khartoum, as Ethiopians, as the Ashanti of Ghana, as the Berbers of the desert" (12). On the place of the human, see Noyes, 49-60 and also Mbembe, 173-211. Frantz Fanon is still a prime source of rethinking humanism.

200 See Makgoba (1999).

201 Hassan, 50.

202 Gyekye K., 158 cited in Moeketsi. For a critical account of *ubuntu* and the TRC see Wilson, 9-13.

203 Fanon, 11.
204 Devèze, n.p.
205 Ndebele (1991).
206 See Mbembe, 102-144.
207 See *Truth and Reconciliation Commission of South Africa Report*, Vols 1-6.
208 For a recent overview see Posel and Simpson. Deborah Posel describes the remit of the Commission thus: "Within parameters very firmly set by the enabling legislation, the TRC embarked on the daunting and formidable" task of "establishing as complete a picture as possible of the causes, nature and extent of the gross violations of human rights which were committed during the period from 1 March 1960 to the cut-off date [10 May 1994], including the antecedents, circumstances, factors and context of such violations, as well as the perspectives of the victims and the motives and perspectives of the persons responsible for the commission of the violations" (147). The Commission comprised three committees: the Human Rights Violations Committee, the Amnesty Committee and the Reparation and Rehabilitation Committee. It also had an Investigative Unit, a Research Unit, and powers of subpoena. The first hearings were held in April 1996 and its work formally closed on 30 November 2001. For local responses to the TRC and its aftermath, see Krog (1998 and 2003), and Goboda-Madizikela.
209 See Soyinka and Rose.
210 See de Kok, 57-71.
211 See Nuttall and Coetzee (1998) and Nuttal and Michael (2000).
212 For more on *ubuntu* see Ramose and Tutu. For an account of Tutu's Christian *ubuntu* see Battle. David Nthubu Koloane curated an exhibition titled 'Ubuntu' held in the National Art Gallery in Kuala Lumpur, Malaysia in 2002; he describes *ubuntu* as "an age-old African term for humanness, incorporating the values of caring, sharing and being in harmony with all creation. As an ideal, Ubuntu espouses selflessness and fairness to all. Broadly, it promotes cooperation between individuals, families, communities, culture and nations. Ubuntu empowers all to be valued for them to reach their full potential in accord to with all that is around them. It is within every human being." (Invitation, exhibition opening, 30 April 2002).
213 The postscript to South Africa's New Constitution contains this reference to ubuntu; see Simpson, 222.
214 Letseka, 182, and see also Kaphagawani, 66-79.
215 *Truth and Reconciliation Commission of South Africa Report*. Vol. 1, 126.
216 *Truth and Reconciliation Commission of South Africa Report*. Vol. 1, 126.
217 This call was supported by Susan van der Merwe, whose husband disappeared in 1978 after allegedly being abducted and killed by an Umkhonto we Sizwe (MK) unit. At the Human Rights Violations hearing at Klerksdorp, on 23 September 1996, she said: "The Tswanas have an idiom which I learned from my husband which goes 'a person is a person by other people, a person is only a person with other people.' We do have this duty to each other. The survival of our people in this country depends on our co-operation with each other" (*Truth and Reconciliation Commission of South Africa Report*. Vol. 1, 127-128). See also comments by Boraine and Bhengu. For a more literary treatment of 'African humanism' see Obee. Es'kia Mphahlele writes, "I am a confirmed African humanist" (288).
218 "During violent conflict and times when violent crime is rife, distraught members of society decry the loss of ubuntu. Thus, heinous crimes are the antithesis of ubuntu. Treatment that is cruel, inhuman or degrading is bereft of ubuntu... We have all been affected, in some way or other, by the 'strife, conflicts, untold suffering and injustice' of the recent past... But all this was violence on human beings by human beings. Life became cheap, almost worthless" (*Truth and Reconciliation Commission of South Africa Report*. Vol. 1, 127).
219 Sanders, 126.
220 As Mark Sanders writes, with *"umuntu ngumuntu ngabantu or as umuntu ngumuntu ngumunte ngabanye...*, one must, in effect, speak of the attainment of human-being through an other and not one's own. One's human-being is folded together with the other, the human-being of the other, and that other is the stranger" (126-127).
221 Crais, 4.
222 For background to the 'African Renaissance,' see Makgoba.
223 The notion of a 'rainbow nation' became a much touted national emblem in the 1990s, eventually becoming something of a cliché. In Mandela's inauguration speech we heard of the "rainbow nation at peace with itself and the world" in *South Africa 1990–1994: The Miracle of a Freed Nation*, 165. For a discussion of 'rainbowism' in art at the time, see Richards (1997) 37-53.
224 Casting creativity in such generalising terms is risky, and as I have already indicated the idea of *ubuntu* is vulnerable to opportunistic and sentimental appropriation. But the point can stand. The TRC report asserts that it is *against* the background of the loss of *ubuntu*, illustrated by the TRC process, that a spontaneous "call has arisen among sections of the population for a return to ubuntu." Of course the idea of 'traditional African values' is similarly open to debate and indeed controversy.
225 Quoted in Appiah (1992) 74.
226 Interesting here is an early critical piece by artist/writer Kendell Geers in which Geers suggested that Zulu's fire works were not original as Yves Klein and others had done similar works earlier. Unfamiliarity with the discourses of mainly Euro-American art was for Geers something of a cultural crime. He used the occasion of this exhibition to spark a polemic about double standards in the artworld; "Zulu is a dead ringer for a series of fire paintings made by the French artist Yves Klein in 1961... In a ruthless international artworld, Zulu would be perceived as nothing more than a decorative clone... tasteful, elegant and pretty, nowhere near the cutting edge. He scorches paper, canvas and wood in monotonous even patterns... In his hands, fire is transformed into a tame circus lion performing tricks in exchange for food. Unlike his predecessor, Zulu covers every single inch of the picture surface with the same mark that by its deadpan monotony ends up producing just another abstract painting" (15). Zulu responded to Geers in a letter, saying Geers's criticism was ill judged and the epitome of "fundamentally cynical views which deprecate the advent of racial equality and equal rights in South Africa.... For generations, racial domination and discrimination placed upon the African the conditions and stigma of a 'peasant' class without intellectual or artistic foundation. And these conditions, just as civic and economic power damages and handicaps, still damage and injure all African artists today. They still discredit and rob African artists of their cultural and intellectual merit, and make their rightful place and position in the culture of their motherland a paradox."
227 Being "just human" is not straightforward, especially considering the European Humanism that Fanon inveighed against; "[w]hen I search for Man in the technique and style of Europe, I see only a succession of negations of man, and an avalanche of murders" (251-252). See also Robert Young on Fanon's "creation of new men" with "a new language and a new humanity" (quoted in Bernasconi, 119). See also Biko. On humanism and (postmodern) anti-humanism see Malik.
228 On some profound if scattered insights concerning violence in post-colonial Africa, see Mbembe. See also Chabani Manganyi and du Toit, and Gutteridge and Spence. For a literary treatment, see Jolly. For accounts of this time of transition in which violence plays a role, see Manganyi.
229 Amongst the more enlightening responses include are Asmal, Asmal and Roberts, Krog (1998), Cochrane, de Gruchy and Martin, Tutu, Boraine, Chubb and Van Dijk, Wilson and Villa-Vicencio and Doxstader.
230 Unpublished discussion/interview, May 2004.
231 Zulu writes; "Fire and water, wind and soil are essential elements for life. These elements... offer not only a context for engaging with socio-historical issues, but also the criteria by which to enter the emotional, theoretical and critical framework for analysis... As psychological elements, fire and water, wind and soil allude to life, to creation and destruction, to colonization and decolonization, to revolution and liberation, to purgation and cleansing, to purification and renewal... My interest is in evoking... the social and psychological struggle for freedom of creative desire and imagining the essentials that stand for life" (15).
232 Galeano, 71.
233 *Diä!kwain*, 18; for an account of the poet, also called Dawid Hoeshaar, see 12.

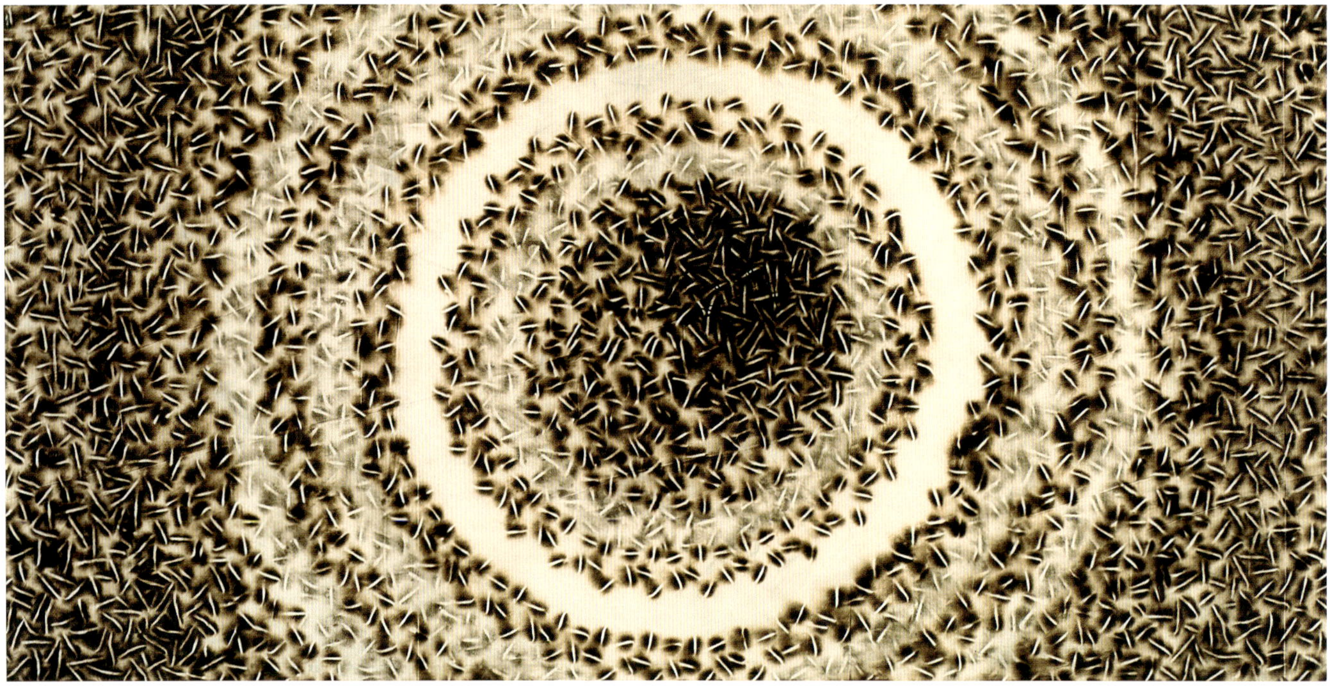

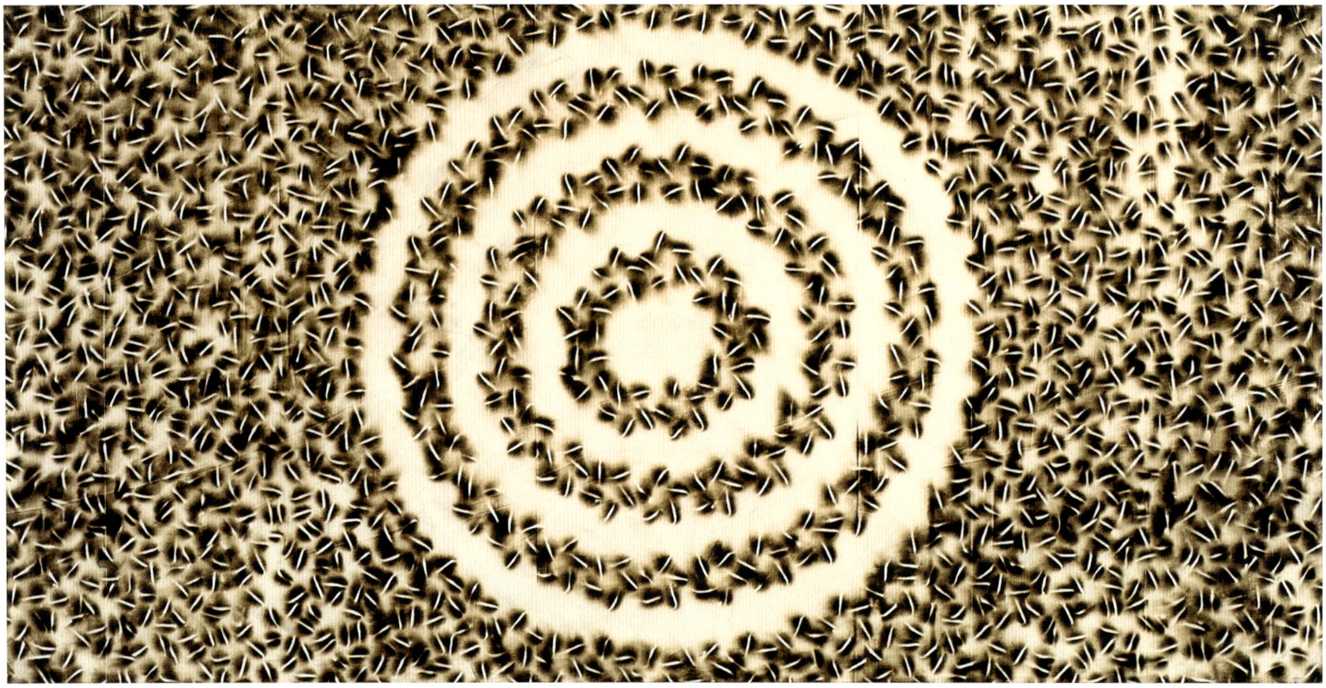

 Galaxy 1 and 2 | (2005) | fire, water, air, earth, wire and canvas | 300 x 160 cm each

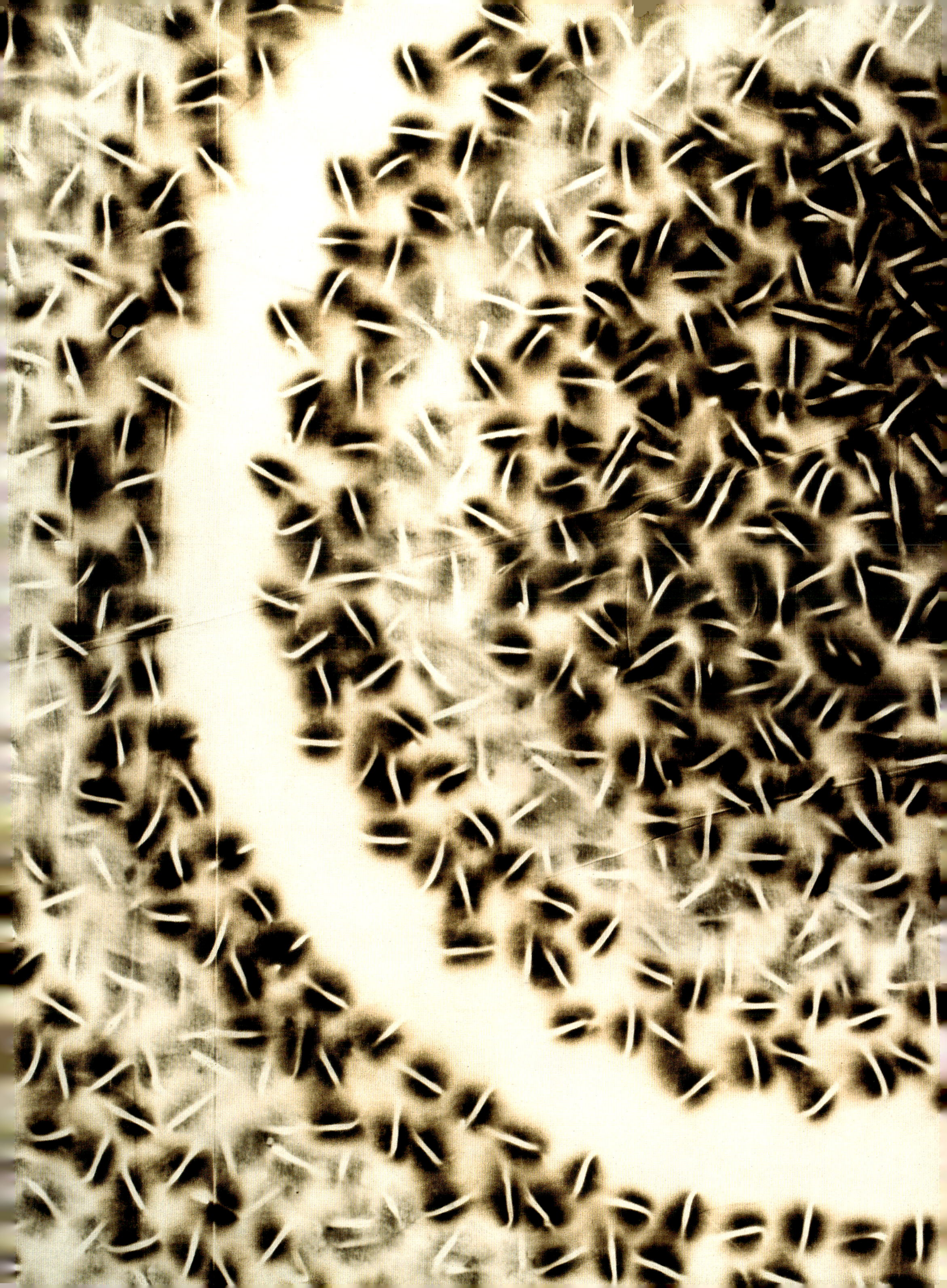

BIBLIOGRAPHY

Abrahams, Lionel, "Place" in Digby Ricci (ed.), *Reef of Time: Johannesburg in Writing.* Craighall: AD Donker, 1986

Alloway, Lawrence, "Systemic Painting" in Gregory Battcock (ed.), *Minimal Art.* New York: E. P. Dutton, 1968

Aniokor, Chike, "Household Objects and the Philosophy of Igbo Space" in Mary-Jo Arnoldi, Christraud Geary and Kris Hardin (eds) *African Material Culture.* Bloomington: Indian University Press, 1996

Appiah, Kwame Anthony, *In My Father's House: Africa in the Philosophy of Culture.* Oxford: Oxford University Press, 1992

Appiah, Kwame Anthony, "Why Africa? Why Art?" in Tom Phillips (ed.), *Africa: The Art of a Continent.* London: Royal Academy of Arts and Munich: Prestel, 1995

Arnoldi, Mary-Jo and Christine Mullen Kreamer (eds), *Crowning Achievements: African Arts and Dressing the Head.* Los Angeles: University of California Press, 1995

Arnoldi, Mary-Jo, Christraud Geary and Kris Hardin (eds), *African Material Culture.* Bloomington: Indian University Press, 1996

Asmal, Kadar, Louise Asmal and Ronald Suresh Roberts, *Reconciliation Through Truth: A Reckoning of Apartheid's Criminal Governance.* Cape Town: David Philip, 1996

Bachelard, Gaston, *The Psychoanalysis of Fire.* London: Quartet, 1987

Bal, Mieke, "Sticky Images: The Foreshortening of Time in an Art of Duration" in Carolyn Bailey Gill (ed.), *Time and the Image.* Manchester: Manchester University Press, 2000

Battle, Michael, *Reconciliation: The Ubuntu Theology of Desmond Tutu.* Cleveland: The Pilgrim Press, 1997

Bedford, Emma (ed.), *A Decade of Democracy: South African Art 1994–2004 from the Permanent Collection of Iziko.* Cape Town: Iziko and Double Storey, 2004

Bell, Paul and Riaan de Villiers (eds), *An End to Waiting: The Story of South Africa's Elections: 26 April to 6 May.* Johannesburg: The Independent Electoral Commission, 1995

Behrens, Roy R., *False Colours: Art, Design and Modern Camouflage.* Bobolink, 2002

Bernasconi, Roberto, "Casting the Slough" in Lewis R. Gordon, T. Denean Sharpley-Whiting and Renée T. White (eds), *Fanon: A Critical Reader.* Oxford: Blackwell, 1996

Bernal, Martin, *Black Athena: The Afroasiatic Roots of Classical Civilization.* New Brunswick: Rutgers University Press, 1991

Bewes, Timothy, *Cynicism and Postmodernity.* London: Verso, 1997

Bhabha, Homi K. (ed.), *Locations of Culture.* London: Routledge, 1994

Bhengu, Mfuniselwa, *Ubuntu: The Essence of Democracy.* Cape Town: Novalis, 1996

Biko, Steve, *I Write What I like.* Harmondsworth: Penguin, 1988

Blanchard, Marc, "Post-Bourgeois Tattoo: Reflections on Skin Writing in Late Capitalist Societies" in Lucien Taylor (ed.), *Visualizing Theory: Selected Essays from V. A. R. 1990–1997.* London: Routledge, 1994

Boraine, Alex, *A Country Unmasked: Inside South Africa's Truth and Reconciliation Commission.* Oxford: Oxford University Press, 2000

Brain, C. K., *Swartkrans: A Cave's Chronicle of Early Man.* Pretoria: Transvaal Museum, 1993

Breytenbach, Breyten, *The Memory of Birds in Times of Revolution.* Cape Town: Human and Rousseau, 1996

Bright, Richard, "Uncertain Entanglements" in Siân Ede, *Strange and Charmed: Science and the Contemporary Visual Arts.* London: Calouste Gulbenkian Foundation, 2000

Brink, André, *SA 27 April 1994: An Author's Diary.* Pretoria: Queillerie, 1994

Brink, André, *27 April: One Year Later.* Pretoria: Queillerie, 1995

Brink, Elsabé, Ghandi Malungane, Steve Lebelo, Dumisani Ntshangase and Sue Krige (eds), *Soweto 16 June 1976: It all started with a Dog....* Cape Town: Kwela Books, 2001

Brown, Duncan and Bruno van Dyk (eds), *Exchanges: South African Writing in Transition.* Pietermaritzburg: University of Natal Press, 1991

Buskirk, Martha, *The Contingent Object of Contemporary Art.* Cambridge, MA: MIT Press, 2003

Butler, Judith, *Excitable Speech: A Politics of the Performative.* London: Routledge, 1997

Campbell, Aidan. *Western Primitivism: African Ethnicity: A Study in Cultural Relations,* London: Cassell, 1997

Camphausen, Rufus, *Return to the Tribal: A Celebration of Body Adornment, Scarification, Body Painting.* Rochester: Inner Traditions, 1997

Canetti, Elias, *Auto da Fé.* London: Picador, 1978

Chubb, Karin and Lutz van Dijk, *Between Anger and Hope: South Africa's Youth and the Truth and Reconciliation Commission.* Johannesburg: Wits University Press, 2001

Cochrane, James, John de Gruchy and Stephen Martin (eds), *Facing the Truth: South African Faith Communities and the Truth & Reconciliation Commission.* Cape Town: David Philip, 1999

Coetzee, J. M., *Age of Iron.* London: Secker and Warburg, 1990

Coetzee, J. M., *The Lives of Animals.* Princeton: Princeton University Press, 1999

Coetzee, J. M., "Man's Fate in the Novels of Alex la Guma" in David Atwell (ed.), *Doubling the Point: Essays and Interviews.* Cambridge, MA: Harvard University Press, 1992

Coetzee, J. M., *Waiting for the Barbarians.* London: Penguin, 1980

Coetzee, J. M., *White Writing: On the Culture of Letters in South Africa.* Sandton: Radix, 1988

Colpitt, Frances. *Minimal Art: A Critical Perspective.* Seattle: University of Washington Press, 1997

Connor, Stephen, *The Book of Skin.* London: Reaktion, 2004

Crais, Clifton, *The Politics of Evil: Magic, State Power, and the Political Imagination of South Africa.* Cambridge: Cambridge University Press, 2002

Crowther, Paul, "Violence in Painting" in *Journal of Philosophy and the Visual Arts.* New York: Academy, 1989

Dart, Raymond, "The Osteodontokeratic Culture of Australopithecus prometheus" in *Transvaal Museum Memoir.* No.10

De Bord, Matthew and Rory Bester (eds), *Trade Routes: History + Geography 2nd Johannesburg Biennale 1997.* Johannesburg: Greater Johannesburg Metropolitan Council and the Prince Claus Fund for Culture and Development, 1997

De Kok, Ingrid, "Cracked Heirlooms: Memory on Exhibition" in Sarah Nuttall and Carli Coetzee (eds), *Negotiating the Past: The Making of Memory in South Africa.* Cape Town: Oxford University Press, 1998

De Kok, Ingrid and Karen Press, Karen (eds). *Spring is Rebellious: Arguments About Cultural Freedom by Albie Sachs and Respondents.* Cape Town: Buchu Books

Diä!kwain, "Death" in Antjie Krog (ed.), *The Stars say 'Tsau'. /Xam Poetry of Diä!kwain, Kweiten-ta-//ken, / A!kúnta, /Han ...kass'o, and //Kabbo.* Cape Town: Kwela Books, 2004

Dissanayake, Ellen, *Homo Aestheticus: Where Art Comes From and Why.* New York: Free Press, 1992

Du Preez, Max. *Pale Native: Memories of a Renegade Reporter.* Cape Town: Zebra Press, 2003

Edmunds, Paul, "Jeremy Wafer and Sandile Zulu at Michael Stevenson Gallery" in *ArtThrob* (August 2003)

Edelstein, Jillian, *Truth and Lies.* London: Granta, 2001

Eilberg-Schwartz, Howard and Wendy Doniger (eds), *Off with Her Head: The Denial of Women's Identity in Myth, Religion and Culture.* Berkeley: University of California Press, 1995

Elkins, James, *Pictures of the Body: Pain and Metamorphosis.* Stanford: Stanford University Press, 1999

Elliott, David (ed.), *Art from South Africa.* Oxford: Museum of Modern Art and Thames and Hudson, 1990

Erasmus, Zimitri, "Hair Politics' in Sarah Nuttall and Cheryl-Ann Michael, *Senses of Culture: South African Culture Studies.* Cape Town: Oxford University Press, 2000

Fanon, Frantz, *Black Skin, White Masks.* London: Pluto, 1967, 1993

Fanon, Frantz, *The Wretched of the Earth.* London: Penguin, 1967

Favazza, Armando, *Bodies Under Siege: Self-Mutilation and Body Modification in Culture and Psychiatry.* Second edition. Baltimore: Johns Hopkins University Press, 1996

Foster, Hal, *Return of the Real.* Cambridge, MA: MIT Press, 1996

Friedman, Hazel, "Art Comes Through the Flames" in *Mail & Guardian* (November 3–9, 1995)

Friedman, Hazel, "On the Verge of Optimism" in *Mail & Guardian* (August 2–9, 1996)

Frost, Lola, *Taxi-003 Jeremy Wafer: Artist's Book.* Johannesburg: David Krut Publishing, 2001

Fudge, Erica, *Animal.* London: Reaktion, 2002

Gable, Eric, "Bad Copies: The Colonial Aesthetic and the Manjaco-Portuguese Encounter" in Paul S. Landau and Deborah D. Kaspin (eds), *Images and Empires: Visuality in Colonial and Postcolonial Africa.* Berkeley: University of California Press, 2002

Galeano, Eduardo, *Memory of Fire: Genesis.* New York: Pantheon, 1985

Gates, Henry Louis, "Europe, African Art and the Uncanny" in Tom Phillips (ed.), *Africa: The Art of a Continent.* London: Royal Academy of Arts and Munich: Prestel, 1995

Garlake, Peter, "The African Past" in Tom Phillips (ed.), *Africa: The Art of a Continent.* London: Royal Academy of Arts and Munich: Prestel, 1995

Geers, Kendell, "Double Standards Damage All Artists" in *The Star* (June 24, 1997)

Gill, Carolyn Bailey (ed.), *Time and the Image.* Manchester: Manchester University Press, 2000

Goldberg, David Theo, *Racist Culture: Philosophy and the Politics of Meaning.* Oxford: Blackwell, 1993

Goldhammer, Johann G. and Cornelius de Ronde (eds), *Wildland Fire Management Handbook for Sub-Saharan Africa.* Freiburg and Bredasdorp: Global Fire Monitoring Centre, 2004

Gottlieb, Carla, *Beyond Modern Art.* New York: E. P. Dutton, 1976

Graves, Robert, *The Greek Myths: 1.* Harmondsworth: Pelikan, 1955

Grosz, Elizabeth *Space, Time and Perversion.* St Leonards: Alan & Unwin, 1995

Gustafson, Mark, "The Tattoo in the Later Roman Empire and Beyond" in Jane Caplan (ed.), *Written on the Body: The Tattoo in European and American History.* London: Reaktion, 2000

Guthrie, W. K. C., "Flux and Logos in Heraclitus" in Alexander Mourletos (ed.), *The Pre-Socratics: A Collection of Critical Essays.* New York: Doubleday, 1974

Gutteridge, William and J. E. Spence (eds), *Violence in Southern Africa.* London: Frank Cass, 1997

Gyekye K., *Tradition and Modernity: Philosophical Reflections on the African Experience.* Oxford: Oxford University Press, 1997

Harker, Joseph (ed.), *The Legacy of Apartheid.* London: Guardian, 1994

Hassan, Salah M, "The Modernist Experience in African Art: Towards a Critical Understanding" in Philip G. Altbach and Salah M. Hassan (eds), *The Muse of Modernity: Essays on Culture as Development in Africa.* Asmara: Africa World Press, 1996

Harrison, David, *The White Tribe of Africa.* Braamfontein: Macmillan, 1981

Harrison, Stephen, Steve Pile and Nigel Thrift (eds), *Patterned Ground: Entanglements of Nature and Culture.* London: Reaktion, 2004

Haymans, Riana, *The Voortrekker Monument, Pretoria.* Pretoria: The Board of Control of the Voortrekker Monument, 1986

Herreman, Frank and Mark D'Amato (eds), *Liberated Voices: Contemporary Art from South Africa.* Munich: Prestel, 1999

Higgs, P., N. C. G. Vakalisa, T. V. Mda, and N. T. Assie-Lumumba (eds), *African Voices in Education.* Landsdowne: Juta, 2000

Hobbs, Philippa and Elizabeth Rankin, *Rorke's Drift: Empowering Prints.* Cape Town: Double Storey, 2003

Hofmeyr, Isabel, *We Spend Our Years as a Tale that is Told: Oral Historical Narrative in a South African Chiefdom.* Portsmouth: Heinemann, Johannesburg: Wits University Press and London: James Curry, 1994

Hug, Alfons and Sabine Vogel (eds) *Colours: Kunst aus Südafrika.* Berlin: Herausgeber Verlag, 1996

Jameson, Frederic, *The Political Unconscious: Narrative as a Socially Symbolic Act.* London: Methuen, 1981

Jamison, Kay Redfield, *Touched with Fire: Manic Depressive Illness and the Artistic Temperament.* New York: Simon & Schuster, 1993

Jansen, E. G., "The Growth of an Idea" in *The Voortrekker Monument: Official Guide.* Sixth edition. Pretoria: Board of Control, 1954, 1969

Johannes Mashego Segogela: 'Devils, Angels and Other Things.' Exhibition catalogue. Johannesburg: Goodman Gallery, 1995

Jolly, Rosemary Jane, *Colonization, Violence, and Narration in White South African Writings.* Johannesburg: Wits University Press, 1996

Kaphagawani, Didier, "Some African Conceptions of Person: A Critique" in Ivan Karp and D. A. Masolo (eds), *African Philosophy as Cultural Inquiry.* Bloomington: Indiana University Press, 2000

Kertzer, David, *Ritual, Politics and Power.* New Haven: Yale University Press, 1988

Khan, Charles H., *The Art and Thought of Heraclitus.* Cambridge: Cambridge University Press, 1981

KKNK Catalogue, Cape Town: Bell-Roberts, 2002

Klopper, Sandra, "Mobilisation of Cultural Symbols in 20th Century Zululand" in *African Studies Forum.* No.8 (23 September 1988)

Klopper, Sandra, "Lexicons and Labyrinths" in *Art South Africa.* Vol.1 No.4 (Winter 2003)

Koloane, David Nthubu, "The Spirit of Ubuntu as a Creative Dynamic" in Shireen Naziree (ed.), *Ubuntu.* Kuala Lumpur: Balai Seni Lukis Negara and National Art Gallery of Malaysia, 2002

Krauss, Rosalind, "Grids You Say" in *Grids: Format and Image in 20th Century Art.* New York: Pace Gallery, 1978

Krell, Alan, *The Devil's Rope: A Cultural History of Barbed Wire.* London: Reaktion, 2002

Kris, Ernst and Otto Kurz, *Legend, Myth, and Magic in the Image of the Artist: An Historical Experiment.* New Haven: Yale University Press, 1979

Krog, Antjie, *Country of My Skull.* London: Jonathan Cape, 1998

Krog, Antjie, *A Change of Tongue.* Johannesburg: Random House, 2003

Kruger, Nellie, *The Voortrekker Tapestry in the Museum of the Voortrekker Monument.* Silverton: Board of Control, 1972

Laband, John, *A Rope of Sand.* Cape Town: Jonathan Ball, 1995

Laband, John and Paul Thompson, *An Illustrated Guide to the Anglo-Zulu War.* Pietermaritzburg: University of Natal Press, 2000

Letseka, Moeketsi, "African Philosophy and Educational Discourse" in P. Higgs, N. C. G. Vakalisa, T. V. Mda and N. T. Assie-Lumumba (eds), *African Voices in Education.* Landsdowne: Juta, 2000

Lippard, Lucy, *Overlay: Contemporary Art and the Art of Prehistory.* New York: Pantheon, 1983

"Lize van Robbroeck" in Anitra Nettleton, Julia Charlton and Fiona Rankin-Smith, (eds), *Voice Overs: Wits Writings on African Artworks.* Johannesburg: Standard Bank African Art Collection and University of the Witwatersrand Art Galleries, 2004

Lodge, Tom, *Consolidating Democracy: South Africa's Second Popular Election.* Johannesburg: Wits University Press, 1999

Lucretius, *De Rerum Natura: A Poem of Nature.* Manchester: Carcanet, 1976

Lynn, William S., "Animals, Ethics, and Geography" in Jennifer Wolch and Jody Emel (eds). *Animal Geographies: Place, Politics and Identity in the Nature-Culture Borderlands.* London: Verso, 1998

Maharaj, Gitanjali (ed.), *Between Unity and Diversity: Essays on Nation-Building in Post-Apartheid South Africa.* Claremont: David Philip and Idasa, 1999

Makgoba, Malegapuru William (ed.), *African Renaissance: The New Struggle.* Sandton: Mafube and Cape Town: Tafelberg, 1999

Makoni, Sinfree, "African Languages as European Scripts: The Shaping of Communal Memory" in Sarah Nuttall and Carli Coetzee (eds), *Negotiating the Past: The Making of Memory in South Africa.* Cape Town: Oxford University Press, 1998

Malik, Kenan, *The Meaning of Race: Race, History, and Culture in Western Society.* New York: New York University Press, 1996

Malik, Kenan, "The Mirror of Race: Postmodernism and the Celebration of Difference" in Ellen M. Wood and John Bellamy Foster (eds), *In Defense of*

History: Marxism and the Postmodern Agenda. New York: Monthly Review Press, 1997
Manganyi, N. Chabani and André du Toit (eds), *Political Violence and the Struggle in South Africa.* London: Macmillan, 1990
Mangon, Marian (ed.), *Ubuntu: Arts et Cultures d'Afrique du Sud.* Paris: de la Réunion des Musées Nationaux, 2002
Mazibuko, Zanele, "Local Artist to Exhibit in New York after Biennale Win" in *City Vision* (Friday 22 January 1999)
Mbeki, Thabo, *Africa: The Time has Come.* Cape Town: Tafelberg and Johannesburg: Mafube, 1998
Mbembe, Achille, *On the Postcolony.* Berkeley: University of California Press, 2001
Mbiti, John S., *Introduction to African Religion.* Second Edition. Oxford: Heinemann, 1990
Mercer, Kobena, "Black Hair/Style Politics" in Erica Carter, James Donald and Judith Squiers (eds), *Cultural Remix: Theories of Politics and the Popular.* London: Lawrence Wishart, 1995
Mitchell, Peter, *The Archaeology of Southern Africa.* Cambridge: Cambridge University Press, 2002
Mnyaka, Nolizwe, "Am I Hallucinated" in *Like a House on Fire: Contemporary Women's Writing, Art and Photography from South Africa.* Compiled and edited by the COSAW Women's Collective. Johannesburg: COSAW, 1994
Mogale, Dikobe wa, "Baptism of Fire" in Sisa Ndaba (ed.), *One Day in June.* Craighall: AD Donker, 1986
Morris, Michael, *Every Step of the Way: The Journey to Freedom in South Africa.* Cape Town: HSRC Press, 2004
Mphahlele, Esk'ia, "Afrika, My Music" in Digby Ricci (ed.), *Reef of Time: Johannesburg in Writing.* Craighall: AD Donker, 1986
Mtshali, Mbuyiseni Oswald, "Hector Petersen – The Young Martyr" in Sisa Ndaba (ed.), *One Day in June.* Craighall: AD Donker, 1986
Mtshali, Mbuyiseni Oswald, *Fireflames.* Pietermaritzburg: Shuter and Shooter, 1980
Mudimbe, V. Y., "The Power of the Greek Paradigm" in his *The Idea of Africa.* Bloomington: Indiana University Press and London: James Curry, 1994
Murdoch, Iris, *The Fire and the Sun: Why Plato Banished the Artist.* Oxford: Oxford University Press, 1977
Mutwa, Credo, *Indaba My Children: African Tribal History, Legends, Customs and Religious Beliefs.* London: Payback Press, 1998
Mzamani, Mbulelo (ed.), *Hungry Flames and Other Black South African Stories.* London: Longman, 1986
Naidoo, Jay, "Was the Makapans Cave Siege a Massacre and a Trekker Victory?" in his *Tracking Down Historical Myths: Eight South African Cases.* Craighall: AD Donker, 1989
Ndebele, Njabulo, *The Cry of Winnie Mandela: A Novel.* Cape Town: David Philip, 2003
Ndebele, Njabulo, "Multi-Lingual Fictions: Writing, Language, and Identity" in *Connect ! Art ! Politics ! Theory ! Practice. Arts International* (Fall 2000)
Ndebele, Njabulo, *The Rediscovery of the Ordinary: Essays on South African Literature and Culture.* Fordsburg: COSAW, 1991
Ndlazi, Mandla, "June's Blaze" in Sisa Ndaba (ed.) *One Day in June.* Craighall: AD Donker, 1986
Nettleton, Anitra, Julia Charlton and Fiona Rankin-Smith (eds), *Engaging Modernities: Transformations of the Commonplace.* Johannesburg: University of the Witwatersrand Art Galleries, 2003
Nixon, Rob, *Homelands, Harlem and Hollywood: South African Culture and the World Beyond.* New York: Routledge, 1994
Noyes, John, "The Place of the Human" in Sarah Nuttall and Cheryl-Ann Michael (eds), *Senses of Culture: South African Culture Studies.* Oxford: Oxford University Press, 2000
Nuttall, Sarah and Carli Coetzee (eds), *Negotiating the Past: The Making of Memory in South Africa.* Cape Town: Oxford University Press, 1998
Nuttall, Sarah and Cheryl-Ann Michael (eds), *Senses of Culture: South African Culture Studies.* Oxford: Oxford University Press, 2000
Obee, Ruth, *Es'kia Mphahlele: Themes of Alienation and African Humanism.* Athens: University of Ohio Press, 1999
Oliphant, Andries, *TAXI-009 Kagiso Pat Mautloa.* Johannesburg: David Krut Publishing, 2003
Osborne, Peter, *The Politics of Time: Modernity and the Avant-Garde.* London: Verso, 1995
Out of Step: War Resistance in South Africa. London: CIIR, 1989
Panoramas of Passage: Changing Landscapes of South Africa. Johannesburg: Wits University Art Galleries and Washington: Meridian International Center, 1995
Papane, Matime, "Soweto is Burning" in Sisa Ndaba (ed.), *One Day in June.* Craighall: AD Donker, 1986
Papastergiadis, Nikos, "Languages for Landscape" in his *Dialogues in the Diasporas: Essays and Conversations on Cultural Identity.* London: Rivers Oram Press, 1998
Park, Robert, *Voodoo Science: The Road from Foolishness to Fraud.* New York: Oxford University Press, 2000
Parrinder, Geoffrey, *African Mythology.* London: Paul Hamlyn, 1967
Paton, Alan, *Cry the Beloved Country: A Story of Comfort in Desolation.* London: Penguin, 1958
Pauw, Jacques, *Into the Heart of Darkness: Confessions of Apartheid's Assassins.* Johannesburg: Jonathan Ball, 1997
Peires, J. B., *The Dead Will Arise: Nongqawuse and the Great Xhosa Cattle-Killing Movement 1856–7.* London: Ravan Press, 1989
Penn, Nigel, "Robben Island 1488–1805" in Harriet Deacon (ed.), *The Island: A History of Robben Island 1488–1990.* Claremont: David Philip and Bellville: Mayibuye, 1996
Perryer, Sophie (ed.), *10 Years 100 Artists: Art in a Democratic South Africa.* Cape Town: Bell-Roberts and Struik Publishers, 2004
Pesci, Peter, *Labyrinth: A Search for the Hidden Meaning of Science.* Cambridge, MA: MIT Press, 2000
Phillips, Tom (ed.), *Africa: The Art of a Continent.* London: Royal Academy of Arts and Munich: Prestel, 1995
Plaatje, Sol Tshekisho, "An Inflammatory Bioscope Film" in Digby Ricci (ed.), *Reef of Time: Johannesburg in Writing.* Craighall: AD Donker, 1931 and 1986
Posel, Deborah and Graeme Simpson (eds), *Commissioning the Past: Understanding South Africa's Truth and Reconciliation Commission.* Johannesburg: Wits University Press, 2002
Pranger, M. B., "Monastic Violence" in Hent de Vries and Samuel Weber *Violence, Identity, and Self-Determination.* Stanford: Stanford University Press, 1997
Pyne, Stephen J., "Frontiers of Fire" in Tom Griffiths and Libby Robin (eds), *Ecology and Empire: Environmental History of Settler Societies.* Edinburgh: Keel University Press and Pietermaritzburg: University of Natal Press, 1997
Pyne, Stephen, "Fire" in Stephan Harrison, Steve Pile and Nigel Thrift (eds), *Patterned Ground: Entanglements of Nature and Culture.* London: Reaktion, 2004
Ramose, Mogobe, "'African Renaissance': A Northbound Gaze" in P. H. Coetzee and A. P. J. Roux (eds), *Philosophy from Africa: A Text with Readings.* Second edition. Cape Town: Oxford University Press, 2002
Rampley, Matthew, "Anthropology at the Origins of Art History" in Alex Coles (ed.), *Site-Specificity: The Ethnographic Turn.* London: Black Dog Publishing, 2000
Rankin, Elizabeth, *Images of Wood: Aspects of the History of Sculpture in 20th Century South Africa.* Johannesburg: Johannesburg Art Gallery, 1989
Razac, Olivier, *Barbed Wire: A Political History.* New York: The New Press, 2002
Reynolds, Andrew (ed.), *Election '94 South Africa: The Campaigns, Results and Future Prospects.* London: James Curry and Cape Town: David Philip, 1994
Richards, Colin, "Kendell Geers" in Sophie Perryer (ed.), *10 Years 100 Artists: Art in a Democratic South Africa.* Cape Town: Bell-Roberts and Struik Publishers, 2004
Richards, Colin, "Looking at What we See" and "Biting the Mother Tongue" in *Special Supplement to The Star* (Saturday June 16, 2001)
Richards, Colin, "Sandile Zulu: Incendiary Devices" in Frank Herreman and Mark D'Amato (eds), *Liberated Voices: Contemporary Art from South Africa.* Munich: Prestel, 1999
Richards, Colin, "Tropics of Ice" in Marith Hope (ed.), *Contemporary Art from South Africa.* Oslo: The National Touring Exhibitions, 1997
Ridgeway, James, *Blood in the Face: The Ku Klux Klan, Aryan Nations,*

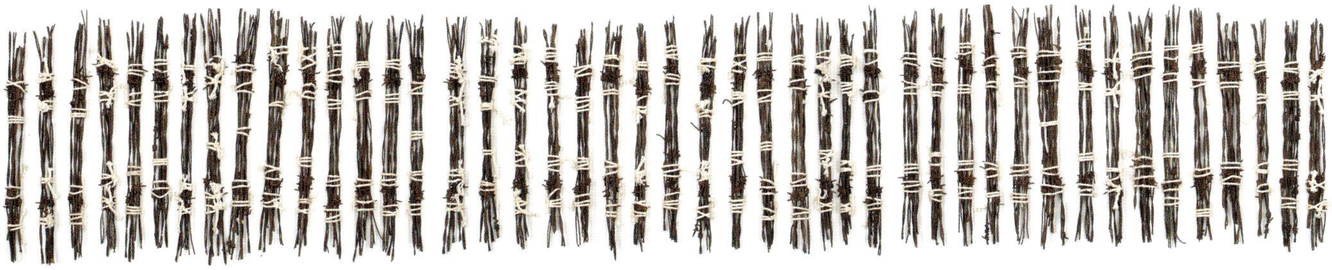

Nazi Skinheads, and the Rise of a New White Culture. Second edition. New York: Thunder's Mouth Press, 1995

Rose, Jacqueline, "Apathy and Accountability: The Challenge of South Africa's Truth and Reconciliation Commission to the Intellectual of the Modern World" in her *On Not Being Able to Sleep: Psychoanalysis and the Modern World.* London: Chatto & Windus, 2003

Rubin, Arnold (ed.), *Marks of Civilization: Artistic Transformations of the Human Body.* Los Angeles: University of California Press, 1995

Rush, Michael, *New Media in Late 20th-Century Art.* London: Thames and Hudson, 1999

Sachs, Albie, "A Conceited Look at Creating Free Space for the Artist: Texts, Subtexts and Contexts" in Els van der Plas, Malu Halasa and Marlous Willemson (eds), *Creating Spaces of Freedom: Culture in Defiance.* The Hague: Prince Claus Fund and London: SAQI Books, 2002

Sanders, Mark, *Complicities: The Intellectual and Apartheid.* Pietermaritzburg: University of Natal Press, 2002

Saunders, Christopher and Nicholas Southey (eds), *A Dictionary of South African History.* Cape Town: David Philip, 1998

Schärf, Wilfried and Baba Ngcokoto, "Images of Punishment in the People's Courts of Cape Town, 1985–7" in Manganyi, N. Chabani and André du Toit (eds), *Political Violence and the Struggle in South Africa.* London: Macmillan, 1990

Schrire, Carmel, *Digging Through Darkness: Chronicles of an Archaeologist.* Johannesburg: Wits University Press, 1995

Schnapp, Jeffrey T., "The Fabric of Modern Times" in *Critical Inquiry.* Vol.24 No.1 (Autumn 1997)

Schwartz, Hillel, *The Culture of the Copy: Striking Likenesses, Unreasonable Facsimiles.* New York: Zone Books, 1996

Searle, Bernie, *Vapour.* Exhibition catalogue. Cape Town: Michael Stevenson Gallery, 2004

Sharp, Guy Willoughby, "Luminism and Kineticism" in Gregory Battcock (ed.), *Minimal Art: A Critical Anthology.* New York: E. P. Dutton, 1967

Sieber, Roy and Frank Herreman (eds), *Hair in African Art and Culture.* New York: The Museum for African Art and Munich: Prestel, 2000

Simpson, Graeme, "'Tell No Lies, Claim No Easy Victories': A Brief Evaluation of South Africa's Truth and Reconciliation Commission" in Deborah Posel and Graeme Simpson (eds), *Commissioning the Past: Understanding South Africa's Truth and Reconciliation Commission.* Johannesburg: Wits University Press, 2002

Singer, Ronald in Philip Tobias (ed.), *The Bushman: San Hunters and Herders of Southern Africa.* Cape Town: Human and Rousseau, 1978

Soyinka, Wole, "Reparations, Truth, and Reconciliation" in his *The Burden of Memory, The Muse of Forgiveness.* New York: Oxford University Press, 1999

Steinberg, Jonny, *Midlands.* Jeppestown: Jonathan Ball, 2002

Stevenson, Michael and Anabel Rosholt, *Moving in Time and Space: Shifts Between Abstraction and Representation in Post-War South African Art.* Cape Town: Michael Stevenson, 2003

Stewart, Susan, *On Longing: Narratives of the Miniature, the Gigantic, the Souvenir, the Collection.* Durham: Duke University Press, 1993

Straker, Gill with Fatima Moosa, Risé Becker and Madiyoyo Nkwale, *Faces in the Revolution: The Psychological Effects of Violence on Township Youth in South Africa.* Claremont: David Phillip and Athens: Ohio University Press, 1992

Taylor, Jane, "Holdings: Refiguring the Archive" in Carolyn Hamilton, Verne Harris, Jane Taylor, Michele Pickover, Graeme Reid and Razia Saleh (eds), *Refiguring the Archive.* Dordrecht: Kluwer Academic Publishers, 2002

Teffo, Lesiba, "Africanist Thinking: An Invitation to Authenticity in African Voices in Education" in P. Higgs, N. C. G. Vakalisa, T. V. Mda and N. T. Assie-Lumumba (eds), *African Voices in Education.* Landsdowne: Juta, 2002

Tembo, Mwizenge, *Legends of Africa.* New York: Friedman Fairfax, 1999

Thorpe, Jo, *It's Never Too Early: African Art and Craft in Kwazulu-Natal 1960–1990.* Durban: Indicator, 1994

Tisdall, Caroline, *Joseph Beuys.* New York: Thames and Hudson and the Solomon R. Guggenheim Foundation, 1979

Torgovnick, Marianna, *Primitive Passions: Men, Women, and the Quest for Ecstasy.* Chicago: University of Chicago Press, 1996

Tutu, Desmond, *No Future Without Forgiveness.* London: Random House, 1999

Villa-Vicencio, Charles and Eric Doxstader (eds), *The Provocations of Amnesty: Memory, Justice and Impunity.* Cape Town: David Philip, 2003

Virilio, Paul, *Art and Fear.* London: Continuum, 2003

Walker, Clarence, *We Can't Go Home Again: An Argument About Afrocentricism.* Oxford: Oxford University Press, 2001

Waller, Margaret, *A Bigger Picture: A Manual of Photojournalism in Southern Africa.* Kenwyn: Juta, 2000

Weinberg, Eli, *Portrait of a People: A Personal Photographic Record of the South African Liberation Struggle.* London: IDAF, 1981

Wheelhouse, F., *Raymond Arthur Dart: A Pictorial Profile.* Sydney: Transpareon Press, 1983

Wicomb, Zoë, "Five Afrikaner Texts and the Rehabilitation of Whiteness" in Robert Kriger and Adebe Zegeye (eds), *Culture in the New South Africa After Apartheid: Vol. 2.* Cape Town: Kwela Books and SA History Online, 2001

Willan, Brian, *Sol Plaatje: A Biography.* Johannesburg: Ravan Press, 1984

Willcott, Ben, "Truth and Reconciliation" in *The Austin Chronicle* (June 2, 2000)

Wilson, Richard, *The Politics of Truth and Reconciliation in South Africa: Legitimizing the Post-Apartheid Space.* Cambridge: Cambridge University Press, 2001

Williamson, Sue, *Resistance Art in South Africa.* Cape Town: Catholic Institute for International Relations, 1989

Williamson, Sue and Ashraf Jamal, "Sandile Zulu: Fire!" in their *Art in South Africa: The Future Present.* Cape Town: David Philip, 1996

Wolch, Jennifer, "Zoöpolis" in Jennifer Wolch and Jody Emel (eds), *Animal Geographies: Place, Politics and Identity in the Nature-Culture Borderlands.* London: Verso, 1998

Woodward, Christopher, *In Ruins.* London: Vintage, 2002

Younge, Gavin, *Art of the South African Townships.* London: Thames and Hudson, 1988

Zulu, Sandile, "Artist's Statement" in *FNB Vita Art Prize and Exhibition.* Exhibition catalogue. Sandton: FNB and Sandton Civic Gallery, 1998

ARTIST'S CV

Born 1960 in Ixopo, KwaZulu-Natal. Lives and works in Johannesburg

1982 Diploma in Fine Art, Rorke's Drift Art School, KwaZulu-Natal
1983 Fine Art, Technikon Natal, Durban
1993 Bachelor of Fine Art, University of the Witwatersrand, Johannesburg

Solo Exhibitions

1995 *Fire!* Rembrandt Van Rijn Gallery, Johannesburg
1997 *Artomic Project I*, Sandton Gallery, Johannesburg
1997 *Artomic Project II*, Gallery Zola, Aix-en Provence, France
1998 *Camouflage*, Millennium Gallery, Pretoria,
2003 *Points of the Delta,* Michael Stevenson Contemporary, Cape Town

Group Exhibitions

1983 *Art Communication*, Executive Hotel, Umlazi, Durban
1995 *Identification*, St. Denis, Réunion Island
1996 *Common and Uncommon Ground*, City Gallery East, Atlanta, GA, USA
South Africa I: At the Forefront, October Gallery, London
FNB Vita Art Exhibition, Johannesburg Art Gallery
1997 *New Art from South Africa*, Talbot Rice Gallery, Edinburgh, Scotland
Graft: 2nd Johannesburg Biennale, South African National Gallery, Cape Town
1998 *6th Biennale of Contemporary Art*, National Gallery, Victoria, Seychelles
Isintu, South African National Gallery, Cape Town
Dreams and Clouds, Kulturhuset, Stockholm, Sweden
FNB Vita Art Exhibition, Sandton Gallery, Johannesburg
1999 *Liberated Voices*, Museum for African Art, New York
Celsius: (new) Art from (new) South Africa, IFA Gallery, Bonn, Germany
2001 *Land,* Unisa Art Gallery, Pretoria
Frank, Millennium II Gallery, Johannesburg
2002 *Lexicons and Labyrinths*, South African National Gallery, Cape Town
Once Were Painters, Klein Karoo Nasionale Kunstefees, Oudtshoorn, South Africa
2003 *Coexistence: Contemporary Cultural Production in South Africa*, Rose Art Museum, Brandeis University, Waltham, MA, USA and South African National Gallery, Cape Town
2004 *Personal Affects: Power and Poetics in Contemporary South African Art*, Museum of African Art and Cathedral of St. John the Divine, New York
Tremor: Contemporary South African Art, Palais des Beaux Arts, Charleroi, Belgium
A Decade of Democracy: South African Art 1994–2004 from the Permanent Collection of Iziko: South African National Gallery, Cape Town
In-team: Schloss Ausstellung der KVD, Dachau, Germany

Public Collections

South African National Gallery, Cape Town
Johannesburg Art Gallery
Sandton Art Gallery, Johannesburg
Gauteng Legislature, Johannesburg
Michael Stevenson Contemporary, Cape Town
Irma Stern Museum, Cape Town
Vodacom Collection, Johannesburg
MTN Art Collection, Johannesburg
Billiton Collection, Johannesburg
Deutsche Securities, Johannesburg
Sasol Collection, Johannesburg
Arabella Sheraton Hotel, Cape Town
Dimension Data, Johannesburg
The Museum for African Art, New York

Awards and Workshops

1994 Art/Omi, New York
1995 Identification – 7 Artists, 7 Countries, St. Denis, Réunion Island
1996 Nominated for National FNB Vita Art Award, Johannesburg
1998 Nominated for National FNB Vita Art Award, Johannesburg
1998 The President's Award, Grand Prize, 6th Biennale of Contemporary Art, Seychelles
2000 Civitella Ranieri Fellowship Award and Residency, Perugia, Italy

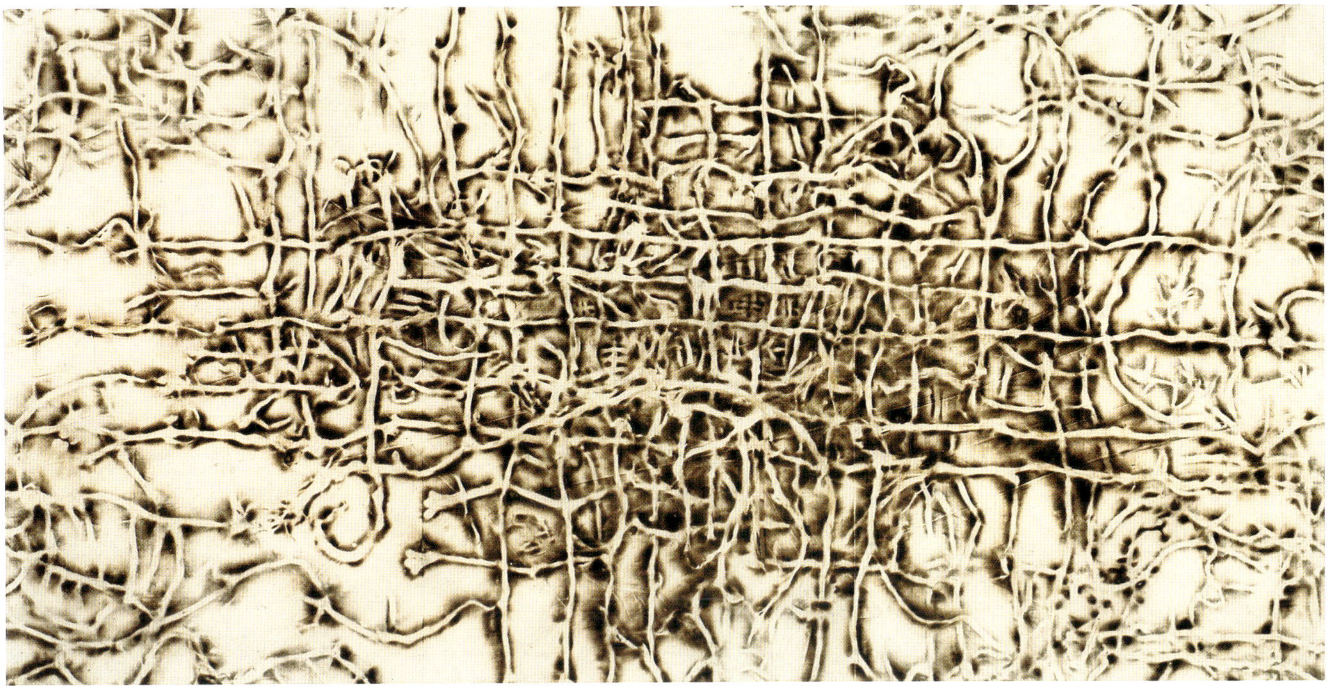

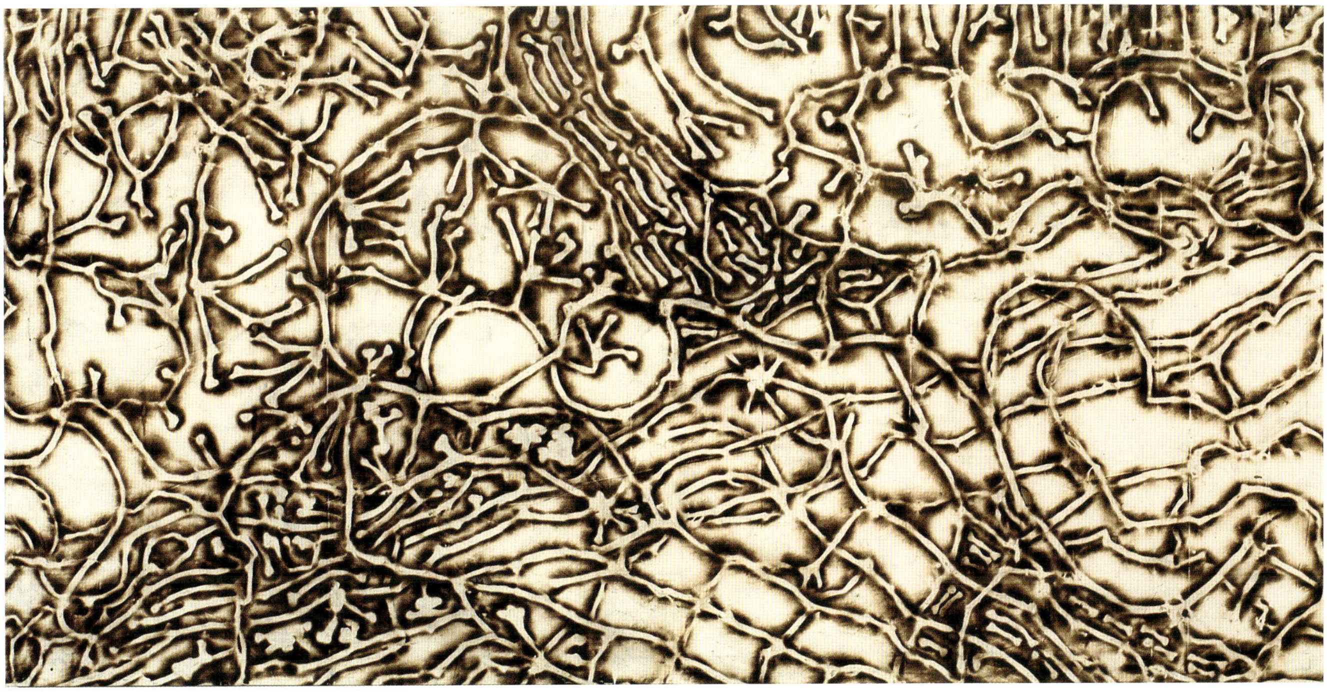

Dendrogram 1 – Dendritic Branching Entanglements	(2005)	fire, water, air, earth, plants and canvas	300 x 160 cm
Dendrogram 2 – Regenerate and Degenerate Life Cycle Forms	(2005)	fire, water, air, earth, plants and canvas	300 x 160 cm

SIGNAUX DE FUMÉE

Sandile Zulu, comme nous tous peut-être, est ébloui par le feu, par sa richesse et par les risques auxquels il nous expose. "Dès que le papier s'enflamme, je suis fasciné. Je peux maîtriser le feu et créer un ordre." De cette fascination, l'artiste tire vitalité et sérénité. Le feu est un intermédiaire avec la contingence totale, le hasard, le chaos. "Le feu est un élément difficile à maîtriser... La flamme offre la possibilité d'une démarche autre... Je cherche à ressentir la relation entre le matériau, le medium utilisé, et moi-même." Ces mots expriment la relation souvent précaire entre le medium et le corps, l'ordre et le désordre, l'émerveillement et la banalité, la réflexion et les risques pris dans son travail. Les brandons volent de-ci, de-là. Un incendie qui se propage est dangereux : le feu, littéralement parlant, est contagieux. Les coupe-feu, ménagés sur le veld quand on décide de brûler la végétation, tiennent le feu en lisière, contiennent le danger de propagation : on combat le feu par le feu. Dans le monde électronique virtuel, on dresse des pare-feu pour empêcher le pillage des données et le sabotage par virus. Comme Paul Edmunds le souligne, "Dans son traitement des processus organiques, Zulu nous donne l'impression qu'ils sont tout juste contenus et qu'ils menacent d'anéantir la géométrie qu'il impose."

Pour Zulu, l'utilisation du feu procède du sens aigu qu'il a de la communauté humaine à la fois dans la nuit des temps et dans le temps présent. Le philosophe Friedrich von Schlegel disait : "Il n'est rien de plus ordinaire que le feu." Le feu permet aussi d'appréhender le temps avant l'avènement du temps historique et de ses traumatismes, le temps du monde idyllique d'avant la chute : "Il n'y avait pas encore d'Europe, mais il y avait déjà le feu." Dans l'introduction d'un ouvrage scientifique sur le contrôle du feu en milieu naturel, Stephen Pyne et ses collègues font cette remarque sur les sources africaines du feu :

> L'Afrique est un continent de feu... En Afrique, le feu crépite plus fort et plus vif que sur toute autre terre. Mais ce que le feu africain signifie ne vient pas seulement de son omniprésence, mais aussi de son ancienneté. Sur ce continent est né le feu lié à l'anthropogenèse et il s'y est maintenu plus longtemps que partout ailleurs... L'Afrique subsaharienne offre un environnement propre à nourrir le feu... Durant les saisons humides, la terre produit des combustibles ; les saisons sèches les préparent à la combustion.

Pour Zulu, le feu est un phénomène social et spirituel qui unit les communautés humaines dans l'espace et dans le temps. Héraclite disait : "On échange le feu contre toutes choses, et toutes choses s'échangent contre du feu." On se partage le feu comme une forme d'énergie purificatrice, qui nous réchauffe et nous anime dans ce que Zulu appelle "la conflagration culturelle." Pour lui, le feu est aussi lié à la foudre, phénomène à valeur métaphysique, et parfois fatal dans certaines parties de l'Afrique du Sud, dont l'oiseau-foudre, l'*impundulu*, agent du mal et des forces magiques, est la forme mythologique. L'historien Clifton Crais, entre autres, évoque un incident qui remonte à 1856 : "le chasseur de sorcières découvrit dans la case de la femme accusée de sorcellerie, de petites réserves de graisse, peut-être de la graisse d'*impundulu*, l'oiseau magique qui assiste les sorcières dans leurs menées malfaisantes." Mais la plupart du temps, Zulu associe la foudre, source spontanée et non humaine du feu, à la révélation, à la vie, à la mort et la (re)naissance, et à la résurrection. Cette conception trouve peut-être son expression la plus explicite dans l'œuvre *Birth of a New World* qui date de 1996.

Le feu est une force anarchique et ambivalente, à la fois créatrice et destructrice, comme la violence elle-même. M.B. Prangler, par exemple, réfléchissant sur ce qu'il appelle le "paradoxe" de la violence, pose la question suivante : "Alors que nous avons tendance à penser que la civilisation est un processus qui permet d'éliminer peu à peu la violence physique, le prix à payer pour exclure la violence de nos œuvres d'art n'est-il pas une certaine atonie dé-vivifiante?" C'est à une telle question que Zulu s'efforce de répondre dans son utilisation du feu et autres formes d'énergie naturelle.

Si l'on considère l'histoire de l'art sur le plan international, l'usage le mieux connu du feu se trouve dans l'œuvre du Français Yves Klein, notamment dans ses *Peintures de feu* (1961) et ses recherches sur *l'Architecture pneumatique*. On peut citer de nombreuses autres œuvres d'art d'après guerre dans le monde anglo-saxon : *TV as a Fireplace* (1969) de Jan Dibbets, *Cremation Project* (1970) de John Baldessari, *Firecracker Silueta* (1973-1977) d'Ana Mendieta. On trouve une représentation plus explicite du feu rituel dans *Hearth 1* (1974) et *Hearth 2* (1978) de Joseph Beuys, dans *Where is our Fire?* (1979) de Mary Beth Edelson et *The Crossing* (1996) de Bill Viola.

Dans le contexte local, le feu continue à être utilisé dans la soi-disant "traditionnelle" pyrogravure sur bois en Afrique australe. Image ou élément iconique, le feu apparaît dans de nombreuses œuvres d'art sud-africaines. *Kaffirs Watching for the Return of their Dead Warriors* (non daté) de Frederick l'Ons représente quasiment le paradigme du colonialisme. On y voit un paysage au lever du soleil avec des silhouettes qui dansent autour d'un arbre en flammes au sommet d'une colline. L'œuvre présente une image de ce qui s'est passé le 18 février 1857 : les Xhosa attendaient le lever du soleil qui annoncerait la réalisation des prophéties de salut proférées par Nongqawuse et Mhlakaza. On trouve aussi des représentations du feu dans les œuvres de nombreux artistes "modernistes," comme dans *Untitled* (three men fighting a fire at night) (1940 environ) de Gerard Bengu et *Untitled* (witchdoctor outside his hut with lightning) de Simon Mnguni, qui date de 1943 environ.

Plus près de nous, citons *The Fire Place* (1985 environ) de Durant Sihlali, *Blaze* (1994) de Nthubu David Koloane, *Fires of the Truth Commission* (1998/9) de Kim Berman, et la récente série de Bernie Searle "Vapour" (2004), "Heat" (2004), et "Torch" (2004) dont chaque œuvre est une représentation du feu. Le feu comme phénomène physique et moyen de représentation est utilisé abondamment par Clive van den Berg, notamment dans *Mine Dump Project* (1995), *Small Excavations* (1996) et *Metal* (1998).

L'œuvre exemplaire à cet égard est peut-être *Brazier* (1992), dans laquelle Kagiso Patrick Mautloa monte un assemblage à partir d'un réel brasero. L'écrivain et chercheur Andries Oliphant décrit le brasero, le mbaula, comme un contenant improvisé, un gril de fortune qui à la fois contient le feu et émet sa chaleur, un récipient qui fait office "de cheminée autour de laquelle se chauffent les sans-abri et de fourneau pour ceux qui vivent dans les cabanes des bidonvilles." Oliphant souligne aussi la fonction sociale du brasero, point de rencontre mobile et instrument de travail pour les vendeurs des rues qui y font cuire ce que les passants achètent en vitesse." Mais si le brasero émet et contient la chaleur, il a aussi un côté néfaste : "les gaz émis et autres éléments toxiques produits par la combustion du charbon peuvent être nocifs voire mortels dans les lieux clos." Des bougies qu'on ne surveille pas ou d'autres sources de lumière et de chaleur dans des locaux sans électricité sont cause d'incendies qui souvent dévastent les cabanes dans les bidonvilles et font des victimes.

Dans l'œuvre de Zulu, le feu et la violence fonctionnent sur un mode presque homéopathique : similia similibus curantur – les semblables se guérissent par les semblables. Dans une étude remarquable sur la recherche scientifique dans l'antiquité, Peter Pesic fait remarquer que "si l'on soumet pendant un temps dûment calculé une roche de nature fondamentalement inerte à un feu modéré, on en modifie le comportement pour déclencher des réactions magnétiques. Il s'agit d'exploiter des relations délicates qu'un feu modéré peut promouvoir et qu'un feu trop intense détruira." Zulu "combat le feu par le feu" d'une manière qui rappelle ces "relations délicates," et c'est là en partie que l'élan psycho-social vers la "rédemption" trouve son dynamisme. En déclarant qu'une dose minime de poison est bénéfique, et, partant, que les blessures et les violences historiques peuvent être mises au service de la beauté, de la vitalité et du développement intellectuel, l'artiste adopte un credo homéopathique. "J'aspire à produire des œuvres qui affirment la vie."

Le feu brûle au plus profond de notre imaginaire culturel, de nos métaphores, de notre vie matérielle. En utilisant le feu comme élément essentiel de son art, Zulu se donne accès à un riche héritage universel d'idées, d'objets et d'événements. Le feu est l'élément primordial d'où naît toute création et toute destruction, qui nourrit l'opposition de l'apparence et de la réalité, de l'histoire et du temps présent. On peut évoquer à ce propos quelques récits anciens significatifs et bien connus : Héraclite qui considère l'âme comme le feu, le souffle vital inspiré à la naissance et exhalé à la mort, la caverne de Platon où le feu projette des ombres, et Prométhée qui aurait volé le feu aux dieux pour en faire don aux hommes et fut châtié de son méfait. Le feu marque les débuts de la maîtrise de l'homme sur la nature et fournit peut-être la première étincelle d'une vie de l'esprit et de l'expression de l'imagination.

C'est le soulèvement de Soweto, le 16 juin 1976, qui est devenu le jour gravé en rouge dans nos archives du feu historique. Zulu était alors tout jeune homme. Le feu fait rage dans le poème de Mandla Nalazi, "June's blaze" – Juin embrasé. La conflagration du soulèvement a vivement inspiré de nombreux écrivains et poètes, qui tous ont cherché à capter la force rhétorique et poétique du phénomène. Mbuyiseni Oswald Mtshali, par exemple, offre une image saisissante dans "Hector Peterson : The Young Martyr," publié dix ans après les événements : "le ghetto était en feu, les langues gigantesques des flammes se dressaient pour lécher les ventres mous des hélicoptères qui tournaient au-dessus du brasier." L'écrivain Matsemala Manaka a aussi recours à des métaphores incendiaires pour exprimer la résistance : "Les flammes de votre feu se cabraient et faisaient rage, votre ennemi contemplait, interdit, le brasier sans pouvoir l'éteindre." Le poète Nolizwe Mnyaka, quant à lui, préfère voir le feu en se détournant de la violence de ce moment historique, violence que l'on peut faire remonter, à travers méandres et relais, jusqu'aux visées des Lumières en Europe. Les Lumières et l'entreprise du colonialisme raciste avaient, après tout, partie liée. Une fresque destinée à fournir la toile de fond d'une pièce du collectif Imvaba en 1989, pour la manifestation commémorant le 16 juin, comporte la photo symbolique du jeune Hector Peterson, mortellement blessé, sur fond de flammes. Cette œuvre évoque l'iconographie du martyre des Chrétiens.

Mais l'image la plus significative des terribles années quatre-vingts est le pneu qui brûle. Dans le roman éponyme de Njabulo Ndebele, Winnie Mandela profère les paroles incendiaires de ces années-là, qui se sont fait entendre quasiment dans le monde entier : "Nous n'avons pas d'armes, nous n'avons que des pierres, des allumettes et de l'essence. Tous ensemble, la main dans la main, avec nos boîtes d'allumettes et nos pneus passés en collier, nous libérerons ce pays." Le pneu en flammes, associé au supplice du collier, a marqué la dernière décennie de la lutte pour la libération de l'Afrique du Sud, et a laissé la marque de son ardente brûlure dans la conscience de millions de Sud-africains.

ACKNOWLEDGEMENTS

Author:	Colin Richards
Editor:	Julia Charlton
Design and layout:	Adele Prins
Photographic Consultant:	John Hodgkiss
Managing Editor:	Bronwyn Law-Viljoen
Publishing Co-ordinator:	Suzanne du Preez
French translation:	Katherine Lauga du Plessis, edited by Xavier Person and Bénédicte Alliot
Advisory Committee:	Sophie Perryer, Julia Charlton, Charles Nkosi, David Koloane and Brenton Maart
Scanning:	Man Repro
Printing.	Keyprint
Paper:	137 gsm Millennium matt

All photography by John Hodgkiss except:

Wayne Oosthuizen	pp. 8-9, 10-11. 16-17, 18, 22-23, 26-27, 28, 31, 32-33, 34, 37, 40-41, 56, 57
Tracy Murinik	p. 19

Artist's Dedication:
For Ayanda my daughter so that she may grow in creative strength and happiness.

Author's Acknowledgements:
In writing this essay I incurred great debts. My thanks to Sandile Zulu for his openness, commitment and willingness to discuss his work with me. And also his encouragement. Working with him has been a great privilege. To Penny Siopis, only she knows the extent of her support. To Alexander and Khadija, thanks for all the excitement and dragging me away from 'work' at crucial moments. Thanks too to Julia Charlton without whom this text would not have happened. Julia gave sage editorial advice throughout and brought my attention to some important references. Suzanne du Preez was an indefatigable, patient and careful project manager, going well beyond what I could reasonably expect. My thanks too to David Krut for suggesting the project and persisting with it.

David Krut Publishing would like to thank the following for contributing to this book: Ayanda Zulu, Michael Stevenson Contemporary, South African National Gallery, Natasha Christopher and David Andrews at the WITS School of Arts, the Deutsche Securities, SASOL Art Collection, Mark Young, Renska Louw and Bernard Malauzat.

Collections:
pp. 10-11, 16-17, 22-23, 25, 26-27, 40-41, 43, 50-51, 53, 54, 58-59, 60, 68, private collections; p. 20, South African National Gallery, Cape Town; p. 28, Irma Stern Collection; pp. 38-39, Sasol Collection; p. 49, Billiton Collection.

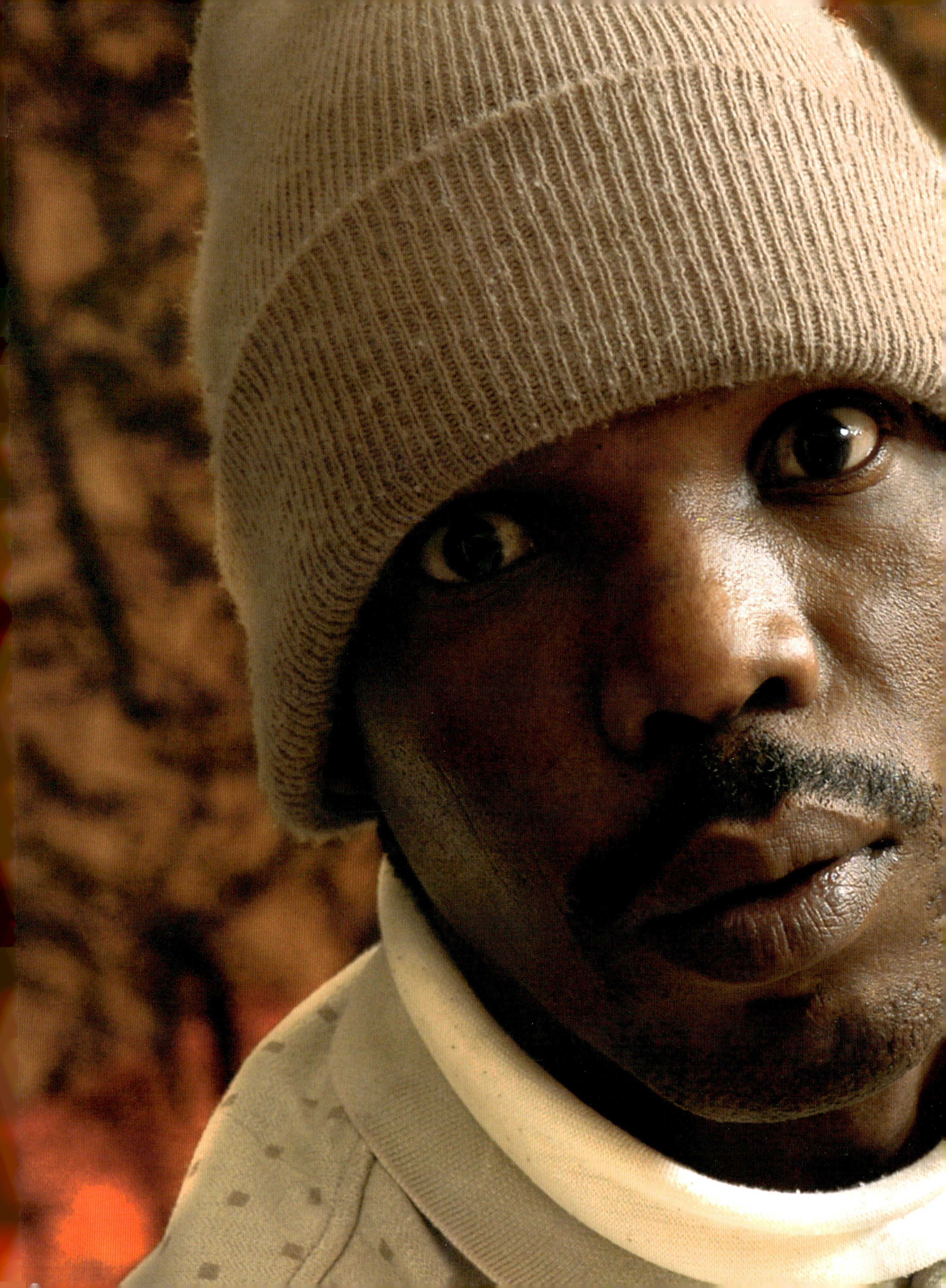